GUARDIANS OF PRIVACY

A COMPREHENSIVE HANDBOOK ON DPDPA 2023 AND DGPSI

Certifiable Audits, Maturity Assessments, and BIS Standards for Data Protection Practitioners in India

Naavi (Vijayashankar Na)

notionpress.com

INDIA • SINGAPORE • MALAYSIA

ISBN 979-8-89186-818-2

What this Book Contains

This book contains a detailed discussion on the newly introduced Data Protection Act in India namely DPDPA 2023 in India which was passed with effect from August 11, 2023.

It also discusses the DGPSI Framework for Implementation, Certifiable Audit and Maturity Assessment in an organization.

The unique DGPSI or Digital Governance and Protection Standard of India developed by the author and adopted by FDPPI, is the Gold Standard that focusses on the compliance of DPDPA 2023 along with relevant aspects of ITA 2000 and Data Governance standard introduced by the Bureau of Indian Standards in August 2023(released as a draft on August 10 2023).

The book also contains a copy of DPDPA 2023 and would make an excellent handbook for Privacy and Data Protection Lawyers, as well as professionals who practice Data Protection in organizations and as DPOs or independently as Data Auditors.

Contents

Preface

Passing of the long-awaited Personal Data Protection Act in India in the form of DPDPA 2023 (Digital Personal Data Protection Act 2023) with a Presidential assent on August 11, 2023 has been a significant development in the domain of personal data protection in India. This Act changes the way our business functions whether we identify ourselves as operating in IT or Manufacturing or Trading or function as NGOs, Educational Institutions, SMEs or MSMEs. Even the "Instrumentalities of the State" will have to watch their backs despite the many exemptions that may be available.

This law will also create, new career opportunities for professionals besides many business opportunities for the enterprising businesses. Hence the market should be generally happy with the passage of the Act.

Professionals will have three kinds of opportunities namely an employment opportunity as Data Protection Officer (DPO), Consultancy opportunity as Implementation consultants and as Data Auditors. Some of the organizations like the KPMG, Deloitte, E&Y, PWC, Deloitte, DNV or FDPPI will take up Data Auditor work in the name of the organization and would use the services of individual specialists either as employees or freelance consultants.

The business opportunities are expected to be generated in the form of Consent Manager, Dispute Resolution, Management of Data Inheritance etc.

This Book addresses the requirements of professionals who would like to study the law or implement or audit compliance. It will be a handbook for company executives also. Additionally, the Business Managers in Companies who are expected to manage Data as an asset will also find the book extremely useful since it addresses the draft requirement standard which was released by the Bureau of Indian Standards (BIS) on 10th August 2023.

For students of Law and students of Management, this will be the first book on the subject of DPDPA 2023 and the Data Protection Management standard of BIS. The contents of this book released in E Book format was already used by students of a law college in Nagpur as well as IIM Udaipur who went through certification programs in the last month.

This book covers the framework of "Data Governance and Protection Standard of India" (DGPSI) which is the only compliance framework in India today available for compliance of DPDPA 2023. DGPSI is a revolutionary concept that extends DPDPA 2023 to relevant aspects of

ITA 2000 in terms of Data Protection law and incorporates the Data Privacy Risk Management requirements included in the BIS standard along with relevant aspects of ISO 27001 and ISO 27701. DGPSI also includes the assessment of maturity of compliance through Data Trust Score (DTS) evaluation Since the DGPSI also incorporates a data classification and jurisdiction based data tagging system the framework can simultaneously be used for multiple data protection law compliance in an organization.

The nature of DGPSI therefore makes it the only framework of its kind and there are no other national or international frameworks that compare with it.

DGPSI has been adopted as a certifiable standard by FDPPI (Foundation of Data Protection Professionals in India), a Not for profit Section 8 Company created by Data Protection Professionals.

This book will therefore be a handbook for all Auditors in India who are required to undertake Data Audit. Since there are many books on GDPR and other international laws, this book does not discuss the international laws in detail. A separate E book is made available by the author for discussing GDPR, US Privacy Laws, Singapore and DIFC laws.

To facilitate different segments of readers making use of this book effectively, it is divided into different parts. The first part is on DPPDA 2023 and would be directly of interest to law students. The second part of the book will be on implementation in Business environment and the third part will be focussed on the DGPSI for Auditors.

Readers are advised to keep track of www.naavi.org as well as well as any supplementary E Books that may be released by the author on changes that may be made to the Act in the form of notifications or with the introduction of a new Digital India Act replacing Information Technology Act 2000 or any refinements that may be announced by BIS on its Governance standard.

At the time of going for print, MeitY has not yet constituted the Data Protection Board and other rules. A supplement in E Book form would be released if the rules are released immediately.

I presume this book will be a useful addition to the libraries of all educational institutions whether in Law, Engineering or Management.

– Naavi

28th November 2023

Chapter I

Legislative History behind DPDPA 2023

(Kindly refer to www.dpdpa.in for a clause-by-clause version of the Act)

The legislative history for a Personal Data Protection law in India goes back to the Bill titled "Personal Data Protection Bill 2006" along with the Information Technology Amendment Bill (ITAA 2006) introduced in the Parliament in December 2006. The bill however could not be passed. The next wave of activity started with the petition in the Supreme Court of India in 2015 spearheaded by Retired Justice Sri K S Puttaswamy about the potential harm that may be caused to Privacy Right through the use of Aadhaar. This led to the formation of a 9-member bench headed by the Chief Justice of India Honourable Sri J.S. Kehar which on 24th August 2017 came up with the historic judgement stating that "Privacy is a fundamental Right in India under the Constitution".

During this debate the Government constituted the expert Committee under the Chairmanship of Retired Justice Sri B N. Srikrishna which came up with its report and a draft law in 2018. The suggested bill was titled PDPB 2018 (Personal Data Protection Bill 2018). The Government collected public comments and presented it as PDPB 2019 in the following new Parliament. This went through the Joint Parliamentary Committee and emerged as DPB 2021 (Data Protection Bill 2021).

While there was an expectation that DPB 2021 will finally become a law, the Government withdrew the Bill on 3rd August 2022 and started working on a new version. In November 2022, Government released a draft DPDPB 2022 (Digital personal Data Protection Bill 2022) for public comments. This had only 30 sections. This was however fine-tuned, and a 44-section version was presented in the Parliament on August 3, 2023. This was passed by Lok Sabha on August 7th, Rajya Sabha on August 9th and signed by the President on August 11th.

This book discusses the DPDPA 2023 as gazette notified on August 11, a copy of which is available as an appendix to this book. It is understood that new notifications and new interpretations will keep emerging as the Government responds to various queries and an attempt is made to capture the relevant interpretations that can be considered as favoured interpretations based on our experience.

Preamble:

The DPDPA 2023 starts with the Preamble that this is "An Act to provide for the processing of digital personal data in a manner that recognises both the right of individuals to protect their personal data and the need to process such personal data for lawful purposes and for matters connected therewith or incidental thereto.

The Preamble avoids the word "Privacy" and directly speaks of "Protection of Personal Data" as the purpose of the Bill.

Even in the rest of the Act, the focus is only on Personal Data and not on "Privacy".

This has naturally given raise to the criticism that this Act is not a "Privacy Protection Act" as was required under the Supreme Court's intentions.

While it must be admitted that DPDPA 2023 is not a Privacy Protection Act, we may also argue that the Supreme Court interpreted Right to

Privacy as Fundamental right under Article 21 of our Constitution but did not define "Privacy" in unambiguous terms. One of the judges in the nine member bench in the K S Puttaswamy case, went on to say that there is no need to resolve all definitional concerns on Privacy while the majority of judges debated the Privacy concerns in the context of Personal Information and "Informational Privacy".

Hence the Government seems to have avoided providing a definition of Privacy such as "Right to Privacy means...." and focussed directly on protection of Personal data as the choice of the data principal to be protected under the Act.

Academicians can however continue to discuss what is Privacy and what are the different types of Privacy etc and we shall discuss these in the coming paragraphs of this book. But the Government has decided that they will provide a framework for the processing of Personal data to ensure protection of "Information Privacy". This is more feasible through legislation and meet the expectations of the individuals. On the other hand, defining "Privacy" as a "State of Mind" of an individual and trying to bring a legislation for third parties to outguess the mental state and protect it, is considered avoidable.

This law therefore is a law that regulates the "Personal Data Processing Industry". To the extent "Personal Data" is also "Data" under Information Technology Act 2000 (ITA 2000), this law namely DPDPA 2023 is an extension of ITA 2000. Though one key section in ITA 2000 namely Section 43A which dealt with "Reasonable Security Practices required during the processing of Sensitive Personal Data" has been removed, there are several other sections of ITA 2000 which can be considered as continuing to apply for Personal Data and hence DPDPA 2023 remains an extension of ITA 2000 and the two need to be studies together.

While we discuss DPDPA 2023 through this book at relevant places we will present the provisions of ITA 2000 as may be relevant. ITA 2000 refers to "Intermediaries" and "Due Diligence". Data Processors are "Intermediaries" and hence many aspects of ITA 2000 apply to them.

"Data Fiduciaries" also in many circumstances process personal data as an "Intermediary" and hence ITA 2000 remains relevant to them.

Though Privacy Protection is not part of DPDPA 2023, since it is the foundation on which the principles of personal data protection are built, we shall cover the "Concept of Privacy" in the next Chapter, followed by the Concept of "Data" under the author's "Theory of Data" before going back into the discussion of DPDPA section by section.

Chapter II

Concept of Privacy and Protection of Privacy through Data Protection

Though DPDPA 2023 is a legislation that tries to set rules for Data Processing industries and does not directly address the issue of "Protecting Privacy of Individuals", protection of "Privacy" as a fundamental right of a Citizen of a democratic society remains the legislative intent behind DPDPA 2023.

The Concept of Privacy per-se is related to "Human Rights" in a democratic society. Most of the democratic societies consider that "Privacy" is a right of an individual without which the right to life and liberty has no meaning. Since Right to life and Right to Liberty are considered fundamental rights, Privacy also is considered as a "Fundamental Right".

But when we discuss "Data Privacy" or "Data Protection" in the industry, we may wonder why protection of a human right is important for a corporate entity whose main goal is to do business, make money and pay dividends to its shareholders.

Emergence of Privacy Protection as an obligation of the industry:

In India, the concept of Privacy has been as ancient as the 12th or 14th century text, "Hitopadesha", a series of stories attributed to one Narayana Pandit. However, in the modern days we look at our Constitution and the Supreme Court to trace the development of the concept of Privacy as a Right.

In the Indian constitution, Privacy was not mentioned as a Fundamental Right. However, article 21 on "Protection of life and personal liberty" has been interpreted by the Supreme Court as inclusive of the "Right to Privacy" (Right to be left alone).

Evolution of Privacy as a Right in India:

In 1954 when the concept of Privacy was still in its infancy, an 8-member bench of the Supreme Court in the case of M.P. Sharma Vs Satishchandra had said that.

"Search and seizure are a temporary interference with the right to hold property and did not offend Article 19(1) of the constitution."

This was a case where the law enforcement wanted to conduct search of a private premises and objections were raised on infringement of Privacy. The Court held that such a right was not a fundamental right and refused to accept the contention that the search was offending the right of the petitioner.

In 1964 however, a Six-member bench of the Supreme Court in the case of Kharaksingh Vs State of UP, held that

"An unauthorised intrusion into a person's home and the disturbance caused to him thereby, is as it were, the violation of a common law right of a man, an ultimate essential of ordered liberty, if not of the very concept of civilisation. An English Common Law maxim asserts that every man's house is his castle".

In arriving at this decision, the Supreme Court referred to the concept of Privacy as derived from English Courts. Many others attribute the origin of the concept of Privacy Greek philosophy or US Courts.

But the Court missed to recognize that our own ancient text, Hitopadesha one of the 12th Century texts in India had provided the exact quote used in the Kharaksingh case when it stated.

"Sarve, Sve Sve gruhe Raja" (Meaning every man is a king in his own house).

It is also stated that Hitopadesha has given 9 types of personal data as relevant to the Privacy of a human in a verse.

Ayurvittam gruhachchidram mantramaushada maithuna I

Danam manapamanau cha nava gopyani karayet II

Meaning "One's age, finances, problems in the house, mantras, medicines and sex, Charity, respect gained, insults borne are nine things to be kept secret."

This view that "Right to Privacy" was part of the "Right to life and liberty" has prevailed since then and was reinforced in other cases at Supreme Court such as Gobind Vs State of Madhya Pradesh (1975), R Rajagopal Vs State of Tamil Nadu (1994) and People's Union of Civil Liberties (PUCL) vs Union of India (1996).

In 2017, during a discussion of the validity of Aadhaar in the Supreme Court on a petition filed by Justice K.S.Puttaswamy and others, the Government pointed out that as per the M P Sharma Vs Satishchandra, "Privacy is not a fundamental right". At this time, the 5-member bench headed by Chief Justice J.S.Kehar stopped the hearings of that case and made a reference to a 9-member constitutional bench to first decide on the view whether Privacy was a fundamental right or not. This nine-member bench of the Supreme Court was constituted under Chief Justice J S Kehar to examine whether Right of Privacy was a fundamental right or not and whether the M.P.Sharma Vs Satishchandra ruling should be overruled.

The result was the historic 547-page judgement delivered on 24th August 2017 by the Court which stated.

1. The decision in M P Sharma which holds that the right to privacy is not protected by the Constitution stands over-ruled.

2. The decision in Kharak Singh to the extent that it holds that the right to privacy is not protected by the Constitution stands over-ruled.

3. The right to privacy is protected as an intrinsic part of the right to life and personal liberty under Article 21 and as a part of the freedoms guaranteed by Part III of the Constitution

This settled the legal question on whether Privacy is a fundamental right or not. Today, in India, Privacy is a fundamental Right under the Constitution under Right to life and personal liberty. With this Supreme Court underscored the need for a comprehensive Privacy Protection Law for India.

The Government of India (even before the judgement) constituted an expert committee under the chairmanship of Justice B.N.Srikrishna which in 2018 submitted along with its report, a draft legislation titled PDPB 2018 (Personal Data Protection Bill 2018). This was released for public comments and after incorporating the suggestions, this was presented again in the next Parliament in 2019 as PDPB 2019. This was vetted through the joint Parliamentary Committee (JPC) and finally in 2021, another version namely the DPA 2021 (Data Protection Act 2021) was presented in the Parliament.

However, considering the many changes suggested by the JPC, Government decided to introduce a new version replacing the DPA 2021 with DPDPB 2022 which was revised to DPDPB 2023. This Bill was passed by the Lok Sabha on 7th August 2023, by the Rajya Sabha on 9th August 2023 and given the President's assent on 11th August 2023.

Presently Digital Personal Data Protection Act 2023 (DPDPA-2023) is gazetted and considered as operational. **The Government is expected to come out with a series of notifications for giving effect to different parts of the Act. One of the first such notifications could be the notification** of the constitution of the Data Protection Board (DPB). Other notifications will follow.

The Information Technology Act 2000 (ITA 2000) which was notified on 17th October 2000 and amended in 2008 (amendments notified on 27th October 2009) was hitherto the law that governed the collection, processing, storage, transmission, usage, deletion etc. of electronic document which included Personal Data and Sensitive Personal data. In 2008, amendments were specifically made to this law to introduce sections such as Section 43A and 72A to bring the data protection regulations into the ITA 2000. It was therefore the Data Protection law of India.

Now DPDPA 2023 has become the other Cyber Law that specifically addresses the issues of how electronic data recognized as Personal Data should be handled by the Data Users.

ITA 2000/8 refers to a concept called "Due Diligence" which is a mechanism to ensure that law remains dynamic and keeps pace with the developments in the society and technology, before formal amendments may be made in the law.

The definition of "Due Diligence" goes beyond what is written down in the statutory law and extends to the "Ethics" or "Best Practices" in the interest of the society. It is a grey area and often subject to judicial interpretations which become part of the development of "Jurisprudence".

The fact that Privacy is a guaranteed fundamental right, it imposes the responsibilities on the Government to ensure that the right is not infringed except through a due process of law. Normally the constitution is a direction to the Government and the public are directed by the statutes created by the Government. Hence the Privacy judgement needs to be implemented through the laws such as DPDPA 2023.

However, the Kerala High Court in a judgement related to Oomen Chandy stated that the implications of the Privacy judgement are such that Privacy can be an obligation even on private corporate entities. Once the DPDPA is effective, the law for establishing such obligations by private persons flows through this Act.

The Privacy judgement in the Puttaswamy case did not in its final order incorporate a definition of Privacy. However, in the individual judgements of the members of the bench which formed the 547 pages of the judgement, there were discussions and reflections on the definition of Privacy, and these are now the indicators that guide us today as to the definition of Privacy and to establish a link between Privacy Protection and Data Protection.

Definition of Privacy:

In the M P Singh or Kharak Singh cases, Privacy was discussed in terms of the freedom from being physically disturbed. This was the concept of "Spatial Privacy" or "Physical Privacy".

However, Privacy is more a "State of Mind" rather than a Fact of physical proximity to others. A person may joyfully enjoy "privacy" amidst a crowd where there is no spatial privacy. At the same time, he may feel miserable when he is in isolation and plenty of spatial privacy.

Hence the kind of "Privacy" an individual wants to enjoy as a "Right" is not spatial privacy. It can be referred to as "Mental Privacy". It is the enablement of an individual to mentally feel that he is left alone, and nobody can enter his mental proximity except when he wants.

In practical terms, how does a person exercise his "Privacy"? Obviously, he has to first state his preference of privacy to others who may then respect his privacy and stay away.

In a digital society where all communications are digital, this concept of Privacy boils down to "Privacy Right" being a choice of an individual to let someone come near him or not into either the physical space or the mental space through a communication of his choices. Since a part of this is to not let others know about a person's identity or where he is present at a given time or what he is doing etc., the requirement is recognized as "Information Privacy".

While we can define that "Privacy" is a "Choice" exercised by a person on how much of his personal information he wants to share with people around him, we should recognize.

i. A person's choice may vary from time to time.

ii. Choices of different persons may vary from each other.

iii. A person may himself not know all information about himself to exercise the choice in full.

Despite this state of uncertainty, world over, efforts are being made to recognize Privacy as a Right. This runs on the belief that Privacy can be regulated across the country through a legislation by trying to control the choice of distribution of personal information. It is therefore an uphill task and will continue to be so in future also.

Data Protection legislations try to use the provision of obtaining consent at the time of collection of personal information along with a freedom to withdraw consent as the means of providing the "Choice" to an individual to express his "State of mind and preferences regarding being let alone".

There is also a possibility that a person's choice may be manipulated by others through clever deceit or direct interference in the activity of the brain of an individual extending the argument of Privacy form "Information Privacy" to "Neuro Privacy".

With the development of Neuroscience and the Brain-Computer interface devices, it is possible today to change the "Choice" of an individual artificially. This risk is sought to be mitigated by extending protection of mental privacy to the domain of neuro privacy.

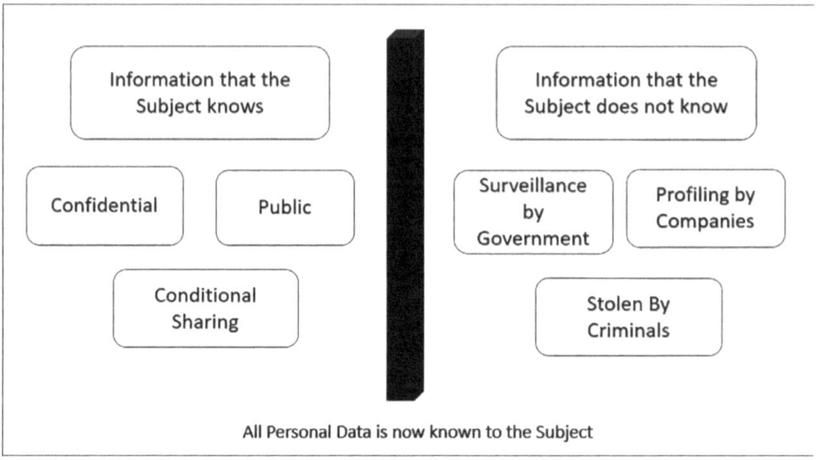

Artificial Intelligence, Virtual Reality, Augmented Reality and Neuroscience has created complex influences on the human exercising "Right of Choice". Hence protection of Privacy Right is incomplete without the regulation of AI, Metaverse and Neuro Rights.

For better understanding of the difficulties involved in understanding the personal data, the different kinds of personal information that can be identified on the basis of knowledge of the self and others are depicted in the personal information grid above.

As this grid indicates, the regulation of "Right of Choice" can only apply to "Information that the subject knows" and not to information that he may not know. Since Privacy can be infringed by the information that the subject may not know, there is a need for Cyber Crime and other laws to support the Privacy protection laws.

The uncertainties of the knowledge of personal information even by the individual himself as well as its propensity to differ between persons and in different times, render creation of Privacy protection laws extremely tough.

The Relation with Data Protection:

On the definition part, the K.S. Puttaswamy judgement made a few interesting observations.

Justice Chelmeshwar who was one of the members of the bench in the Puttaswamy case said (in his detailed judgement not included in the final order)

"Whether it is possible to arrive at a coherent, integrated and structured statement explaining the right of privacy is a question that has been troubling scholars and judges in various jurisdictions for decades."

And …

"In my opinion, there is no need to resolve all definitional concerns at an abstract level to understand the nature of the right to privacy.… Definitional uncertainty is no reason to not recognize the existence of the right of privacy.…".

He then concluded that.

"For the purpose of this case, it is sufficient to go by the understanding that the right to privacy consists of three facets i.e., repose, sanctuary and intimate decision. Each of these facets is so essential for the liberty of human beings".

"Repose" refers to freedom from unwarranted stimuli, **"Sanctuary"** to protection against intrusive observation, and **"Intimate decision"** to autonomy with respect to the most personal life choices.

Justice D Y Chandrachud (and two other judges who gave a common judgement) gave a more precise definition (again contained in the judgement but not part of the final order) and spoke.

*"Privacy, in its simplest sense, allows each human being **to be left alone** in a core which is inviolable."*

He also highlighted the importance of Digital Privacy by pointing out.

"In an age where information technology governs virtually every aspect of our lives, the task before the Court is to impart constitutional meaning to individual liberty in an interconnected world. While we revisit the question whether our constitution protects privacy as an elemental principle, the Court has to be sensitive to the needs of and the opportunities and dangers posed to liberty in a digital world."

This recognition of the "Interconnected world" gave rise to the discussion of the term "Information Privacy" in the judgement. In this context, judges quote a foreign judgement which states.

"This notion of privacy derives from the assumption that all information about a person is in a fundamental way his own, for him to communicate or retain for himself as he sees fit... In modern society, especially, retention of information about oneself is extremely important. We may, for one reason or another, wish or be compelled to reveal such information, but situations abound where the reasonable expectations of the individual that the information shall remain confidential to the persons to whom, and restricted to the purposes for which it is divulged, must be protected."

With these arguments Justice Chandrachud (along with two other judges) gave a concept of Privacy as follows:

*"Privacy postulates the **reservation of a private space** for the individual, described as the right **to be let alone.***

The age of information has resulted in complex issues for informational privacy. These issues arise from the nature of information itself.

Information has three facets: it is ***nonrivalrous, invisible*** *and* ***recombinant.***

Information is nonrivalrous in the sense that there can be ***simultaneous users*** *of the good – use of a piece of information by one person does not make it less available to another.*

Secondly, ***invasions of data privacy are difficult to detect*** *because they can be invisible. Information can be accessed, stored and disseminated without notice. Its ability to travel at the speed of light enhances the invisibility of access to data, information collection can be the swiftest theft of all.*

Thirdly, information is recombinant in the sense that ***data output can be used as an input to generate more data output.***

This argument has brought the Privacy Protection into the domain of the "Data Protection".

Naavi's Theory of Data:

In developing the Jurisprudence of Data Protection, it has been recognized that there is a glaring difference in the concept of data as per the perspective of a technology person and the community of lawyers and public. Naavi's "Theory of Data" emerged in this context.

This theory recognizes that given the fact that Privacy and Personal Data are linked to each other, there is a need that we have a common understanding of what is "Data" whether it is viewed by a Privacy Activist in the context of Privacy Protection, or a Data Protection professional in the context of data protection.

If differences exist, then they will reflect in the technologist criticising the law that the laws are made without understanding the domain and are therefore impractical. At the same time, the law makers will accuse the technologists that they do not respect the law and hence are always trying to innovate new ways by which the objective of privacy protection is defeated.

If such differing perspectives are not bridged, "Compliance" will not be voluntary and has to be forced. Forcing compliance of law will lead to technologists challenging the law. Building a harmonious consensus between technologists and Privacy Activists on basic concepts which the Data Protection law tries to address is essential for a smooth roll out of the implementation.

In this context, there appears to be a need for a "New Theory of Data" which will create a common platform for the technologists and the privacy activists to understand "Data" in each other's perspectives. The author has created some concepts around this new theory of data that tries to bridge the gap in perception between the technologists and the privacy activists. (P.S: Since this theory is a new thought yet to be widely accepted, it may be referred to as "Naavi's Theory of Data" for the time being rather than by any other name.).

A detailed discussion on the theory may help in a critical analysis of some of the provisions of the Act.

This theory is built on three hypotheses namely.

a. Interpretation Hypothesis

b. Reversible Lifecycle hypothesis

c. Additive Value hypothesis

Interpretation hypothesis states "Data is created by technology and interpreted by humans" or "Data is in the beholder's eyes".

What this means is that "Data" is a sequence of binaries and for a human it will be meaningful only if the sequence of binaries is arranged into bytes and interpreted using a protocol with associated software and hardware and converted into a human experience such as the text or image or sound.

What is converted into a human experience is then perceived by different people differently based on their own knowledge. For example, if you go a remote village school in Karnataka and ask people to read 'Xi' they are unlikely to read it as the personal name of the Chinese premier. Hence even after the binary is converted into text in an understandable language the meaning is still not perceived, and it is not adopted as "Personal Information". For you and me it may be a personal information but for those who do not know Mr Xi as a person it is just two letters of English alphabet.

The Interpretation hypothesis therefore suggests that every data has to be interpreted in the context of who is an observer. What is personal data to one may be non-personal data to another.

The second hypothesis in Naavi's Theory of Data states that data exists in a "Reversible life cycle".

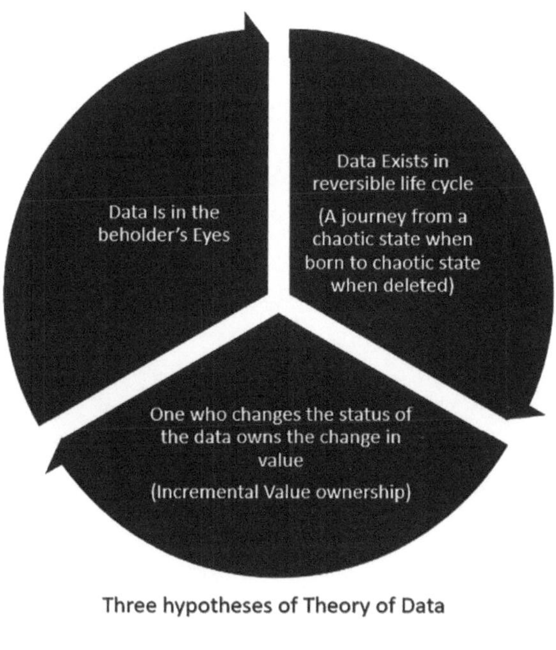

Three hypotheses of Theory of Data

What this means that all data is a meaningless sequence of binary which is distributed in a data holding device such as the hard disk in a chaotic manner. No protocol can read it and convert it into a meaningful data. From this state of chaotic data is born one set of data where bits are organized into sequence of 8 bits or a byte. This sequence can be read using the available protocols and converted into numbers or letters in one language or the other. These bytes can also be fed into a system which takes it as an instruction to do something and convert it into human experience such as displaying on a monitor or render sound or image.

When we say "Data is erased " we mean that the binary data sequence is jumbled up again to merge with the chaotic surroundings. Thus, from the chaotic distribution back to chaotic distribution, binary elements keep on changing shape, and we call it personal data, non-personal data, anonymous data, name, phone number, address IP address, educational information, Health information, financial information etc.

Just as a human is born, develops as a child, as an adult, is a student, is a husband or wife and finally dies, data is born, takes different meanings and later dies. However, unlike a human life cycle, data life cycle is reversible in the sense that personal data can be made non personal data by anonymisation and converted back to personal data through de-anonymization etc.

At any point of time what we observe as data is the then status of the binaries as interpreted by the used software/hardware by the observer. Data is neither absolute nor static and it has to be used by the observers in whatever status one can catch it.

The third hypothesis extends the "Life Cycle" concept to say that conversion of data from one state to the other requires efforts which means money and the expense involved represents the cost of converting data from one state to another. This value addition should be recognized as the property of the person who makes the change.

In other words, this hypothesis challenges the popular concept that personal data belongs to a data subject and the profile built over it is also part of his property which can be claimed by the data subject.

The situation is similar a land being leased out to a person who constructs a building in the premises which under law belongs to the landowner when the lease expires unless the contract is to return the land in the same state in which it was given by demolishing of the structure and removing the debris.

The hypothesis under Naavi's theory states that the value addition (positive or negative) belongs to the person who caused the change of state of data.

For example, if I have collected personal data from 1000 people and created a report about how people of a particular age or gender behave to a stimulus, the report constructed over the original personal data belongs to me and even when the consent for use of the data is withdrawn by the data subjects, I am still entitled to own and use the report.

These thoughts could be expanded further to explain different Privacy principles to develop Data Protection Jurisprudence.

Similarly, when two people converse or a team goes into a group discussion, what comes out is a conversation that is stitched together by all, and the ownership has to be shared jointly.

This theory of Data helps us understand the subject of Data Protection, as we go forward.

In the digitized economy, organizations have become "Data Oriented" in the sense that managerial decision making is more dependent on "Data". Many organizations are proud to call themselves "Data Driven" and underplay the significance of the "Human Resources" which not only create the data but also manage the data as well as the algorithms that use the data and create automated decisions in an organization.

There is one school of thought that believes that Artificial Intelligence will lead to decisions better than what humans can take on their own and hence in due course the role of humans in business would be diminished.

Probably this is true but while the society tries to reduce the dependence on the human skills for management, the dependence on Data and the

Process that converts data into business decisions is increasing to a level where wrong decisions will now be justified.

In a simple example, if we ask a child today about the meaning of a word, the first reaction that comes to mind is "Google it". In case Google gives a wrong answer or a less than optimum answer, it still becomes the "Google Standard". In future our writing skills will also be subordinated to ChatGPT, and literature may become mechanised.

In such a scenario of "Critical Dependence" on data for all out activities, it becomes necessary for us to understand the concept of "Data" as deeply as possible before we start interpreting "Data Protection" or "Information Privacy".

If we fail to understand "Data" properly, our interpretation of Data Protection Laws will not be perfect, and we will be fighting in a Court room to decide what different aspects of Data mean.

For example, in the world of Meta Verse, a digital Avatar can marry another digital avatar. There are jurisdictions such as Utah which provide for online marriage. Such marriages may be recorded with much fanfare before virtual attendees, and we can all enjoy the innovative manner in which they have tied the marriage knot.

However, when there is an issue of divorce of the Meta Verse Marriage, the matter has to be adjudicated by the physical Court since we have still not recognized Meta Society as a different society which can have its own Netizens and their rule of law. Hence the issue of whether a Meta Verse marriage is a legally recognized marriage, whether it is a marriage under Hindu Marriages Act or Special Marriages Act, what will be the implications of the marriage on property settlement, progeny etc become areas of adjudication by the physical courts. To understand and interpret the implications of the operation of law on activities in the Cyber society, jurisprudence has still not reached its maturity.

Similarly, when we try to protect the "Right of Privacy" by "Information Privacy" we are trying to protect a right of one society with a solution in another society. If we could have distinguished "Digital Privacy" from physical world Privacy, it would have been easier to introduce laws for Privacy protection.

Today we are suggesting "Pseudonymization" as a solution for protecting "Privacy". But "Pseudonymization" is essentially "Misrepresenting one's identity". One has to consider if this should be considered as an offence in normal parlance.

We recall that in the US case of Megan Meir, the mother of one girl who was a classmate of Megan Meir, created a pseudo identity as a 16-year-old boy, befriended the young girl Megan Meir only to unfriend her later to cause a disappointment.

Unfortunately, it ended up in Megan Meir committing a suicide and escalating the impersonation into a crime. In Data Protection, we use Pseudonymization as a means of data protection but unintended similarity of names of identity may cause problems to some because of the use of pseudonymization.

The ethics of this approach therefore requires to be taken into account just like we try to incorporate principles of ethics in Artificial Intelligence.

Data Protection as a Choice Protection:

When we discuss Data Protection, as part of Privacy Protection, the objective is to capture the choice of the data subject (Data principal) on how he/she prefers the personal data to be used by another person and what we call as "Data Protection" is the protection of this choice.

In order to effectively capture the "Privacy Choice" of the data principal, we need to have a clear understanding of what is "Personal Data", "Who is the Data Principal", "What are the preferences of the Data Principal" etc.

Once the "Intentions" of the data principal are captured effectively, it is possible to introduce the controls that enable the processing to be compliant with the intentions.

However, a perfect adherence to protection of Choice may be difficult as there could be some differences in the way terms such as "What is Personal Data" and "What protects the expressed choice", "Whether the notice for collection of consent is clear and precise" etc are interpreted.

Hence the understanding of how we interpret "Personal Data" is extremely important for going ahead with the Data Protection measures.

Law normally mentions that "Data Related to an identifiable living natural person" is considered as "Personal Data".

Some laws may not restrict the data to that of the "Living natural persons" but include deceased individuals. Data of Non-natural persons is also data, but they are not referred to as "Personal Data". Protection of such "Non-Personal Data" is also necessary but it is a subject different from "Privacy Protection".

In the context of "Privacy Protection", there has to be an "Individual" whose "Privacy" is in the need of protection.

The dead person does not have an enforceable right of "Privacy" and hence normally the Data Protection law restricts its scope to protection of data about a living individual only.

However, when law makers forget the fundamental objective of the law and deviate from the principle of "Protection of Privacy" to "Protection of personal information", whether the information is that of a living person or a person who is deceased, ceases to have meaning.

In identifying an individual, law often states that if there is a Data "D" and the holder of the data can identify that "D" belongs to an individual "I" then "D" is considered as "Personal data". Sometimes "D" on its own may not be able to identify any person. But the receiver of the data may already have other information say "E" which if combined with "D" can lead to the identity of the person. Then the possibility of "D+E" being able to identify "I" makes both "D" as well as "E" as personal information.

This means that it is not only the incoming non personally identifiable data "D" that gets converted into a personal data set, but the already available non personally identifiable data "E" also gets converted into personal data.

This principle means that "Data which is non personal may get converted into Personal Data because of other information floating around".

In a way, "D" interacts with "E" and becomes a compound "D+E" and properties of D and E are that they are "non-personal" while "D+E" is personal.

Such occurrences are common in Chemistry. For example, Hydrogen and Oxygen are both gasses at normal temperature whereas two atoms of hydrogen combined with one atom of oxygen makes H_2O a liquid.

In such a scenario should we recognize Hydrogen or Oxygen also as "Liquids"? Scientists do not think it is necessary.

But Data Protection law makers think differently. A GDPR practitioner will call an IP Address as a personal identity even if it is just an IP address without any link to who is actually using it for accessing any data object on the internet.

The defining of 18 identity parameters as "Identifiers" under HIPAA also is a similar approach though it calls these as "Identifiers" and does not call them as PHI. GDPR practitioners however consider that any element of identity such as a name, or an email address or an IP address or a Cookie as "Personal Information".

Perhaps we need to take a re-look at the definition of "Personal Information" and accept that "All Identifiers are not Personal Information" whereas "A combination of identifiers may create personal information when they are seen together".

Current definition of personal data under GDPR is as follows:

'Personal data' means any information relating to an identified or identifiable natural person ('data subject').

-an identifiable natural person is one who can be identified, directly or indirectly, in particular by reference to an identifier such as a name, an identification number, location data, an online identifier or to one or more factors specific to the physical, physiological, genetic, mental, economic, cultural or social identity of that natural person.

Under DPDPA 2023, personal data is defined as

"Personal data" means any data about an individual who is identifiable by or in relation to such data".

Jurisprudence has to develop on whether the above definitions should stay or need to be modified perhaps as follows.

"Personal data" means a combination of data elements available to a common data custodian which together can identify as related to a natural person with a reasonable level of certainty.

This definition recognizes that "Personal Data" is always a set of attributes which together identify the elements of data with an individual.

For example, naavi@naavi.org is an e-mail address. By itself it may not clearly identify to whom it belongs to. If the holder of the email address explores the web and finds out what is naavi.org, he may be able to get more information. But this is an additional data gathering exercise and is not present initially when the data naavi@naavi.org is available with a data processor. The email address is an identifier and one of the attributes in a set of attributes. If it is associated with a name Vijayashankar together

"Vijayashankar,naavi@naavi.org" becomes a better identifiable personal information. If it is further associated with a PAN card number or Aadhaar Number or a biometric information, the information becomes increasingly more certain.

This will introduce the concept of "degree of certainty" with which a set of data elements together can be considered as personal data of an individual. This means that there could be different levels of personal data such as Level 1 personal data, Level 2 personal data etc.

These will be like the "Quantum levels" of a molecule which has different levels of energy embedded there in.

This will have a role in "Data Valuation" which we shall discuss elsewhere where the "Depth" of data may determine the valuation of a data set.

This definition of "Personal Information" being a set of attributes which can identify a person with a reasonable level of certainty means that when an organization is in the process of collection of different attributes, it first will have "Un identified personal data attributes or Identifiers". At this state, it is "Personal Data element but Not Identified reasonably with any individual". When a critical set of attributes accumulate, the data gets upgraded into "Personal Data". This process of identifying floating personal data attributes in an organizational data lake and matching it with some logic with other elements and finally getting confirmation that the set is identifiable with reasonable certainty with an individual is the process of "Discovery of Personal Data". This is critical when a law like DPDPA 2023 needs to be implemented in an organization which already has legacy data.

Right To Privacy Under Artificial Intelligence Environment:

Artificial Intelligence (AI) is invading every aspect of data processing and has naturally come into relevance even for data protection.

AI in Data Protection can be used for "Recognition of Personal Data" for Discovery purpose as well as for "Automated Processing" of personal data.

Automated Processing leading to an actionable decision about an individual is not permitted without a specific consent in most data protection laws.

Mere collation of different data elements into a set may not be considered as an "Automated Decision-Making Process" but since "Intelligence" is involved in identifying personal data and such identification could arise out of a Machine Learning process which may be not free from bias, use of AI even for discovery of personal information needs some kind of monitoring.

Some data protection laws have started mandating more transparency for the automated processing. The DPDPA 2023 may in detailed regulations propose "Algorithmic Transparency" when final rules are formulated for the Act.

So far, laws discuss the use of algorithms by human beings as a tool. In such cases, the personal data is accessed by a human being then fed into a software and output is again taken over by a human being for some kind of decision making.

Let us take a situation where a human being does not have access to personal data, but a software accesses it and after processing, lets out only such data that does not carry the "Identifiable data". One example could be a CCTV which captures the data including the face of an individual, processes it and identifies individual faces with specific traits and develops a prediction something like persons with long noses are likely to behave in a particular manner.

In such cases, do we say that there has been a profiling of personal data in violation of the privacy of the individuals?

In AI algorithms, the personal data is viewed by the software, interpreted and processed for decision making. The entire process is a substitution of a human who collects the data, processes it and uses it for his decision making. However, it is possible to configure the system in such a manner that personal data is anonymized within the algorithmic process and no identifiable processed data is generated by the algorithm as an output.

When we look at the "Right to Privacy", as a "State of Mind of a data principal to be left alone", a question arises whether the "Being Left alone" refers to human beings or even the inanimate objects.

This distinction of whether "Privacy" is infringed when data is visible to a software but not any other human being is a grey area. India has developed a DEPA (Data Empowerment and Protection Architecture) in which it is proposed that there could be intermediaries (called Consent managers under DEPA as different from Consent mangers under DPDPA 2023) who with the consent of data principals, receive the request for personal data from Data Requesters, connect to Data Providers through an API, pull the required data and pass it on to the data requesters. In the process the Consent manager does not have "Visibility" of the personal data and hence no infringement of privacy is envisaged.

It is difficult to say if the supervisory authorities under GDPR would accept the DEPA framework as not involving processing of personal data in violation of GDPR "Automated processing" provisions.

On the other hand, the Consent Manager under DPDPA 2023 is a Data Fiduciary who has visibility to personal data of its clients and takes the full responsibility for the same as a Data Fiduciary.

The GDPR framework and the DPDPA 2023 Consent Manager framework is compatible with each other as it requires consent from the data principal/subject and accountability.

However, the DEPA framework could be considered as incompatible with the principle of Privacy as interpreted by GDPR.

If we consider that DEPA concept of "No Visibility" processing and DPDPA 2023 concept of Processing with visibility, are different, then we need to define the two as two different concepts of Privacy.

The GDPR concept is "Privacy 1.0" where processing by a software is considered as "Infringement of privacy" unless there is an express consent.

Processing by DEPA Framework should be considered as "Privacy 2.0" where the processing by a software is not considered as an "Infringement of privacy" as long as there is no visibility to the personal data to a human being.

India is now trying to work with both these concepts simultaneously and needs to resolve this sooner or later.

Naavi's theory of data first published in October 2019 tried to create a common philosophy of data that could address some of the concerns regarding the emergence of data as a human experience, the concept of reversible lifecycle and how to recognize value during the lifecycle of data.

The concept of "Visibility to a human being" vs "Visibility only to a software" was not specifically explained earlier in discussing the three hypotheses in the Naavi's theory of data.

However, this concept was embedded in the first hypothesis which said, "Data is created by technology and interpreted by humans" and "Data is the beholder's eyes".

In explaining this hypothesis, it was argued that Data is a structure of binary expressions and depending on the alignment of the Zeros and Ones, humans use different protocols and protocol interpreters to give meaning to data at one level which is further interpreted by a human being at the next level.

For example, let us take a scanning of a human eye. The picture which constitutes "scanning" is a bundle of binary data arranged in such a manner that an image viewing software can render a picture out of it. However, when an expert ophthalmologist views the picture, he may draw an instant profile of the person behind the scanned eye as having some eye related problem such as cataract or general health condition such as diabetes or that there is a vision issue. In case the same picture is accessed by as security person who has access to the iris scan of the person in his data base, he can use the medical scan of the eye also to identify the person.

When does the binary data of the scanned image become an identity? Or A "Profile"? Obviously scanning is not a sufficient development to make the binary data as personal data or a profile. It is the knowledge of the viewer or the tools he uses that converts the original binary data to a meaningful identity or profile.

Because of this principle, no data is "Personal or Non-Personal" per-se. In fact, what we call as "Deletion of Data" is just removing the arrangement of binaries in a manner which the reading tools can interpret as either a number, letter or a pixel density etc. A Data holding device such as a Hard Disk initially exists with all the binaries in a chaotic state and unable to be interpreted by the computing device. When it is formatted the device can perhaps view the disk and still consider the chaotic data distribution as "Empty disk". When the data in the empty disk gets further organized, the device may be able to interpret the data as a text or an image or a sound etc which can be rendered if the device is connected with appropriate data processing components of the computer system.

Thus "Chaotic binary arrangement" is "Empty Data" and "Arranged binary" is "Data" and finer arrangements make distinctions between personal and non-personal data as well as special categories of data which we may call sensitive.

The current data protection law makers have not fully assimilated this philosophy of data and have tried to create a law based on imperfect understanding of the data.

Perhaps in future this "Philosophy of data" will be discussed more in academic circles and a new vision of data will emerge along with a more refined data protection law.

For the time being we shall try to study what law is before us and keep some of the infirmities that are visible when you go deeper into the philosophy for a future day.

Just as the Indian philosophy has Dvaita, Advaita and Vishistadvaita as different philosophies under which we try to understand the world, we shall try to understand the Data World with whatever concepts we are familiar with today and keep developing the Data Jurisprudence applying the new philosophical thoughts.

Conflict Between Privacy With Other Rights:

Yet another basic conceptual understanding that is necessary for understanding the data protection law is an understanding that the "Right to Privacy" of an individual which the data protection law is expected to protect, is not an "Absolute Right".

The Puttaswamy judgement observed,

"Like other rights which form part of the fundamental freedoms protected by Part III, including the right to life and personal liberty under Article 21, privacy is not an absolute right.

A law which encroaches upon privacy will have to withstand the touchstone of permissible restrictions on fundamental rights. In the context of Article 21 an invasion of privacy must be justified on the basis of a law which stipulates a procedure which is fair, just and reasonable. The law must also be valid with reference to the encroachment on life and personal liberty under Article 21. An invasion of life or personal liberty must meet the three-fold requirement of

i. *legality, which postulates the existence of law.*

ii. *need, defined in terms of a legitimate state aim; and*

iii. *proportionality which ensures a rational nexus between the objects and the means adopted to achieve them;"*

In order to appreciate the "Legitimate state claim" and "proportionality" the "reasonable restrictions" provided under Article 19(2) with reference to the Right to Freedom of Expression is broadly interpreted as applicable to all the fundamental rights covered under Part III of the constitution including Article 21 related to Privacy.

Hence the reasonable restrictions as provided in Article 19(2) of the Indian Constitution which includes.

a. interests of the sovereignty and integrity of India,

b. the security of the State,

c. friendly relations with foreign States,

d. public order,

e. decency or morality or

f. in relation to contempt of court,

g. defamation or incitement to an offence

are also considered to be applicable to the application of the Right to Privacy.

Hence the Right to Privacy of one person has a conflict with the Right to the Freedom of Expression or the Right to Information of another person. Similarly, if National security is a duty of the Government, then restricting the right to privacy on the grounds of national security also become a legitimate state aim.

Apart from the national security being a legitimate state aim, it can be argued that "expecting the State to provide security" is a fundamental right of a citizen and hence appropriate measures initiated by the State for national security reasons is the collective protection of the individual rights to security of other citizens.

Exceptions to the Right to Privacy translated into Data Protection will therefore apply to meeting the legitimate needs of right to information as well as right to security and duty of the Government for national security.

Current Data Protection Law in India:

While we are discussing the data protection law in India in the form of the DPDPA 2023, we must not forget that at present we have the Information Technology Act 2000 (ITA 2000) in place which had all the ingredients of a "Data Protection Act" and even after the introduction of DPDPA 2023 and removal of a critical section 43A in the ITA 2000, ITA 2000 continues to have provisions that apply to Personal Data and compliment DPDPA 2023.

ITA 2000 was enacted with an objective of E Commerce Promotion and included the Cyber Crime issues. It defined that unauthorized access to data is an offence and whoever creates a wrongful harm needs to pay compensation and face prosecution.

When ITA 2000 was amended in 2008, more aspects of personal data protection was added with Section 43A specifically speaking of Data Protection, definition of sensitive personal information, reasonable security practice etc. Section 72A made personal data breach a punishable offence. Additionally, Section 67C spoke of data retention, Section 69/69A/69B/70B spoke of powers of agencies for surveillance etc. and Section 79 with the rules clearly defined the responsibilities of an intermediary to protect privacy of individuals whose personal information is collected by the organization.

Additionally, Section 65B of Indian Evidence Act brought through ITA 2000, endorsed a certain concept of interpretation of Data which is relevant in the current context of Data Protection as explained later in this book under the "Interpretation hypothesis" of the Theory of Data.

As regards the regulatory functions, any person aggrieved by a contravention of the ITA 2000 could approach the Adjudicator. There was no provision for registration of data processors nor administrative fines purely for noncompliance of ITA 2000. It could be invoked only when somebody claimed having suffered a wrongful loss. The regulation of the implementation was left to the "Adjudicator" and the "Criminal Justice System" and there was no separate Data Protection Authority

Rules under Section 43A which defined the "Reasonable Security Practice" and provisions of 72A provided that data management by the processor was to be determined mostly by the "Contract" between the data supplier and the data receiver. In a way this was the "Consent" based data management system that ITA 2000 represented.

The concept of "Due diligence" working with the "Reasonable Security Practice" ensures that there are some responsibilities that every organization needs shoulder in processing, storing, securing personal data.

But for these minor gaps, ITA 2000/8 had most of the ingredients of what one can expect as a data protection law.

With the DPDPA 2023 becoming effective, Section 43A of ITA 2000/8 has been deleted indicating the direct relationship between ITA 2000 as it is present now as a predecessor of DPDPA 2023.

Since ITA 2000 continues to address other issues of misuse of data, it will continue to be relevant even after DPDPA 2023 becomes effective and the two laws together will be often used to bring relief to the victims of Cyber Crimes involving personal data.

DPDPA 2023 should therefore be considered as a continuation of ITA 2000/8.

International Developments:

Internationally, Privacy has been a concept which has arisen as a "Human Rights" concept desired in democratic societies.

The international human rights conventions such as

- The Universal Declaration on Human Rights (Article 12) (1948)
- The European Convention on Human Rights (Article 8), (1950)
- The Treaty on Civil and Political Rights (Article 17) (1980)

have established the "Right to Privacy" as an important ingredient of Governance for all UN members.

The European countries have been always championing the cause of Privacy and through OECD directives and later the EU Data Protection directive followed by individual data protection laws in countries like UK, the Privacy Protection and the consequential Data Protection requirements across the globe have been led by the EU countries. This has now reflected in GDPR becoming a defacto global standard for data protection.

US on the other hand does guarantee Privacy as a constitutional right through a series of Judicial pronouncements and has been addressing the issue under different sectoral laws such as HIPAA (For Health Care) COPPA (For Children), GLBA (For financial information) etc. as against the generic Privacy Protection law adopted by the EU Countries which cut across different business domains. In recent days individual states like California have led the way to formulate GDPR like "General Data Protection laws" which provides some protection to "Consumers" sharing their personal data with third parties.

When there was a need to harmonize its laws with the EU countries, US developed "Safe Harbor" principles, "Privacy Shield", and EU-US Data Protection framework as instruments for providing assurance beyond "Standard Contract Clauses", "Binding Corporate Rules" etc suggested under GDPR.

The Problem of Determining the "Choice":

As discussed in the earlier paragraphs, Privacy is defined as the "Right to be left alone". While the Right to be left alone physically could be considered as one aspect of Privacy, it is essential to recognize that this "Feeling of being let alone" is a "State of Mind" of an individual.

"Data Protection" therefore means protecting the information relevant to Privacy as per the "Choice" of the data owner in such a manner that the individual feels that he is free of interference physically and mentally.

As a "State of Mind", human behaviour is such that the "Choice" of what a person wants differs from person to person and also what a person wants also changes from time to time.

Some people are by nature extroverts and would like to be more expressive of themselves with others. Some others are introverts and would like to hold back sharing of their personal information with others.

Sometimes people want to be with others and some other time, they want to be left alone.

Some time we speak of "Spatial Privacy" meaning the preference to keep a physical distance with others. But people do not complain about lack of privacy when they are in the midst of a crowd in a mall or in a train as long as they know there is nobody in the crowd who know who the person is. At the same time, a person may not relish if he is alone in an unknown place or when there are a few strangers around.

When "Privacy" and the "Choice" of an individual of what he wants is so inconsistent, it becomes extremely difficult to make a law that is applicable to the entire country trying to protect the Privacy Right of every citizen.

This is one of the key aspects that makes framing of a Privacy Law complicated.

Most of the Privacy regulations recognize that the data owner has a choice by which he would like part of his personal information to be kept confidential and part to be made available with a choice that he wants to exercise on a case-to-case basis. At the same time, some of his personal information may be already in the public domain and is out of the privacy debate.

At the same time, the privacy laws need to also take into account the fact that part of the personal information is required to be available to the Government for purposes of national security or public interest through what the data owner may recognize as "Surveillance" or "Interception".

Further there are always criminals who have scant respect for law and would steal the personal information where possible. They often know more about us than we know.

A law that tries to protect the Privacy of an individual through regulating how his personal information is to be processed covers all the above different types of personal data.

Conflicts in understanding the concept of Privacy also arise while drawing boundaries on Privacy Rights with other rights such as "Right to Information" or "Right to Freedom of Expression" as well as "Right to Security".

Profiling a "Deviant Mind" in an organization or the society is a requirement of security of the society. Can this right be curbed in the argument of "Privacy"?

Can Right to Privacy be considered a right to remain anonymous when harm has been committed or believed to have been committed to another individual?

Can the "Right to Privacy" of a person prevent the right of the people who need to work with him to know if he has any communicable deceases? Or other vices?

In a public health emergency scenario like the Covid situation, the need to publish the identity of affected persons is often discussed as to whether it is a violation of the privacy rights or not.

These are some of the issues that often make Public disagree with hard core Privacy Right supporters and the regulations need to balance the requirements of such disparate requirements under one platform.

In the past there have been many attempts to draft Privacy protection laws in India, but all such attempts have failed to be converted into a legislative act. But the latest attempt in the form of DPDPA has become a law.

Privacy Rights of Artificial Persons:

Today the "Right to Privacy" is recognized for individuals and not for Companies or organizations. "Privacy" of an organization is covered under other laws of "Information Security", "Protection of trade secrets and IPR", etc.

Even the identity parameters associated with individuals are distinguished as "Personal identity" and "Business Contact" to distinguish what is owned by the individual and what is owned by an employer.

In the coming days, Artificial intelligence is developing as a semi-intelligent species with ability to make cognitive observations, unsupervised learning and automated decision making. Whether such entities which may be algorithms or humanoid robots need to be recognized as "Artificial Individuals" with their own Privacy Rights will be a matter of debate in the future. Since at least in one instance, a humanoid robot, namely Sophia, manufactured by a Hong Kong firm has been bestowed with "Citizenship" of Saudi Arabia, and one humanoid robot has been appointed as the CEO of a company in USA, the possibility of the humanoid robots claiming their own privacy is not unthinkable.

Indian law such as Information Technology Act 2000 (ITA 2000) interprets activities of any automated software to the "Person who caused" the automated functioning and hence the responsibility for the actions of humanoid robots or automated software actions are attributed to a human being. Similarly, interpretation of any electronic document as judicially acceptable evidence is also made dependent on a human interpretation in the form of a certification. (Section 65B of Indian Evidence Act). Thus there is some clarity on the legal status of AI and AI led humanoid robots.

However, in the coming days there could be some "Due Diligence" responsibilities that may be hoisted on AI so that the society is not misled by a humanoid robot or an AI output.

We need to however be ready for different interpretations of current laws in the Tech Space as well as new laws coming up which disrupt our current understanding of what is Privacy and how it is to be protected.

Managerial Perspective of Data:

Perceiving data as an element of personal identity and a subject of Privacy Protection is the legal perspective of data. Perceiving data as a sequence of binaries is the technical perspective of data. However, for a business manager, "Data" is an asset which generates revenue to the organisation.

We often hear the statements like "Data is the new Oil" from the perspective of the tremendous unexplored financial benefits that an organization can derive from the processing of data.

Essentially there is an agreement that "Data" has financial value and hence is a business asset. It would be interesting to debate whether Data is a current asset or a fixed asset or both depending on the context.

Data can be considered as a "Fixed Asset" if it retains its form over a time (except for a depreciation over time) but helps in generating more value out of other business assets. For example, consider a social media company like Twitter. The main asset of twitter is the data which is in the form of tweets contributed by the customers. The vast amount of data aggregated and published on the twitter server attracts visitors. Visitors do not change the data but may add further data. As the data accumulates and visitors find it interesting to read, Twitter gets an opportunity to carry advertisements and make money out of the advertisements. In this context data is a fixed asset for Twitter which generates value out of the advertisements.

Similar value accretion occurs in any blog or website where articles accumulate, attract visitors and create value. In this process the original data (Tweets or the articles) does not change like a machine which churns out finished goods out of raw material. However, just as a Machine wears out over time and depreciates, the data on twitter or a blog may also lose public interest due to lapse of time when the interest of the visitors on the content wears out. This is like depreciation.

However, not all data is subject to depreciation. Some data such as say, "Artistic data", or "Scientific data" may actually gain value over time just as vintage cars gain a value larger than current functional cars. This could mean that even those assets which are like "Fixed assets" may have different rates of depreciation.

In an interesting case of "Vintage Value" of data, Jack Dorsey the founder of Twitter put his first tweet to auction which was sold for $2.9 million. In this instance the tweet remained in store as a fixed asset and was part of the content on which some advertising revenue was also generated. But when it was monetized and sold for $2.9 million, the data was converted to money. This was a case of a fixed asset which got some exceptional value because of its historical importance.

There are other cases where data becomes a "Current Asset" which is acquired in "Raw" form, processed and later sold as a "finished good". In such a scenario, data is like a current asset.

An example of Data as a current asset can be a case where a company collects some information from the market, makes an analysis and converts it into a research report and sells the research report to a company which uses it for selling its products or services.

Thus "Data" as an industrial asset can assume both the characteristic of a current asset or a fixed asset.

In the industry 4.0 scenario, we can visualize a shop floor with robotic arms undertaking the series of operations where the raw material is processed into a finished goods. In such a scenario, there is one set of data which is the software loaded onto the robotic arms and directs its operations. There is another set of data which is collected by the sensors attached to the robotic arms which send feedback to the central processor about the status of the operation, so that the central processor can issue further instructions. If the operation is a robotic lathe, the sensor in the tip of the tool will give feedback of the distance between the blade and the object being machined and accordingly adjusts its position. Similarly in a chemical process the sensors provide feedback on the temperature or viscosity of the processed material so that the process can be continued or stopped or modified.

The data which is loaded as software is like a fixed asset since it does not change over time but helps in the revenue generation. On the other hand, data which the sensors provide are like "Consumables" which have temporary but useful purpose.

Thus, processing of data is similar to processing of any other physical asset and in terms of valuation, it can be considered either as a current asset or as a fixed asset.

Virtual Nature of Asset:

Data asset has another interesting character which the industrial manager needs to appreciate. Data is a sequence of binaries which exist on a certain data holding surface. It may exist as a magnetic field at pixel levels on a surface of a hard disk or as pits and lands on the surface of a compact disc. But there is a dependency between the data as it exists and the surface which holds it.

If for any reason, the surface of a hard disk gets demagnetised, then data simply vanishes. We recognize this as "Corruption of data" in normal parlance. In managing data assets, we should therefore recognize the relationship between the data and the dependencies that it carries. Such dependency can be extended not only to the physical asset such as the hard disk but also to the software that can read that data and the operating system that can host the software.

Hence data as an asset exists along with the application and the hardware that is required to enable the data to be experienced by a human being.

For example, if we have a floppy disk containing data, and it is generated in an application which is no longer available, then the data may not be recognized by the system or there may be no hardware to run the container like the floppy disk. If we therefore have a data asset which was generated at a point of time, it is necessary for the organization to recognize that its value may suddenly come down to zero if the license for the required software expires or the technology changes and makes it difficult or impossible to read the data through the computer which is currently being used.

We should therefore always have the dependencies of data recognized and controls preserved for the contingent event of the technology changing.

Some of the above thoughts are presented to high light that the perspective of a Business Manager on what is data and how it is to be persevered etc may be different from what an IT expert or a Legal expert may have.

Managers by virtue of their decision-making positions in the organizations need to supervise and direct the technologists and legal experts in the company and the understanding of the existence of different perspectives will help in carrying all types of professionals along harmoniously.

Managerial View of Privacy:

While Privacy has emerged as a human right concept and merged into a Personal Information Security concept, in the corporate domain there has to be a perspective of the management on what is "Privacy" in business.

While colloquially, Privacy can be considered like "Confidentiality" of business aspects, the corporate data does not come under protection of data protection laws such as DPDPA or GDPR. They are to be covered under Intellectual Property laws or Cyber Crime laws.

Though the term "Data Privacy" is often used, it does not refer to "Protection of Data Per-se" but apply to the "Protection of Personal data for the purpose of protecting the Privacy of the person to whom the personal data belongs".

In the current business scenario, the managerial view of Privacy is as a "Risk" that needs to be managed to avoid the penalties associated with noncompliance of relevant laws. It is a Risk that needs to be estimated, insured to the extent possible and mitigated through "Compliance by Design".

The Indian law namely the Digital Personal Data Protection Act 2023 (DPDPA 2023) has recognized this aspect more clearly than any other law and hence not titled the Act as "Privacy Protection Act". At the same time the Bureau of Indian Standards (BIS) has come up with a draft Guidelines for Adequacy of Organizational Data Governance and Management Practices ("Data Governance and Management Standard") as a guidance to the industry to manage Data both for productivity as an asset and for protection in the context of business.

This book follows a pioneering approach by integrating the Data Governance with Data Protection in to one single requirement of Business since they are considered the twin goals of a data driven organization.

Chapter III

DPDPA 2023

Structure of DPDPA 2023:

India entered the set of around 130 of countries having Personal Data Protection legislations with passage of the DPDPA 2023 which got the Presidential assent on 11th August 2023.

This version of the law consists of 44 sections and is divided into IX chapters and a Schedule.

The structure of the Act is as follows.

Structure of DPDPA 2023

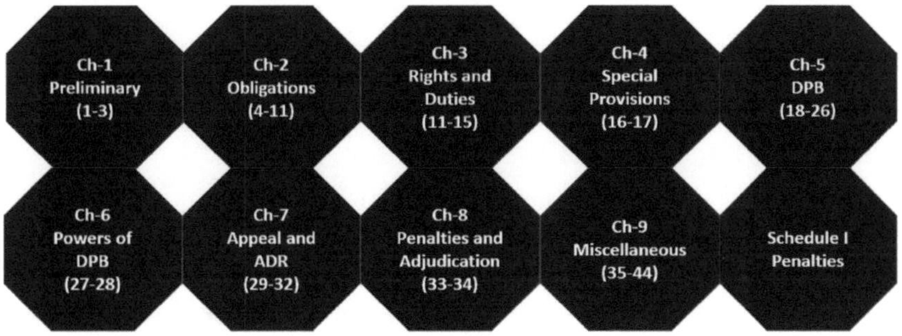

As can be observed, the Act is concise and simple compared to the earlier versions like PDPB 2018/2019/DPA2021 or the GDPR.

It can be stated that this law is a continuation of Information Technology Act 2000 (ITA 2000) which has been in existence since 17th October 2000 and has also been addressing Personal Data Protection since the amendments of 2008 since 27th October 2009. It has not been popularly recognized as a Data Protection law and is considered more a Cyber Crime prevention law, unlike DPDPA 2023.

Chapter	Sections	Descriptions
I	1-3	Preliminary
II	4-10	Obligations of the Data Fiduciary
III	11-15	Rights and Duties of the Data Principal
IV	16-17	Special Provisions
V	18-26	Data Protection Board of India
VI	27-28	Powers, Functions and Procedure to be followed by Board
VII	29-32	Appeal and Alternate Dispute Resolution
VIII	33-34	Penalties And Adjudication
IX	35-44	Miscellaneous
Schedule		Penalty

It is expected that there would be a series **of notifications** that will follow which will provide the detailed clarifications.

Preliminary:

The title of the Act in Section 1 which states that the Act may be called the "Digital Personal Data Protection Act 2023" clearly mentions the scope and the limitation of the Act.

The Nine Member bench of the Supreme Court which gave its decision that 'Privacy was a fundamental right' in India, refused to bite the bullet by defining what is Privacy. Hence it was not possible for the law makers to define what is Privacy and state that this law is meant to protect the Privacy of individuals. Instead of attempting the impossible, the Government has limited the scope of the Act stating that it is meant to protect Digital Personal Data.

In comparison, if we look at Article 1 of GDPR, it states that.

"This regulation (GDPR) lays down the rules relating to

a. The protection of natural persons with regard to the processing of personal data and

b. Rules relating to the free movement of personal data. "

Hence GDPR states that it protects "Right to protection of personal data" as a right by itself and makes it applicable to activities of a data subject in the EU region.

GDPR also promotes the business in the EU region stating that the free movement of personal data within the EU shall not be restricted for reasons connected with the protection of personal data of natural persons.

However, GDPR also has not given a definition of "Privacy" and most of the provisions of GDPR are related to the protection of Personal Data just like DPDPA 2023.

Instead of trying to make a law to protect a concept which cannot be defined easily, the Indian law has pitched itself as a law for managing of personal data in a manner which could be considered as required for protection of "Information Privacy" of an individual.

This is both a strength and limitation of the Act.

Section 1.2 of DPDPA states that the Act will come into force on such date as the Government may by notification appoint and different dates may be appointed for different provisions.

It is considered that the Act which has been published in the gazette for general information as of 11th August 2023 may be considered as having notified with effect from 11th August 2023 though it would have been better if the notification had been worded more specifically.

In the case of Information Technology Act 2000, (ITA 2000) it may be recalled that it was signed by the President on June 9, 2000, but the law was further notified for effectiveness on October 17, 2000. A similar approach is possible in the case of DPDPA 2023, and the Government may issue a notification of provisions becoming effective when they notify the constitution of the Data Protection Board (DPB).

In the event of any breach of personal data before the DPB is formed, we may consider that liabilities under ITA 2000 will be applicable but penalties under DPDPA may be considered only after DPB comes into existence.

Individual data principals can invoke adjudication under Section 46 recognizing the data breach under Section 43 or any other applicable sections of ITA 2000. Hence any delay in the publication of specific dates of effectiveness of DPDPA 2023 does not adversely affect the interest of the public. At best it may delay the imposition of fines as a deterrent to the noncompliance.

Applicability:

According to Section 3, the Indian Data Protection Act (DPDPA 2023) would be applicable to the processing of digital personal data within the territory of India where the personal data is collected—

i. in digital form; or

ii. in non-digital form and digitised subsequently.

It will also apply to processing of digital personal data outside the territory of India, if such processing is in connection with any activity **related to offering of goods or services to Data Principals** within the territory of India.

However, the Act will not apply to personal data processed by an individual for any personal or domestic purpose; and more importantly it will not apply to personal data that is made or caused to be made publicly available by the Data Principal or by any legal authority.

When data is processed outside India and not related to offering any goods or services to data principals in India, such processing is considered as out of scope of DPDPA 2023 even if the entity involved in the processing is established in India. Also processing of personal data of data principals outside India by a processor in India under a contract is exempt from some of the provisions of this Act.

Since the applicability of the Act is limited to "Digital Personal Data", it is important for us to recognize the definition of "personal data" under Section 2(t) and definition of "data" under section 2(h)

As per section 2(t), "Personal Data" means any data about an individual who is identifiable by or in relation to such data.

This means that any data which does not make the individual identifiable in relation to the data is not considered as "Personal Data".

It is obvious that "Anonymous Personal Data" including such data which was "identifiable personal data" before anonymization as well as the data which came to the hands of a person only in an "Anonymous" state or any kind of non-personal data does not come under the provisions of this Act.

According to the Act, data which is collected in non-digital form and subsequently digitized is also within this Act. It appears that if data obtained in physical space and used for making telephone calls in a digital network can be considered as data.

Personal data processed by an individual for any personal or domestic purpose is outside the scope of the Act. This means that personal data processed even by an individual can be within the provisions of this Act if the processing is for non-domestic purpose.

At this point we need to note that the word "Person" is used by the Act in two contexts. Firstly a "Person" could be a "Data Principal" and is subject to certain rights related to protection of his personal data. In another context a "Person" may be a data fiduciary who is processing the personal data of other data principals.

It would be incorrect to consider that personal data of a business entity owner as "Personal Data". We may however recognize a category of personal data as "Business Contact Data" which is personal data but shared for business contact purpose. The business contact personal data can be processed without a specific consent as a legitimate use for the business purpose. It is obvious that the same data will not be usable for a different purpose without a different consent.

A Business Contact data is not specifically defined but it is incorrect to consider that @gmail.com ID is always a personal email ID but @domain.com is always a business ID. The distinction is for the data principal to make. If I designate naavi9@gmail.com as my business email address, it must be considered as a business contact ID. If I designate abc@naavi.org as a personal email address, it must be considered as personal ID.

It is interesting to note that only such data which is made or caused to be made publicly by the data principal is considered as "Publicly available data". If personal data becomes available in public space without the data principal making it public, such data may be considered as coming within the Act.

It would be interesting to debate on what constitutes "Public Data", since the Act itself does not define what is Public Data. Generally, data can be considered public if it can be accessed by a person without restriction such as prior authorization. If there is any information the access to which is restricted by say a password and the person wanting to access is expected to make a request etc., it may not be considered as "Publicly Available". Such data would not be available even for search engines.

There are some data which is available for browsing on the web, but a search engine access is blocked with a "No Robot" code. Most of the websites also restrict the access through a mandatory requirement of acceptance of Cookies and some form of information provision. It is debatable whether websites which require acceptance of cookies before access can be considered as "Public".

Data such as what is available on social media websites such as Linked-in or Twitter or Face Book may appear to be publicly available data, but they would not allow parsing of the data or scraping of the data without specific licensing.

What is visible is not always to be considered as "Publicly Available". In most cases it would be better to seek confirmation from the data principal whether the data can be used for processing which is like seeking consent for further processing.

While looking at "Applicability" we may also remember that there are certain exemptions available for some data from some provisions of the Act. We shall discuss this separately since "Exempted" data is also within the "applicability" of the act and are exempted as part of the provisions of the Act itself.

Data to which the Act is not applicable remains outside the purview of the Act unless it changes its state once again and becomes a type of data to which the Act is applicable.

Before we go further, we need to also flag the issue of difference between an "Identifier" and "Identity". All identifiers are not identities and therefore are not "personal data". For data to be considered as "Personal" it should be capable of identifying an individual to whom the data relates. Hence a "Session Cookie" or a "Session IP address" do not in our opinion qualify as "Personal Data" though under GDPR it may be a common perception.

Definitions:

Section 2 of the Act covers definitions and some of the key definitions to be noted are as follows.

Person: Person as per Section 2(s) is defined as including

i. an individual;

ii. a Hindu undivided family;

iii. a company;

iv. a firm;

v. an association of persons or a body of individuals, whether incorporated or not;

vi. the State; and

vii. every artificial juristic person, not falling within any of the preceding sub-clauses.

This definition of a person is in the context of a person being a data fiduciary.

Personal Data:

The definition of personal data is not data related to the person as defined in section 2(s). Instead, personal data is defined separately under 2(t) as data about an individual who is identifiable by or in relation to such data. "Digital Personal data" is defined under Section 2(n) as personal data in digital form.

"Digital Form" is not defined in the Act, but "Data" is defined under Section 2(h) a representation of information, facts, concepts, opinions or instructions in a manner suitable for communication, interpretation or processing by human beings or by automated means.

This definition appears to cover both data in digital form and non-digital form, and we do not know if this was intentional since the rest of the Act applies only to "Digital Personal Information" and there is no specific definition of "Digital Form" such as data in binary form or data suitable for processing by a computer like the definition used in ITA 2000.

We may have to derive the meaning of "Digital Form" from the section 2(b) which defines the word "Automated" as any digital process capable of operating automatically in response to instructions given or otherwise for the purpose of processing data.

This definition uses the word "Operating automatically in response to instructions given" which seem to define a software but the words that follow namely "Or otherwise" introduces an element of ambiguity which needs to clarify over time.

The critical word used in the definition of personal data is "Individual".

The act at present does not indicate that the "Individual" should be "Living". Hence it may be in order for us to interpret that this Act may apply to the personal data of deceased persons. More on this would be discussed in a subsequent chapter on "Rights of Nomination".

The Individual who is the subject matter of personal data processed by another agency is referred to as the "Data Principal".

Under Section 2(j),

"Data Principal" means the individual to whom the personal data relates and where such individual is—

i. a child, includes the parents or lawful guardian of such a child;

ii. a person with disability, includes her lawful guardian, acting on her behalf.

In the case of a Child which according to section 2(f) means an individual who has not completed the age of eighteen years, the Act recognizes the parent as not simply as a representative of the minor but as the "Joint Data Principal". This treatment is extended to the legal guardians of a person with disability.

This treatment of a Minor and his guardian being "Joint Data Principals" introduces some unique jurisprudential principles as to how the data under process can be treated at the transition time when a minor turns

18 years when the parental consent should cease and a new consent from the erstwhile minor who is now a major has to be taken. During this time there could be a need to discontinue processing of the data of the erstwhile minor. However, if the data of the erstwhile minor is considered as also the data of the guardian, there would be no discontinuity. The Government may specify a reasonable period of time when the consent may be switched in future notifications.

A "Data fiduciary" is defined under 2(i) as any person who alone or in conjunction with other persons determines the purpose and means of processing of personal data; In contrast, a Data Processor is defined under 2(k) as any person who processes personal data on behalf of a Data Fiduciary.

It is presumed that the "Data Processor" does not determine either the purpose or means of processing. In cases where one person determines the purpose and another the means of processing, they should be considered as "Joint Data Fiduciaries".

It must be noted however that the recognition of a person as "Data Fiduciary" or "Data Processor" is in the context of a "Process" involving personal data and it is possible that the same person can be a data fiduciary in one context and a data fiduciary in another context.

Hence the obligation under the Act has to be applied "Process wise" and cannot be applied as a common implementation across the enterprise.

The word "Fiduciary" indicates a trustee like responsibility which is far wider than the meaning of the term "Data Controller" used in GDPR and many other international data protection laws. In Jurisprudential terms this has the effect of imparting responsibility for a Data Fiduciary to take decisions which protect the data principal when the law is unclear or the situation on the ground requires an out of box decision.

The Act also defines two other categories of "Data Fiduciaries" namely the "Significant Data Fiduciary" and the "Consent manager". The criteria for recognizing a data fiduciary as a "Significant Data Fiduciary" as per section 2(z) will be notified later under Section 10.

A "Consent Manager" is defined under Section 2(g) as follows:

"Consent Manager" means a person registered with the Board, who acts as a single point of contact to enable a Data Principal to give, manage, review and withdraw consent through an accessible, transparent and interoperable platform.

The exact nature of the "Consent Manager" whether it will be only a "Platform", in which case it will also be an "Intermediary" under ITA 2000 or be an organization that will use the "platform" as a tool and act as a Data fiduciary by itself will be clear when the Government comes out with the necessary guidelines.

In the definition clause there are definitions related to the "Board", "Chairperson", "Member", "Digital office" which are related to the Data Protection Board.

There is also a definition of "State", as defined under article 12 of the Constitution. Under this definition, the term "State" includes the government and Parliament of India, the government and Legislature of each of the states, and all local or other authorities within the territory of India or under the control of the Government of India. In other words, local authorities like the Municipal bodies and Corporations may also be considered as "State" under this Act.

The term "Appellate Tribunal" has been defined to mean the "Telecom Disputes Settlement and Appellate Tribunal" (TDSAT) and there is no other special Appellate Tribunal or Adjudication authority under the Act.

An important definition that we should take note of is the definition of "Processing" under Section 2(x) which is defined as under

"processing" in relation to personal data, means a wholly or partly automated operation or set of operations performed on digital personal data, and includes operations such as collection, recording, organisation, structuring, storage, adaptation, retrieval, use, alignment or combination, indexing, sharing, disclosure by transmission, dissemination or otherwise making available, restriction, erasure or destruction.

The term “legitimate use” is separately defined with reference to list of activities indicated under Section 7.

The word “Specified Purpose” is defined to mean the purpose mentioned in the notice given by a data fiduciary at the time of collection of personal data.

The Act takes pride in using the term “she” in relation to an individual includes the reference to such individual irrespective of gender.

The section 2(o) and 2(p) define the terms “gain” and “loss” and replace the definition of the term “Harm” which was present in earlier versions of the law.

Accordingly, “gain” means:

i. a gain in property or supply of services, whether temporary or permanent; or

ii. an opportunity to earn remuneration or greater remuneration or to gain a financial advantage otherwise than by way of legitimate remuneration.

and “loss” means:

i. a loss in property or interruption in supply of services, whether temporary or permanent; or

ii. a loss of opportunity to earn remuneration or greater remuneration or to gain a financial advantage otherwise than by way of legitimate remuneration.

This definition seems to ignore the need to define the nature of adverse impact on a data principal in terms of “loss of reputation” or “mental harassment" or "psychological manipulation" etc. This can only be justified under the premise that this law is meant to discipline the industry and any remedy expected by an individual data principal has to be provided by other laws such as ITA 2000 or IPC.

Similarly the lack of definition of the term "Sensitive Personal Information" which is a common term used in many data protection laws as also in the Section 43A of ITA 2000 which is now replaced with this Act needs to be justified by considering that the definition of Significant Data Fiduciary can take into account "Sensitivity" of personal data and hence the need to define special obligations can be incorporated by defining a data fiduciary processing a certain type of sensitive information as a significant data fiduciary. This could obviate the need for first defining "Sensitive Personal Information" and then say data fiduciaries handing sensitive personal information are significant data fiduciaries.

Though we often do not recognize the "Definitions" clause, from the point of view of "Jurisprudence" particularly in a new law, it is important to study "Definitions" in depth since it would be necessary to interpret many other aspects of the law.

Chapter IV

Obligations of a Data Fiduciary: Notice and Consent

The essence of DPDPA 2023 is to ensure that personal data is collected and processed by the industry in a manner that meets the requirements of protection of the right to privacy of individuals.

We have already discussed that the "Right to Privacy" is a right which as "Information Privacy" boils down to enabling that personal data is processed in accordance with the choice of an individual and in a manner that is not detrimental to the individual's interest.

In order to regulate the industry, DPDPA imposes certain obligations on entities involved in data processing and also simultaneously guarantees some rights to the individuals. The rights guaranteed to the individuals also translates as obligations on the data processing industry apart from providing a mechanism to the data principals to exercise their rights.

It would not be incorrect to state that DPDPA is more a Data Processing industry Regulation Act than a Privacy Protection Act. The principle followed is that if the Data Processing as an activity is regulated properly then the protection of Privacy should follow.

For the purpose of such regulation, Data Processors are classified into different types.

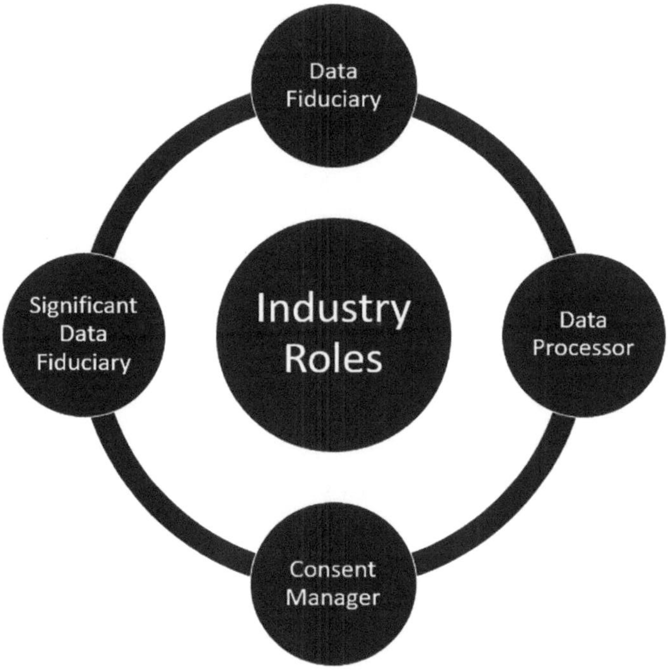

Once Data processors are able to distinguish between what is "Personal Data" and "What is Not Personal Data", they need to self-introspect on what they are doing with the Personal Data.

Those entities who determine the purpose and means of processing of personal data are termed as "Data Fiduciaries". Those entities who only process data as per the instructions of another entity which determines the purpose and means of processing are called "Data Processors".

In certain processing situations more than one entity may determine the purpose of processing and share the personal data collected from a pool or one entity may determine the purpose, but the means of processing may be determined by another entity. In such cases there may be "Joint Data Fiduciaries" in the transaction.

All Data Fiduciaries are however also "Data Processors" since "Processing" includes collection, storage, any kind of juggling with the personal data or even its disclosure or destruction/deletion.

Within the activity of an entity and its relationship with other entities there may be situations where for one process entity A may determine the purpose and means, and entity B may execute the processing and, in another process, B may determine the purpose and A may execute the processing. In a third process both A and B may determine the purpose and/or means.

Hence when we look at the organizational level the status of Fiduciary or Processor or Joint Fiduciary are based on the process.

One example could be that A has a business for which it collects some personal data and engages the services of B for processing as required by him and returning it back to A. In this case A is the Data Fiduciary and B is the Data Processor.

In the same case after processing, A requests and authorizes B to manage the storage of data in its cloud server and means of securing the data being at his discretion. As a manager of stored data B becomes the Data Fiduciary for the Data Store Management which may involve encryption, creating users, granting credentials for users, withdrawing the credentials etc. In another instance A wants the data to be processed for a given purpose but how exactly it is to be done is determined by B who is a having necessary expertise and a proprietary software. B therefore offers that he will process the data in his own way for the purpose determined by A, but the means of processing will be his trade secret. In such case A and B are both data fiduciaries while for data management services B may be alone a data fiduciary and A may take the role of a data processor.

Whenever we use the term Data Fiduciary or Data Processor therefore, we must speak in reference to a context of a specific process.

Just as an entity may be both a Data Fiduciary and a Data Processor in different process contexts, an individual can be a Data Principal as well as a Data Fiduciary or a Data Processor in different circumstances. For example, as a subject of personal data, an individual is a data principal. But if an individual processes personal data of others for non-domestic purposes or business purpose, he may be a data processor. If he also determines the purpose and/or means of processing of personal data, then he can also be a Data Fiduciary.

Chapter II of the DPDPA 2023 under Sections 4-10 discusses the "Obligations of a Data Fiduciary" and Chapter III of DPDPA 2023 under Sections 11-14 discusses the rights of a data fiduciary which also have to be considered as the obligation of the data fiduciary. It is also a right of the Data Principal to expect Data Fiduciaries to meet the obligations under Sections 5-11 of the Act and hence we can look at sections 5-14 as determining both the obligations of a data fiduciary as well as the rights of the data principal.

Section 15 under Chapter III provides that Data Principals shall have certain duties while exercising their rights.

DPDPA imposes all obligations on the Data Fiduciary and any obligation of a Data Processor is through a contract which the Data fiduciary has to enter into with the Data Processor.

Grounds of Processing (Section 4):

The most important obligation of a Data Fiduciary is indicated under Section 4 which provides that.

a person may process the personal data of a data principal only in accordance with the provisions of this Act and for a lawful purpose for which the data principal has given a consent or for purposes which are declared as "Legitimate users".

For the purpose of this section, "Lawful purpose" means any purpose which is not expressly forbidden by law.

This principle is called establishing the "Ground for processing digital personal data" and is considered the fundamental aspect of compliance.

To meet this obligation, an organization needs to first identify if it is processing "Digital Personal Data" and if so whether he is processing it either under a "Consent" or as a "Legitimate use".

Every organization even if it is not collecting the personal data of outsiders, have the personal data of its employees. In the case of manufacturing employees having a retail store or e-commerce operations, there could be personal data of customers who visit their stores or visit their websites or those individuals who buy or sell goods or services. Some of these customers may be non-individuals in which case as a B2B transaction their information is not considered as "Personal Data".

In data generated through a "Transaction", two parties are involved in generation of data. Hence when an entity A sells some goods to an individual B, the transaction contains the name, address and phone number of an individual which is a personal data, but it is also associated with the information that A sold so may units for so many rupees with such and such a discount, a delivery schedule etc. If we consider the entire data set, it is a "Transaction data set" which belongs to both the parties. Hence the customer cannot ask for say deletion of his personal data immediately after the sale as a matter or right saying that he gave the information for the purpose of delivery and now that the delivery is over, the data has to be deleted.

In such cases the "Personal Data" and "Business Data" may be intertwined and both parties may have legitimate use of the data for a certain period of time and hence the rights over the transaction data must be considered as belonging to both. In a way the entire data set can be considered as "Business Data" rather than splitting it to business data of one and personal data of the other. This principle is yet to be widely accepted and must be recognized as debatable at this point of time.

A similar situation arises when data represents a conversation between two persons or a group. Such data cannot be considered as an exclusive data of one of the participants to a discussion and must be considered as belonging to all jointly and severally.

The meaning of "Digital" has to be drawn from the ITA 2000 and we may consider any data which is in such form as being capable of being processed by a computer as "Digital Data". Since Computers can process data in binary language, binary expressions are considered as "Digital data".

In DPDPA, data which is manual but later digitized is also within the scope of the Act. ITA 2000 has a more comprehensive definition of digital/ electronic document and any document which is meant to be processed or is being processed or has been processed by a computer is considered as "Digital Document". Hence a printout or even an OCR sheet can be considered digital data under ITA 2000. Under DPDPA, the OCR sheet containing personal data may still not be under the scope of the Act, but a printout certainly is.

The third aspect addressed by section 4 is whether the purpose of processing of personal data can be considered "Lawful" or "Unlawful". DPDPA considers whatever is not expressly forbidden by law as "Lawful".

The concept of "Consent" and "Legitimate use" is covered separately under other sections.

Notice (Section 5) and Consent (Section 6):

"Notice" and "Consent" are the foundation pillars of protecting privacy of an individual. Consent records the choice of an individual. A consent is not a good consent if the notice is not proper. Hence, we speak of "Informed Consent" where the data principal or the subject receive complete information about the consequences of sharing the personal data with another entity and allowing its process in a given manner.

"Consent" is also dependent on the "Obligations" and the "Rights" that are prescribed in a given law which should get reflected in the communication of the notice and obtaining of the consent.

Section 6 of DPDPA simply says that a,

Consent given by the Data Principal shall be free, specific, informed, unconditional and unambiguous with a clear affirmative action and shall signify an agreement to the processing of her personal data for the specified purpose and be limited to such personal data as is necessary for such specified purpose.

If we try to derive the definition of "Consent" from the above, we can say that "Consent" is a communication of the data principal agreeing to the processing of the personal data for a specified purpose with certain conditions.

The conditions attached to a consent are that it should be purpose oriented and only such personal data as is necessary for the purpose should be processed.

"Consent" should be given through an "Affirmative" action which means that there has to be some gesture that indicates the consent. The word "Free" "informed" and "Signify an agreement" can be interpreted as a requirement that the Data Principal should not be under any obligation such as "Threat", "Coercion", "Undue Influence" or induced by "Mis representation" or "Fraud" and that there should be a "meeting of minds" where the data principal is aware about why the consent is being given and how it is going to be made use of.

The Notice under Section 5 supports the Consent since it has to provide the "Information" necessary for the data principal to take the free decision as to whether he should provide the consent for processing or not.

The Notice under DPDPA 2023 is very simple and essential speaks of just three requirements. Other than the need to inform the Data Principal the manner in which the rights guaranteed under the Act for a Data Principal may be exercised and how a complaint may be filed with the regulatory authority, if need be, the notice is essentially a list of what is the purpose for which the personal data is collected.

When the purpose is indicated, it automatically puts the boundaries on what information is required for the purpose, how long it will be required to be kept. These are often referred to as "Data Minimisation" and "Data Retention Limitation". Though some of the other laws specifically list out the "Data Processing principles" that includes "Data Minimization", "Data Retention", "Data quality", "accountability", "Security" etc., DPDPA 2023 subtly brings in all good practices by using the term "Fiduciary" for the entity that is called a "Controller" by GDPR. Since a "Data Fiduciary" is a "Trustee", an expectation that a "Trustee" will take all steps which are reasonably necessary to safeguard the interest of the data principal would be taken by the Data Fiduciary.

Section 5 makes it mandatory that,

"Every request made to a Data Principal under section 6 for consent shall be accompanied or preceded by a notice given by the Data Fiduciary" informing the data principal the data processed and the purpose.

It is expected that the data Principal shall be given an option to access the notice in English or any language specified in the Eight Schedule of the Constitution.

Section 5(2) also indicates that,

"Where a Data Principal has given her consent for the processing of her personal data before the date of commencement of this Act, the Data Fiduciary shall, as soon as it is reasonably practicable, give to the Data Principal a notice..."

However,

"the Data Fiduciary may continue to process the personal data until and unless the Data Principal withdraws the consent".

This ensures that if the data principal does not expressly withdraw the consent, the data fiduciary may continue processing.

However, it may be necessary for the Data Fiduciary to make a reasonable effort to reach out to the data principal with a suitable notice and keep a record that the notice has been given and no withdrawal has been received back.

The notice shall be presented in clear and plain language providing the contact details of the Data Protection Officer or any other contact person who can be reached out for grievance redressal.

If any part of the consent is in violation of the Act or any other law, then that part of the consent would be considered as invalid. In other words, consent given by the data principal would not be valid if it is unconscionable or in violation of any law.

Consequences of Withdrawal of Consent:

It may be observed that in case of withdrawal of consent the ease of withdrawal has to be similar to the ease of giving the consent.

When the consent given is allowed to be withdrawn, section 6 of the Act also states that the consequences of withdrawal will be borne by the data principal and such processing will not affect the legality of processing of the personal data based on consent before its withdrawal.

Consent Manager:

DPDPA has recognized that the quality of consent often depends on the clarity of the notice and ability of the data principal to understand the implications of providing consent to the purpose for which the fiduciary would like to process the personal data and the means of processing proposed.

When a data principal is trying to download a mobile app or avail a certain service, he is often in a hurry to go through the consent process and is confronted with "Consent fatigue" which makes him accept permissions without understanding its full implications. Data Fiduciaries also often mis-represent and use dark-patterns of communication that misleads the less informed data principal.

India also has the problem of languages and lack of education of the data principals which also may make it difficult for data principals to take an informed decision about permissions.

Taking into these universal problems of consent, DPDPA has proposed that Consent may be provided by trusted agencies of the data principals who will be called "Consent Managers". These consent managers will be "accountable" to the data principals and act as their trusted agents. They are not agents of the data fiduciaries.

According to section 6(9), Every Consent Manager shall be registered with the Board in such manner and subject to such technical, operational, financial and other conditions as may be prescribed.

This indicates that they may be registered as a separate category of data fiduciaries and the Government may prescribe separate obligations for them including the financial requirements for such organizations.

Under the Account Aggregator framework introduced by RBI to enable sharing of financial data for purposes such as KYC like an "Intermediary" which receives request for a certain data from data requesters and transmits it to the data providers, fetch the data and transfer it to the data requester.

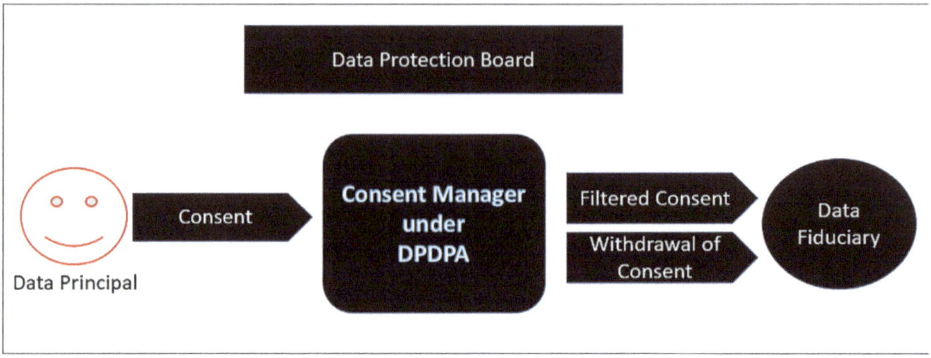

The concept of consent manager under DPDPA is different from the concept used in the Account aggregator framework and is better represented by the following diagram.

Under DPDPA, Consent manager is more like the "Certifying Authority" under ITA 2000. It is an organization with certain technical capabilities and probably with prescribed financial strength such as minimum net worth and capital etc. Like in the case of the Certifying authorities, the Consent Managers need to be regulated so that they do not take the personal data of the public and vanish one day or merge with another foreign entity transferring the effective control of the personal data to another organization, without an opportunity for the data principal to withdraw his mandate and shift his personal data to another consent manager.

We may recall that we have earlier seen a similar instance where under the patronage of RBI, the credit information sharing mechanism such as CIBIL was set up an organization promoted by several Indian Banks. Without any disclosure during one period the equity stakes of Indian Banks were transferred to the US private company namely Trans Union and over 500 million sets of personal data came under the control of the TransUnion CIBIL which is a private US company registered at NY-SE.

In the case of Certifying Authorities there is a restriction that companies need to be registered in India, need to have certain minimum equity capital and minimum net worth and cannot be closed overnight, besides the needs of technical ability, security etc.

A similar condition has to be laid for Consent Managers under DPDPA so that they do not become "Data Laundering" mechanisms through transfer of shareholding.

On the other hand, if the Consent Managers have the right intention of protecting the privacy of "Data Principals", they can provide value added services and ensure that release of personal data of data fiduciaries is regulated by a strict filtering of the consent request and evaluation of the notice. They can also release information based on pseudonymization or anonymization where it would suffice the purpose and provide such services to the data principal.

The "Virtual Aadhar" service of UIDAI could be one example of service that can be replicated by a Consent Manager for which the data fiduciaries need to seek personal information through an API and the Consent manager will release only such information which is required. It can follow the purpose, the end of purpose and exercise withdrawal of consent.

Consent Managers can also ensure that at the data principal's side they can maintain a good KYC and also educate them to get quality consents using the services of "Consent Registration Agents".

Consent Managers can ask questions about the Compliance maturity of the data fiduciaries and ensure that there is discipline in the use of personal data. They can also manage the Grievances of the Data Principal with the Data Fiduciary and take it further either to the Data Protection Board or to the Adjudicator under Information Technology Act.

There is no doubt that the Consent Manager will be an organization where risks will be concentrated and hence, they need to manage the security better than the best data fiduciary.

If properly structured the Consent Manager business would be an interesting proposition where it will become a repository of personal information of the citizens and prevent misuse of personal data by clever manipulation of notice by the Data Fiduciaries.

Onus of Proof for Consent:

According to Section 6(10) of the Act, where a consent given by the Data Principal is the basis of processing of personal data, when a dispute arises in this regard, the Data Fiduciary shall be obliged to prove that a notice was given, and consent was obtained in accordance with the provisions of this Act.

Chapter V

Obligations of Data Fiduciaries-Legitimate Use

While Consent is a mandatory obligation of a data fiduciary in the DPDPA 2023, the Act recognizes that there could be several circumstances in which there would be a requirement for processing of personal data either before a consent is in place or consent cannot be obtained.

Under GDPR, the establishment of legal basis itself is indicated as "Consent" plus five "Other situations" namely.

a. When processing is considered necessary for the performance of a contract to which the data subject is party or in order to take steps at the request of the data subject prior to entering into a contract;

b. When processing is necessary for compliance with a legal obligation to which the controller is subject;

c. When processing is necessary in order to protect the vital interests of the data subject or of another natural person;

d. When processing is necessary for the performance of a task carried out in the public interest or in the exercise of official authority vested in the controller;

e. When processing is necessary for the purposes of the **legitimate interests** pursued by the controller or **by a third party**, except where such interests are overridden by the interests or fundamental rights and freedoms of the data subject which require protection of personal data, in particular where the data subject is a child.

GDPR uses the term "Legitimate Interest" as one of the six ways by which lawfulness of processing can be established. Here the "Legitimate Interest" of either the data controller or by a third party can be used for processing personal data without consent or other reasons for processing. It is essential that when "legitimate interest" is used as a legal basis, care has to be taken to ensure that no other option is available and also that the processing does not adversely affect the interest of fundamental rights of the citizens.

The Indian law however uses the term "Legitimate Use" in a slightly different manner. It is the list of uses for which personal data may be processed without an explicit notice-based consent either by the data principal himself or by a consent manager on behalf of the data principal.

The purposes for which the "Legitimate Use Argument" can be applied are.

a. Voluntary provision of personal data by the data principal

b. Processing by the State for providing citizen benefits.

c. Processing by the State for National Security reasons

d. For meeting legal obligations

e. For compliance with any judgements

f. Medical emergencies

g. For Medical reasons during epidemic

h. During disaster Management situations

i. For the purposes of employment or those related to safeguarding the employer from loss or liability, such as prevention of corporate espionage, maintenance of confidentiality of trade secrets, intellectual property, classified information or provision of any service or benefit sought by a Data Principal who is an employee.

Any organization that would like to use the "Legitimate Use" clause for processing needs to have a clear understanding of the scope of applying of the sub clauses and avoid any misinterpretation which may render any processing as "Without appropriate legal basis".

Hence, we need to study each of these sub clauses in detail and organizations need to develop a clear "Legitimate Use Policy" to guide its employees in understanding what is a legitimate use and what is not.

1. Legitimate use on Voluntary Provision Basis:

The first legitimate use purpose indicated under Section7(a) is that personal data may be processed.

for the specified purpose for which the Data Principal has voluntarily provided her personal data to the Data Fiduciary, and in respect of which she has not indicated to the Data Fiduciary that she does not consent to the use of her personal data.

Two illustrations are also provided in the act itself to clarify this "Voluntary provision" concept namely.

I. X, an individual, makes a purchase at Y, a pharmacy. She voluntarily provides Y her personal data and requests Y to acknowledge receipt of the payment made for the purchase by sending a message to her mobile phone. Y may process the personal data of X for the purpose of sending the receipt.

II. X, an individual, electronically messages Y, a real estate broker, requesting Y to help identify a suitable rented accommodation for her and shares her personal data for this purpose. Y may process her personal data to identify and intimate to her the details of accommodation available on rent. Subsequently, X informs Y that X no longer needs help from Y. Y shall cease to process the personal data of X.

In either of the illustration, it is the individual who makes the first move and provides the data with a request of a service with the use of this data such as the phone number to which the message may be sent. The distinction with the "Notice-Consent" basis and "Voluntary provision basis" is that in the case of Notice-Consent the initiator of the request for transfer of personal data is the data fiduciary while in the case of the "Voluntary Provision Basis", the initiator is the data principal.

In contract situations we often differentiate an "Offer" from "Request for offer". Similarly Voluntary provision is an "Offer" of personal data while "Notice" is a "Request for offer". The difference is very subtle and fraught with the risk of the data principal contending that he/she felt that the service (acknowledgement in the illustration) would not be available without the provision of the information and hence there was an element of compulsion in providing the information. The shopkeeper could have told, we do not acknowledge the receipt of the payment, but you can come back tomorrow and enquire if we have received the payment. In such a case the data principal would find that the option of providing the personal information is obviously forced.

On the other hand, if we consider that this situation is similar to a "Oral Notice" and "Oral consent" it would be fit in more appropriately to the "Notice-Consent" mechanism. Even in a situation where a Privacy Notice is available on a website, it is the Visitor who walks into the website and reads the notice. In a way he/she is the first mover to visit the website and ask for what is your privacy policy and receive it in a document which may be titled either as "Privacy Policy" or "Privacy Notice".

Hence the "Voluntary Provision" may be considered as "Oral Notice and Acceptance" with all the limitations attached to the possibility of some details being missed.

There will be no documentation for such "Oral notice and consent" and hence proving that the consent was there on a later date when the data principal contends that she has not given the consent voluntarily but was forced to oblige in the absence of any other way of the service being received would be difficult.

The data fiduciaries in the situations similar to the illustration are better off by printing a "Privacy Notice" on the back of the bill as has been customary for the terms of service taking care that they are not accused of using a "Fine Print". Alternatively, a prominent notice on the store front could be used to ensure that the customer has received the message.

In practice most stores have "Loyalty incentives" for their customers and the register of members for this purpose is maintained on the basis of the mobile number more than the name. Hence there can be a written consent obtained for the "Loyalty incentive scheme" which will make the use of the vague "Voluntary Provision" redundant.

2. Legitimate use by the State for Governance:

The second legitimate use provided under DPDPA is directed towards the "State" and any "Instrumentalities of the State".

Under Article 12 of the Constitution, "State" includes the Government and Parliament of India and the Government and the Legislature of each of the States and all local or **other authorities** within the territory of India or under the control of the Government of India.

By "Other authorities" we mean authorities who have the power to make rules, regulations etc having force of law. According to Supreme Court the following five tests are laid down to define "Other authority".

1. Entire share capital is owned or managed by State.
2. Enjoys monopoly status.
3. Department of Government is transferred to Corporation.

4. Functional character governmental in essence.
5. Deep and pervasive State control.
6. Object of Authority

A Data Fiduciary which is a "State" and any of its instrumentalities may process personal data under the "Legitimate use clause to provide or issue to the Data Principal such subsidy, benefit, service, certificate, licence or permit as may be prescribed, where—

i. the data principal has previously consented to the processing of her personal data by the State or any of its instrumentalities for any subsidy, benefit, service, certificate, licence or permit; or
ii. such personal data is available in digital form in, or in non-digital form and digitised subsequently from, any database, register, book or other document which is maintained by the State or any of its instrumentalities and is **notified** by the Central Government, subject to standards followed for processing being in accordance with the **policy** issued by the Central Government or any law for the time being in force for governance of personal data.

According to the above provision the Government may notify any digital data and a policy for its processing or prescribe a standard for processing of personal information by the State and its instrumentalities.

The National Data Governance Policy (NDGP) of the Government a draft of which was issued in 2022 and is set to be updated with a new policy which addresses "Anonymization" of personal data could be one such policy which may apply to the processing of notified personal data by the State.

Though the NDGP may be more directed towards Non-Personal Data Governance, the intersection of NDGP with Personal Data would be in the area of "Anonymized Personal Data". Globally there is a debate on whether "Anonymization" of personal data is a type of "Processing of Personal Data" which requires consent of the data principal. One school of thought has an opinion that "Anonymization" is a "reversible process" and hence is a threat to the privacy of the individual.

However, it is necessary to differentiate the processing which is referred to as "Anonymization" from two other processes called "De-Identification" and "Pseudonymisation", both of which are also processes on identifiable personal data and convert them into forms of usage where the privacy of the underlying individuals is protected to a certain extent.

De-identification is a process where the identifiers attached to a core identity of personal data constituting the full set of personal data are removed and a common data ID is introduced to carry the non-personally identifiable part of the total data set. The de-identified data can be effectively used as a "Limited Data Set" for many purposes including research and archival. It can also be used for marketing purpose as long as it is not meant to be used for individually targeted marketing. The mapping data between the fully identified information set and the truncated set is kept separate and can be used for re-building the identified full set of the data if required.

Similarly, in "Pseudonymisation", each of the identifiers are substituted by similar data elements randomly so that the resulting data set appears similar to the original real data set but is not identifiable with the real data principals and therefore protects their privacy. In this case unlike the de-identification which substitutes a set of identifiers with a single master ID, each identifier will have a mapping to a proxy identifier. Mapping of this is also kept separately and can be used for re-identification.

Since the character of the data set is not altered in the pseudonymisation processing, the resulting data set can be used in the existing processes without altering them. For example, if the processing of a particular data column is on the presumption that the data would be a 12-digit numerical, the pseudonymized element will also be a 12-digit numerical and not a hash value or an alphanumeric value.

In the "Anonymization" process the identity mapping of the original identifiers and the proxy identities are destroyed in such a manner that it is no longer available even to the person who carried out the anonymization in the first place under appropriate "Data Deletion Standards".

In such circumstances an anonymised personal data becomes "Non-Personal Data" and can be further processed accordingly.

The question of whether "Anonymisation" requires consent can be answered by considering "Anonymisation" as a process that is accompanied by "Deletion" of identifiable personal data. If "Deletion of Personal data" is considered as "an obligation after the end of the purpose for which data was collected" or "on withdrawal of consent", "Anonymisation" may be considered as equivalent to "Deletion" since the process ensures that the original personal data to be deleted is no longer available as personal data.

Hence "Deletion" of data can be considered as "Making the data unavailable in the form in which it is presently available" and in that context, anonymization can be considered as removal of personal data from processing as personal data and does not require specific consent. Request for deletion of personal data or an obligation to delete personal data is a sufficient requirement that can enable a data fiduciary to use anonymisation instead of deletion and fulfil his legal obligation.

There is an argument that anonymisation of personal data can be re-identified though data analytics and hence it is not equivalent to deletion. However, by this stretch of imagination, even deletion of data is reversible and hence there are standards of deletion to render irreversibility of deleted data. If any person takes efforts to un-delete a deleted data or decrypt an encrypted data or re-identify an anonymised data, it must be considered as an unauthorized modification of data equivalent to a punishable offence under ITA 2000.

These elements of "Anonymisation" can be considered as a "Policy" under which State may be allowed to use personal data under "Legitimate use".

3. Legitimate use by state for National Security:

In addition to the above functional use of personal data for Governance purpose, State and any of its instrumentalities may also apply the legitimate use concept for processing personal data under any law for the time being in force in India or in the interest of sovereignty and integrity of India or security of the State.

This follows the principle of "Reasonable exemption" under Article 19(2) of the Indian Constitution which is extended to all "Fundamental Rights" including the fundamental right of Privacy under Article 21.

Apart from the reasons of sovereignty and integrity of the state under this clause, there are other exemptions under Section 17 which are available for some additional purposes of law enforcement which we shall discuss separately.

4. Legitimate use by any Data Fiduciary for legal obligation:

Yet another recognized legitimate use of processing of personal data without consent is for fulfilling any obligation under any law to disclose any information to the State or any of its instrumentalities, subject to such processing being in accordance with the provisions regarding disclosure of such information in any other law for the time being in force.

Excepting for specific provision such as in the case of Right to Information Act as per Section 44, if any other law requires disclosure of any data as in the case of Criminal Procedure Code where an authority has sought data, it is a legitimate use to fulfil such an obligation.

Hence all disclosure obligations under ITA 2000 under Sections 69,69A,69B,or 70B are covered under this "Legitimate Use" clause.

5. Legitimate use for processing by any data fiduciary for Judicial Purpose:

Legitimate use of processing can also be as a basis by all Data fiduciaries for compliance with any judgment or decree or order issued under any law for the time being in force in India, or any judgment or order relating to **claims of a contractual or civil nature under any law for the time being in force outside India**.

This section appears to provide an un-warranted recognition to extra territorial judicial authorities.

Normally if there is any order of an authority from outside India, the execution of the decree of the order is done through a local authority. This section appears to provide an exception to this rule and includes claims of Contractual or Civil nature adjudicated under any law for the time being in force outside India.

We do not know if the Government wanted to provide easy means of recovery related to "Arbitration" awards from outside India. However, Arbitration may be held outside India, but the operating law may be either Indian law or otherwise. It is surprising that this section seems to blindly accept the rule of law of another country at least to the limited extent of enabling processing of personal data without consent.

One possible spillover of this provision is that if there is a request for processing of personal data of Indians by an external judicial authority or a Contractual beneficiary, the data fiduciary may process the data without specific consent.

If therefore an Indian company enters into a Contract with a website which is subject to laws outside India and there is a claim from that website which requires the processing of personal data of Indian Citizens, this provision seems to suggest that there is no need for specific consent.

This provision may need to be clarified by the Government in due course or suitably modified.

The constitutionality of these provisions is however likely to be read down by the Supreme Court sooner or later.

6. Legitimate Use of Processing in Emergencies:

The legitimate use as a basis of processing without consent is also applicable in emergency situations such as

a. for responding to a medical emergency involving a threat to the life or immediate threat to the health of the Data Principal or any other individual.

b. for taking measures to provide medical treatment or health services to any individual during an epidemic, outbreak of disease, or any other threat to public health.

c. for taking measures to ensure safety of, or provide assistance or services to, any individual during any disaster, or any breakdown of public order.

These are measures that are essential under public safety considerations. It also covers cases where personal data needs to be processed by any person who is let us say trying to save the life of an accident victim or a hospital is giving lifesaving treatment to an unknown person.

The legitimate use under this clause will cover situations that India faced during Covid when the Government introduced the Arogya Sethu app and mandated its use for employees to report for duty which was objected to by some people as infringement of Privacy.

“Breakdown of public order” can be a law enforcement situation where there is a riot, and it is necessary to process CCTV footages to identify the persons involved in the crime.

7. Legitimate use in Employment Situations:

Another important provision under the "Legitimate Use" clause is the recognition that processing in certain employment situations may require to be conducted in the absence of appropriate consent and the Act recognizes this.

Accordingly, Legitimate use covers

"For the purposes of employment or those related to safeguarding the employer from loss or liability, such as prevention of corporate espionage, maintenance of confidentiality of trade secrets, intellectual property, classified information or provision of any service or benefit sought by a Data Principal who is an employee."

This is an important provision since processing of personal data of employees is applicable to 100% of organizations irrespective of whether an organization is big or small or is engaged in IT, Banking or manufacturing etc.

The section identifies two situations "For employment" and "those related to safeguarding the employer".

Personal data is processed for the purpose of employment at several stages such as

a. Recruitment

b. During Employment

c. Post Termination

At the time of recruitment, different types of information are collected from the website of the company as well as from other recruiting agencies. Many times, information is received in an unstructured document that is attached to an e-mail sent either to the HR department or to any of the employees.

When recruitment agencies submit list of prospective candidates, we may have to determine whether the data was submitted at our request or on their own. If data is submitted at our request and the recruitment agency has collected it on our behalf, we may become Data Fiduciaries and be responsible for the data collected. If however the consent has been obtained by the recruiter without our prior clearance, they may be Joint Data Fiduciaries. During this onboarding stage there may be background verification again at our request or at the instance of the recruiting firm and the nature of relationship is always a grey area and determined by the contract of service between the recruiting agency and the Company for whom people are recruited.

Additionally, there is an issue of how long the information of the rejected candidates be retained and whether they need to be informed that their data is being held for future use etc.

Further it is also possible that the data may be old and obsolete and used for automated decision making which could require updating.

Whether the "Legitimate Use" criteria "For Employment" can be used as an omnibus permission to process the data without consent at the time of receiving the information, conducting a background verification, conducting an interview etc is a moot question. In the absence of any clarifications, we can consider that if we can track an information as "Related to the Employment Process", then perhaps it can be brought under the legitimate use both by the employer company as well as the recruiting company.

The second part of the clause is interesting since it applies to employees after their recruitment. During this stage, the personal data of employees can be processed to safeguard the interest of the organization. This may include safeguarding from financial loss or prevention of corporate espionage, maintenance of confidentiality of IPR or for provision of benefits sought by the employee who is also a data principal in a context.

During the employment, employees do have a special relationship with the employer, and they are trusted with information which is otherwise confidential.

The need to safeguard the interest of an organization may require surveillance on the employees both on and off the campus as well as their living styles etc. Hence there could be disputes related to the scope of this clause.

Similarly, after a person submits a resignation there is a phase of relationship during the termination notice period and after the severance of the relationship till all the labilities are settled and thereafter as a "Past Employee". At each of these stages the person retains a special relationship with the organization.

To address all these situations, there is a need to consider an exclusive privacy management system for employees and a separate Privacy policy which is different from the policies used for other customers and other occasions.

The role of contractual employees by whatever name they are called and employees who work at customer place and employees who work from home and using their own devices all present different types of privacy requirements and if Legitimate is to be relied upon, an organization may be exposing itself to unknown risks. It is therefore advisable if the employers try to use "Consents" even with employees to ensure that the risks are under control.

In summary, Legitimate Use is a convenient provision provided in the Act but needs to be used with extreme care.

Chapter VI

Obligations of Data Fiduciaries-General

While Chapter I of DPDPA 2023 describes the applicability of the Act, in terms of the type of data processing of which invokes the Act, and who is a "Data Fiduciary" by definition, Chapter II speaks about the "Obligations of the Data Fiduciary".

From the "Compliance point of view", sections 4 to 10 are important for every data fiduciary since noncompliance could lead to penalty as provided in the table below.

S No	Subject Matter of Breach	Penalty
1	Breach in observing the obligation of Data Fiduciary to take reasonable security safeguards to prevent personal data breach, under sub-section (5) of section 8	May extend to two hundred and fifty crore rupees.
2	Breach in observing the obligation to give the Board or affected Data Principals notice of a personal data breach, under sub-section (6) of section 8	May extend to two hundred crore rupees.
3	Breach in observance of additional obligations in relation to children, under section 9	May extend to two hundred crores rupees.

4	Breach in observance of additional obligations of Significant Data Fiduciary, under section 10	May extend to one hundred and fifty crore rupees.
5	Breach in observance of the duties under section 15 *(P.S:Applicable to Data Principals)*	May extend to ten thousand rupees.
6	Breach of any term of voluntary undertaking accepted by the Board under section 32	Up to the extent applicable for the breach in respect of which the proceedings under section 28 were instituted.
7	Breach of any other provisions of this Act, other than the provisions of section 16	May extend to fifty crore rupees.

Out of the 7different types of violations mentioned above, point no 5 refers to penalty that may be imposed on a data principal in case of failure to observe the prescribed duties and the rest apply to a data fiduciary failing to comply with the obligations imposed under this Act.

The above table reflects the "Financial Risk" for a data fiduciary in not complying with the Act and hence should be the focus of the Top management of any organization. It is expected that all responsible managements should recognize that the DPDPA 2023 has been gazetted on August 11, 2023, and though some of the provisions including the application of penalties may be notified for effectiveness on different days and different compliance deadlines may be prescribed for different types of data fiduciaries based on their size and criticality of operations, in general wise managements have started their compliance activities immediately.

The need to start compliance efforts with a comprehensive "Risk Assessment" or a quick "Business Impact Assessment" has therefore been recognized and actioned by many organizations.

The legal fraternity consisting of lawyers also need to take note that DPDPA 2023 is part of the "Due Diligence" under ITA 2000 and hence the industry needs to take steps for compliance and document it. Otherwise, it should be considered as "Negligence" or "Lack of Due diligence" or even "Assistance for commission of a crime" under Section 43(g) of ITA 2000 as was observed by TDSAT in the Umashankar Vs ICICI Bank case.

All Data Fiduciaries as well as Data Processors as defined under DPDPA 2023 could also be "Intermediaries" under ITA 2000 and are liable under section 79 and Section 85 to observe due diligence. Instituting a proper compliance program for Data Protection is one of the first requirements of such due diligence and not doing so is opening the doors for vicarious liability.

In implementing compliance of a new law like DPDPA 2023 which suddenly descends on an organization that is already in business, there will be serious challenges for handling compliance with respect to past data processing activity. It may be relatively easy to implement new plans for compliance for the future but not so easy to correct the past where personal data collected is spread over hundreds and thousands of systems and even creating a personal data inventory would be almost impossible.

Unfortunately, DPDPA 2023 is not a prospective law. It applies to existing data also. Hence organizations while implementing compliance need to take specific steps in handling the legacy data in addition to the future operations. It is possible that the degree of compliance could be different for future collection of personal data than the existing data.

One strategy to be considered by all large organizations is to set up a brand-new data network to handle the DPDPA compliant data processing from say six months hence while the legacy data system is managed with some corrective measures which may not be fully effective.

When data breaches happen, the DPB may or may not recognize that the breach was from past data or data collected after the law came into effect, but it may be possible for Data Fiduciaries to seek concessions in penalty if there is a good faith implementation of the compliance at least for futuristic activities.

Classes of Data Fiduciaries:

DPDPA 2023 recognizes Data Fiduciaries as any entity that collects and processes personal data in India (Refer to Section 3 for details) for business purposes and determines the Purpose and Means of Processing. If there are multiple such entities with respect to a given data set, they may be recognized as "Joint Data Fiduciaries". Those who process the personal data without determining the purpose and means, at the instance of a data fiduciary are referred to as "Data Processors".

Among the Data Fiduciaries, two special category of data fiduciaries have been identified, they are "Significant Data Fiduciaries" and "Consent Managers".

We have already discussed the role of a "Consent Manager" who is a data fiduciary who represents the data principal and is accountable to the data principal. He can provide consent to data fiduciaries on behalf of a data principal and also withdraw consent. Data Principal may also "Review" the consent through the consent manager which means that the Consent Manager can intervene from time to time on existing consent and try to ensure that the data fiduciary is only processing data as per the consent agreement. He will therefore be monitoring the activities of the data fiduciaries and perhaps may even proactively inform data principals is there is any need to re-consider the consents already given.

We have also discussed that "Consent Manager" under DPDPA 2023 may be more than the intermediary concept of Consent Manager under the Account Aggregator scheme of RBI.

He works more like a power of attorney holder of the data principal and as a "Fiduciary" has the responsibilities of a trustee providing guidance to data principals which are good in their interest.

While this "Fiduciary" nature is applicable to all Data Fiduciaries and all of them are expected to take the interest of the Data Principals into consideration while arriving at any personal data processing decisions, the Consent Managers have a greater responsibility than other data fiduciaries.

While other data fiduciaries may use the "Legitimate use" provision to suit their commercial requirements, Consent Managers may have a very narrow scope for "Legitimate Use".

The DPB/MeitY will come up with separate guidelines on what are the special obligations that may apply only to Consent Managers.

As regards "Significant Data Fiduciaries", section 10 (1) states that the Central Government may notify any Data Fiduciary or class of Data Fiduciaries as Significant Data Fiduciary, on the basis of an assessment of such relevant factors as it may determine, including.

a. the volume and sensitivity of personal data processed.

b. risk to the rights of Data Principal.

c. potential impact on the sovereignty and integrity of India.

d. risk to electoral democracy.

e. security of the State; and

f. public order.

The Ministry (MeitY) and DPB will come up with a more detailed guideline on who are the "Significant Data Fiduciaries", but an indication is available in the above criteria.

One obvious criterion would be the "volume of data processed'. Currently ITA 2000 classifies Social Media intermediaries with more than 50 lakh subscribers from India as "Significant Social Media Intermediaries". This may be an indication of the level at which the volume of data processed may determine the classification of a data fiduciary as a "Significant Data Fiduciary".

However, the Government may decide to combine the "Sensitivity" parameter also as a determinant and combine it with the volume criteria. In that context, data fiduciaries who process sensitive data including data of children, health data, or finance data, Genetic data, biometric data etc may be classified as "Significant Data Fiduciaries" either without any volume criteria or at a very low volume criterion.

The "Sensitivity" goes with the criteria "Risk to the rights of data principal" and any processor who does processing which adversely affects the rights of a data principal may be classified as a significant data fiduciary irrespective of the volume. If we consider "Right to Access", "Right to withdraw consent", "Right to Correction", "Right to Nominate" and " Right to Grievance redressal" as the primary rights available to Data Principal, any processor who provides services which may adversely affect these rights as "Significant Data Fiduciary". The "Consent Manager" by definition would be one such class of persons which should be considered as "Significant Data Fiduciary" and any obligation associated with the Significant Data Fiduciary automatically applies to the Consent Manager also. If a process is such that correction or withdrawal is impossible, it may also be considered as an operation of a Significant Data Fiduciary.

It may be observed that under Section 6(5) the consequences of such withdrawal shall be borne by the Data Principal. In this context if the withdrawal of the consent is subject to some conditions directed by the nature of processing, such data fiduciaries may have to be classified as "Significant Data Fiduciaries".

The next criteria which may determine the status of a data fiduciary as a significant data fiduciary is when the nature of processing is such that it may have a potential impact on the sovereignty and integrity of India or a risk to electoral democracy or security of the state.

Under this criterion many of the "Social Media Intermediaries" including YouTube Chanels, OTT platforms as well as the news portals could be considered as "Significant Data Fiduciaries" irrespective of the volume of data processed.

There is also yet other criteria namely "Public Order" as a relevant factor that may determine the status of a data fiduciary as significant data fiduciary. The nature of impact of data processing on "Public Order" is dynamic and hence there could be a case for declaring an intermediary as "Significant Data Fiduciary" on a limited time basis when the public order is in an adverse state. However, the special obligations required of a significant data fiduciary like a DPO being available or Data Audit being conducted may be more permanent in nature while DPIA can be ordered in respect of a specific process during a public order crisis.

We need to await evolution of the Government thinking on many of these aspects in due course. One thing we can notice is that most Data Protection laws classify information as "Sensitive" and Controllers processing "Sensitive Personal Information" or "Special Category of Personal Information" for prescribing additional obligations. However, DPDPA 2023 directly goes for classification of data fiduciaries as significant data fiduciaries based on the type of the activity of the data fiduciary.

When the Government comes up with a detailed guideline it may still not be a list of individual entities as significant data fiduciaries and only description of types of activities may be contained therein. The need for interpreting the guidance and determining whether an organization is to be classified as Significant or not remains as an exercise which organizations need to do in their initial Business Impact Assessment of the DPDPA 2023 becoming a law before going in for a detailed "Gap Analysis" of what needs to be done.

General Obligations of all Data Fiduciaries:

Under DPDPA 2023 there are list of obligations which are applicable to all Data Fiduciaries and supplementary obligations applicable for data fiduciaries processing Children Data, Data Fiduciaries which are considered as Significant Data Fiduciaries and Consent Managers.

Under the General obligations [Section 8 (1)] A Data Fiduciary shall, irrespective of any agreement to the contrary or failure of a Data Principal to carry out the duties provided under this Act, be responsible for complying with the provisions of this Act and the rules made thereunder in respect of any processing undertaken by it or on its behalf by a Data Processor.

This provision indicates that the obligations are not limited to some specific data processing principles under Chapter II but cover all requirements under this act from Section 1 to Section 44 as well as the rules made there under. The obligation however rests with the "Data Fiduciary" who is also responsible for the acts of his "Data Processor".

However, under Section 8(2), A Data Fiduciary may engage, appoint, use or otherwise involve a Data Processor to process personal data on its behalf for any activity related to offering of goods or services to Data Principals **only** under a valid contract.

Hence the Data fiduciary needs to enter into a valid contract with the Data Processor who is involved in the data processing on behalf of the Data Fiduciary.

The act at this point of time does not indicate what should be the terms of the Data Processor contract. The liability regarding use of a data processor lies with the data fiduciary and therefore it is his responsibility to put such clauses in the contract that are necessary to cover his liability. There would be no relief to the data fiduciary even if there is a failure on the part of the data principal to carry out the duties provided under the Act for which the data principal may be separately penalised.

We must not forget however that DPDPA 2023 will co-exist with ITA 2000 or any of its amended versions and ITA 2000 has appropriate provisions to punish not only Data Processors who by their negligence or design cause any harm to a data principal or even third parties but also Data Principals. If a data principal fails to fulfil the duties under DPDPA 2023 and thereby causes a loss to the Data Fiduciary, the Data Fiduciary can invoke relevant provisions of ITA 2000 or even IPC to either file a criminal case against the data principal or a civil case with the Adjudicator under ITA 2000.

Similarly, even though a Data Processor may not be penalized under DPDPA 2023, he has no immunity on being held responsible under ITA 2000 for any misdemeanour. Either the Data Fiduciary or the Data Principal can invoke either Civil proceedings or criminal prosecution under ITA 2000.

DPDPA 2023 prescribes under Section 8(3) that the data fiduciary processing personal data shall ensure its completeness, accuracy and consistency. But this provision is indicated as "Where the personal data processed by a data fiduciary is likely to be used to make a decision that affects the data principal or is disclosed to another data fiduciary.

Where data is neither disclosed or used for decision making, the requirement of updating for completeness, accuracy and consistency is not indicated. Such data lying in archive and not used for decision making or disclosure may therefore be left without special efforts to update it. However, ITA 2000 has prescribed that the consent for Privacy Policy and Terms of use of an Intermediary service needs to be renewed at least once in a year.

Another obligation of the data fiduciary under Section 8(6) is that in the event of a personal data breach, the Data Fiduciary shall give the Board and each affected Data Principal a notice in the prescribed form and manner to be prescribed.

Here again it may be noted that a data breach of personal data is also a data breach under ITA 2000 and the need for reporting the data breach within 6 hours with the specified format will continue to be applicable.

In GDPR, "Right to Forget" is an important right of the data principal and it leads to deletion of the personal data from all places where it exists in an organization. It is also considered as an obligation that has to be met by the Data Controller religiously.

In DPDPA 2023, there is no mention of "Right to Forget". There is only a "Right to Erasure" along with the right to withdraw consent for processing or after the purpose for which the personal data was collected no longer subsists.

Accordingly, Section 8(7) prescribes that a Data Fiduciary shall, **unless retention is necessary for compliance with any law** for the time being in force, —

a. erase personal data, upon the Data Principal withdrawing her consent or as soon as it is reasonable to assume that the specified purpose is no longer being served, whichever is earlier; and

b. cause its Data Processor to erase any personal data that was made available by the Data Fiduciary for processing to such Data Processor.

One of the illustrations provided in this context is where X, an individual, registers herself on an online marketplace operated by Y, an e-commerce service provider. X has given her consent to Y for the processing of her personal data for selling her used car. The online marketplace helps conclude the sale. In such instance Y shall no longer retain her personal data.

Another illustration quoted for retention of personal data after the purpose is over is an instance where X, an individual, decides to close her savings account with Y, a bank. Y is required by law applicable to banks to maintain the record of the identity of its clients for a period of ten years beyond closing of accounts. In this instance, since retention is necessary for compliance with law, Y shall retain X's personal data for the said period.

We may also note that ITA 2000 had a section 67(C) which stated that data shall be retained for such period and in such form as may be prescribed. However, notification has been made so far specifying the period up to which any kind of data has to be preserved only under the CERT IN Guideline applicable to log records and KYC information. But if SEBI or IRDAI has prescribed any such data retention requirements, they may be considered as necessary to be complied with before deciding on the erasure of the data.

The Kerala High Court in December 2022 (Refer https://www.naavi.org/wp/hats-off-to-kerala-high-court-for-its-treatise-on-right-to-forget/) had provided a complete treatise on the "Right to Forget" and had opined that it is not a universal rule but is applicable in certain instances like the matrimonial cases where the names of the litigants may be redacted from the published judgement. There have been individual decisions of similar nature from High Courts of Delhi and Odissa also.

In view of this background, it is essential for a data fiduciary confronted with a request for erasure to be mindful of the data being evidence of some crime and a request could be made by any law enforcement authority or may be required by the data fiduciary himself for enforcement of his own legal rights.

It is therefore recommended that organisations shall maintain a "Data Erasure Policy" and approve data deletion with appropriate verification and documentation.

Section 8(8) provides that in case a data principal does not approach the data fiduciary to exercise the right to withdraw consent if the Data Principal does not approach the Data Fiduciary for withdrawing of consent and does not exercise any of her rights in relation to such processing, for such time period as may be prescribed, and different time periods may be prescribed for different classes of Data Fiduciaries and for different purposes.

Once the notification under section 8(8) is made by the Government it could become a "Data Retention Norm" where no request for withdrawal of consent has been made.

Under Section 8(9) the data fiduciary shall publish the business contact information of the data protection officer if applicable or a person who can respond to the queries of a data principal.

This section indicates the recognition of "Business Contact Information" which can be interpreted as "Personal Information used for business purpose". Such information does not otherwise constitute personal data under the Act.

A similar requirement exists even under ITA 2000 for publishing the information of a Grievance officer or a Compliance officer particularly in respect of social media intermediaries.

Under section 8(10) it is mandatory for data fiduciaries to establish an effective mechanism to redress the grievances of data principals. For invoking the grievance redressal, the data principal needs to contact the data fiduciary either in person or by way of communication in electronic form or physical form.

A Grievance redressal system needs to more than a technical help centre and be capable of understanding and resolving the issues related to noncompliance of DPDPA 2023. Ideally it should be a graded system involving negotiation between the DPO and the Data Principal followed by reference to an Ombudsman and later to Mediation. Preferably the process has to be an online process.

Under the general obligations of Data Fiduciaries Sections 8(4) and 8(5) address the issues of Compliance and Security which are discussed in a separate Chapter after we discuss the Rights of the Data Principal guaranteed under this Act.

Chapter VII

Rights of the Data Principal

Before we discuss other obligations, let us take a look at the "Rights of Data Principals" protected under DPDPA 2023.

The origin of a data protection law is with the need to protect the human right of "Right to Privacy". Since defining the boundaries of the definition of "Right to Privacy" is difficult, in the "Data Industry", "Right to Privacy" is deduced to the concept of "Right to protect the choice of a data principal on how his/her personal data may be collected, processed and used".

Hence "Rights" of the Data Principal are the foundation of DPDPA 2023 and determine the "Obligations" as well as the Compliance measures.

The DPDPA 2023 under Chapter III, Sections 11-14 specify the "Rights" of data principals that are protected under the Act. Additionally, under Section 15, DPDPA 2023 specifies certain "Duties" of the data principal to be followed while exercising these rights.

The Concept of "Duty" of a Data Principal is unique to India and is a measure of balancing the benefits of law to the community which consists of both the individuals whose personal data has to be protected as well as the business entities for whom "Data is a class of business assets which should be available for monetization without causing harm to the data principal".

There are essentially four rights indicated in the DPDPA 2023.

The first right is the "Right to access information about personal data". This right is to ensure that when the personal data of a data principal is being processed either under a consent given or when the data is being processed under the legitimate use provision, the data principal shall have the right to request for

a. a summary of personal data which is being processed by such Data Fiduciary and the processing activities undertaken by that Data Fiduciary with respect to such personal data.

b. the identities of all other Data Fiduciaries and Data Processors with whom the personal data has been shared by such Data Fiduciary, along with a description of the personal data so shared; and any other information related to the personal data of such Data Principal and its processing, as may be prescribed.

When such a request is made, it would be the obligation of the data fiduciary to provide the information and failure to respond within a reasonable time (which may be prescribed) could be considered as a non-compliance.

When such a request is received, the data fiduciary needs to verify if the information has been received from the concerned Data Principal only or from a consent manager who is authorised by the data principal. In order to ensure the identification of the data principal at the time of collection of the consent itself, there has to be a mechanism for identification of the data principal without which the request for exercise of rights becomes difficult to act upon.

In the simplified Notice format suggested under DPDPA 2023 the details of how the data is being processed and with whom the data is being shared is not required to be included. They can however be requested under this right.

This "Right to information" is subject to the condition that it shall not apply in respect of the sharing of any personal data with any other Data Fiduciary authorised by law to obtain such personal data, where such sharing is pursuant to a request made in writing by such other Data Fiduciary for the purpose of prevention or detection or investigation of offences or cyber incidents, or for prosecution or punishment of offences.

The second right of the data principal is the Right to Correction and Erasure of Personal Data. Under this right, a Data Principal shall have the right to correction, completion, updating and erasure of the personal data.

We may recall that under Section 8(3) there is an obligation on the data fiduciary to keep the data complete and accurate. This obligation goes with the Right to correction of the data principal. Under the obligation it is specified that it applies when the processing is used for decision making or disclosure.

As a right the "Correction" is not subject to the condition that the processing is related to disclosure or decision making and has to be carried out since it is a choice of the data principal. In the earlier version of data protection law there was a provision that the data fiduciary could dispute the request for correction if he has alternate view.

The current provision indicates that the "Right to correction" is restricted to information provided by the data principal and in case of deliberate misleading information provided by him/her it can be questioned as failure of the duty under Section 15 discussed below.

As regards "Erasure", the right is subject to the view of the data fiduciary regarding whether retention is necessary the specified purpose or for compliance with any law for the time being in force. If there is a need to reject the request for erasure, the data principal may take the dispute to the DPB.

The third right of the data principal mentioned under Section 13 is related to the "Grievance Redressal". Accordingly, a Data Principal shall have the right to have readily available means of grievance redressal provided by a Data Fiduciary or Consent Manager in respect of any act or omission regarding the performance of its obligations or the exercise of rights.

The Data Fiduciary or Consent Manager shall respond to any grievances within such period as may be prescribed.

It is also prescribed that the Data Principal shall exhaust the opportunity of redressing her grievance under this section before approaching the Board.

In order to meet this requirement, the data fiduciary should clearly state the procedure for raising the grievance such as sending an e-mail to the DPO or filling up a grievance form etc.

An important right that the DPDPA 2023 grants to the Data Principals is the "Right to nominate" which is unique and has several implications on compliance.

According to Section 14, a Data Principal shall have the right to nominate, any other individual, who shall, in the event of death or incapacity of the Data Principal, exercise the rights of the Data Principal in accordance with the provisions of this Act and the rules made thereunder.

This provision is relevant in two circumstances namely "In the event of death" and "In the event of incapacity of the data principal".

It may be noted that "Incapacity" may be temporary and could be a medical condition that is subject to change. Keeping with the spirit of "Nomination", it should be applied only in the event of an "Irreversible incapacitation" which could mean that there has to be a validation of an authorized medical person like the death certificate in case of death which should be considered mandatory for invoking the nomination.

We may also recognize that "Nomination" of "Personal Data" presupposes the nature of data as a "Property" belonging to a person. In the case of personal data, the property may be deemed to belong to the data principal. In any other case, the property needs to be attributed to a person who creates the property.

Under ITA 2000, an instrument in electronic form of the nature of a Will or any testamentary deposition (an instruction that is contingent to the death of a person) does not have a legal recognition. In the DPDPA scenario, the nomination document cannot therefore be taken as an electronic document or combined with the consent where a “Click” on I Submit button is taken as a “Deemed Contract” though it is not equivalent to an electronic signature under ITA 2000.

Data Fiduciaries may therefore have to obtain written nomination in respect of the personal data held by them. This may be inconvenient and may also be unintentional but considered a legal necessity unless the ITA 2000 is amended.

A nomination facility also requires obtaining the identity of the nominee at the time of nomination during the lifetime of the data principal and establishing the identity when a claim arises. It is common in such situations that the “Nominee” may not be the sole legal heir and hence the data fiduciary may be confronted with objections from multiple claimants which needs to be legally resolved.

The ”personal data” that may be bequeathed may be contents of a website which is hosted by a hosting company, the emails in an e-mail service provider’s server, or data with the cloud service providers.

Each of such data fiduciaries need to establish a process for handling the information about the deceased data principals whose data is with them.

In the event a data principal is reported deceased, and the information is available to the data fiduciary, then he may have to initiate procedures for freezing the access to the account, archive the contents pending settlement of the claim. There needs to be in place to keep tracking the data principals.

The claim settlement process itself could involve "Receipt of Claim", "Verification of Claim" and "Disposal of Claim" for which appropriate policies and procedures need to be set in place.

In the case of claim against a property such as Bank deposits, when multiple claimants make a claim, the Bank normally directs the claimants to produce either a Will with a probate for the executor or a succession certificate or a legal heirship certificate along with an affidavit signed by some relatives. The nominee by law is considered as not necessarily the whole owner of the property and where there is no dispute, the Bank gets discharged by settling the balance in the account with the nominee. If, however a notice of dispute is received, Banks take the safer stand of requesting for a Court document such as probate or succession certificate.

A similar procedure is ideal for personal data transfer after death of the data owner since personal data includes valuable assets such as copyrightable content, crypto currency information, passwords to NFTs, passwords to high value software purchased or subscription to online services etc.

However, unlike other properties, a virtual property such as "personal data" can be shared with multiple claimants and hence it is open to debate if there can be a way of resolving disputes from multiple legal heirs by sharing the data with multiple persons.

This could be a new Jurisprudential issue that may be raised consequent to the DPDPA 2023

Duties of a Data Principal:

For the first time perhaps in a data protection law we observe that DPDPA 2023 speaks of "Duties" of the data Principal.

Under Section 15 of the Act, following duties of the data principal are mentioned.

a. comply with the provisions of all applicable laws for the time being in force while exercising rights under the provisions of this Act.

b. ensure not to impersonate another person while providing her personal data for a specified purpose.

c. ensure not to suppress any material information while providing her personal data for any document, unique identifier, proof of identity or proof of address issued by the State or any of its instrumentalities.

d. ensure not to register a false or frivolous grievance or complaint with a Data Fiduciary or the Board; and

e. furnish only such information as is verifiably authentic, while exercising the right to correction or erasure under the provisions of this Act or the rules made thereunder.

It is interesting to note that persons who have not complied with any law will not have a right under this law. Jurisprudence has to develop if persons convicted of any offence and who has not completed their sentence or say illegal immigrants etc., could be barred from exercising their rights under DPDPA 2023.

If any data principal is not adhering to the duties, there is a provision that DPB may impose a penalty of up to Rs 10000/- for such act.

It may be noted that if a person is in breach of these duties, he would probably be in breach of provisions of ITA 2000 (e.g., Sections 66C) and hence being assessed for failure of duty under DPDPA 2023 by the quasi-judicial body like DPB is evidence for prosecution under ITA 2000.

Chapter VIII

Compliance By Design

Section 8(4) of DPDPA 2023 requires that the Data Fiduciary shall implement appropriate technical and organisational measures to ensure effective observance of the provisions of this Act and the rules made thereunder.

Simultaneously Section 8(5) states that the Data Fiduciary shall protect personal data in its possession or under its control, including in respect of any processing undertaken by it or on its behalf by a Data Processor, by taking reasonable security safeguards to prevent personal data breach.

To understand the scope of 8(5) we need to also refer to the definition of a personal data breach which according to Section 2(u) means any **unauthorised processing** of personal data or accidental disclosure, acquisition, sharing, use, alteration, destruction, or loss of access to personal data, that compromises the confidentiality, integrity or availability of personal data.

The use of the word "Appropriate" means that the "Technical and Organizational Measures" required to be implemented has to be based on a "Risk Assessment" and the requirement is to ensure effective observance of the provisions of this Act and the rules made thereunder. It means that the risk assessment should cover all aspects of compliance requirement under the Act and not merely to protecting the personal data from breach which is covered under Section 8(5).

Section 8(5) requires the data fiduciary to protect the personal data both under its direct control and in the control of a processor who processes personal data on behalf of the data fiduciary and such "reasonable security safeguard" should be reasonable in relation to the "Risk" of noncompliance and be able to prevent personal data breach.

A "Breach" of data under information security consideration includes data being unauthorizedly deleted or modified or prevented from access by an authorized person. This is the concept of CIA triad or preserving the Confidentiality, Integrity and Availability of information.

Under Privacy consideration even unauthorized processing, accidental disclosure, unauthorized acquisition, unauthorized sharing is all considered as breach.

Hence when a risk assessment is undertaken under Section 8(4), it should cover not only the risk of loss of confidentiality, integrity and availability of personal data but also collection without proper notice and consent, collection of information in excess of the purpose for which it is collected, retention of the data beyond a reasonable period and without proper justification, inability to protect the rights of data principal such as receiving the notice in 22 languages, using the services of a consent manager, access to a summary of information processed, correction and erasure of the data the inability to provide nomination or grievance redressal etc.

Risks are associated with the processing of the personal data and hence could be considered as Process Specific. The risks may be different from one process to another. Hence risk assessment as well as the compliance may have to be "Process Oriented", and an aggregation of process-oriented Risks become the organizational risks.

Even the risk mitigation measures and controls have to be process oriented. For that matter, even the fact whether an entity is a Data Fiduciary or Data Processor also is process oriented.

Hence the Section 8(4) obligation of appropriate measures and Section 8(5) obligations of "reasonable Safeguards" are better traced with reference to individual processes.

Within each process, certain personal data is processed and hence the "Personal data inventory" can be traced as part of the Process inventory. The Consent may also be related to the process and the nature of processing and hence needs to be process oriented.

The Data Protection Impact Assessment or Privacy Impact Assessment which is a risk identification exercise is also better done with reference to each process.

It is possible that in a given instance and organization may have 10 data elements of an individual X including his name. Process A may use 4 data elements and Process B may use another 4 data elements and Process C may use all the 10 data elements.

While the collection of 10 data elements is justified because in Process C requires all of them the risks of Process A is related to the 4 elements used in that process and risks of Process B and see are related to the number of personal data elements used in each of the process. If C uses PAN card number and Aadhaar while the other two processes do not use them, the risk of any breach in Process C is far higher than in the other two processes.

Hence Risk assessment is process dependent and "Compliance by Design" has to start with creating an inventory of personal data processing in an organization.

The personal data classification, purpose description and the consent based on the purpose are all related to the different purposes. The risks will differ if the data is EU data or Indian Data since the compliance requirements are themselves different. Hence the personal data classification has to take into account whether the data is DPDPA related or GDPR related or CCPA related etc. It should also classify data as employee and non-employee, Minor and adult etc. This classification goes with the personal data within each of the processes and the nature and purpose of processing should synchronize with the compliance requirements of different processes.

Even for discovery of personal data in an organization, it is more effective if the identified personal data is immediately tagged with the process. If there is any personal data which is an orphan or not associated with any process, it is a candidate for immediate deletion as data no longer required.

Considering an organization as an aggregation of processes also has another advantage since, we can identify "Process Owners" and make them responsible for compliance within the process. Hence the process owner can throw out data which is not required for his process and if it is not required by any other process, it should be discarded.

When an existing company goes into compliance the biggest challenge is to ensure that data which is not related to a process is spotted and discarded. Personal data which remains should be associated with some processing and the owner of that process has to validate the requirement of the data, adequacy of the data, quality of the data, etc.

The essence of "Compliance by Design" which should be addressed in the technical architecture is therefore "Process Based construction of an organization". Since a given set of personal data may be required in multiple processes, it is necessary to maintain data in a Central warehouse and each process may call the required data elements for processing so that data elements not required by a given process is not called by the process at all. This significantly reduces the risk of data leak.

For example, if in a process an employee's travel schedule has to be set, it is not necessary for the process to access the full data of the employee including his spouse's name, his loan liabilities etc. But for booking of ticket, his full name, age, phone number, email address may be required along with the eligibility for travel in a particular class (First class or Economy Class etc), which may depend on his basic salary or designation. If such access is provided to the entire data sheet of an employee, redundant data will get spread at multiple process levels and could be leaked.

Coming to the "Reasonable Security Safeguard" under Section 8(5), again the word "Reasonable" means "Risk Based", and the CIA controls should ensure that data is shared only on a need-to-know basis and restricted to the limited data sets and not to the entire data. The preservation of integrity of data means that no data should be unauthorizedly altered and when altered, the record of who authorised the alteration and what was the data before and after alteration must be available as a version history. Availability of data means that the persons who have a need to access the data should not be denied access either because there is a DOS attack crashing the server or otherwise.

In order to meet the requirements of Sections 8(4) and 8(5) of DPDPA 2023, the technical architecture should enable Central data storage with a suitable Unique Identity of a personal data.

Additionally, use of Encryption for data at rest and data in transit with accompanying key management controls as well as use of De-identification, Pseudonymization/Anonymization or Data Masking should be used. Data in Process may not always be possible to be secured by encryption but where the process is amenable for use of homomorphic encryption it can be considered.

The responsibility for "Compliance by Design" as a combination of policies and technical tools is the responsibility of the DPO with the assistance of the technological department.

Any tool or policy will have to be finally implemented by the people and hence the "organizational measures" of compliance must include management of the people, making them aware of the requirements, motivating them to remain compliant by habit and culture. It may be necessary for building a compliance culture in an organization to use supplementary strategies such as Whistle blowing, sanctions and incentives.

In order to ensure that an organization is able adopt all requirements of compliance by design, certain guidance frameworks are developed and are used by the organizations as best practices. Some of these frameworks can be capable of being used for certification by third party assessment. ISO 27001 is one such framework for managing Information Security. ISO 27701 is another framework for managing Personal Information processing as per GDPR and DGPSI (Data Governance and Protection Standard of India) is another comprehensive framework for compliance to DPDPA 2023.

The use of these frameworks is discussed separately in another chapter.

Chapter IX

Processing of Personal Data of Minors

Section 9 of the Act under Chapter II discusses the obligations of Data Fiduciaries related to the processing of personal data of children.

In every Data Protection law, children's data is considered as a high-risk personal data and classified as "Sensitive Personal data". A Minor is represented by the "Guardian" who could be a "Natural Guardian", or a Court appointed "Legal Guardian".

A Natural guardian is first the father and then the mother.

In India persons below the age of 18 are considered as "Minors" though in case of "Court appointed guardian" the age of attaining majority gets extended to 21 years.

A Court may appoint a guardian for a minor in case there the parents are not alive. In case one of the parents ceasing to be a Hindu or becoming a Sanyasi renouncing the worldly life, the natural guardian status of the person may be considered as terminated.

In case of "re-marriage" stepfather or stepmother are not considered "Natural" guardians.

Under the Hindu Minority and Guardianship act 1956, custody of the minor child up to an age of 5 is normally given to the mother but the father remains the sole natural guardian unless the Court steps in to appoint either the mother or any body else as a legal guardian. A mother can be considered as a natural guardian and vested with the rights of managing the property of the minor provided there is a consent from the father.

These issues affect the processing of data of a data principal who is not of 18 years of age. In such cases, the consent for processing has to be provided by the guardian.

DPDPA 2023 has a unique provision that the definition of a "Data Principal" itself in the case of a "Child" (minor) includes the parents or lawful guardian.

This means that the "Children's Data" belongs to the guardian and therefore he can provide the consent.

This provision raises a compliance issue of how to determine if a data principal is a minor or not. If there is a service meant for kids, such as online comics, should any body who registers there be considered as a minor? Can an adult be allowed to be a subscriber? Are issues to be resolved.

Secondly in any service meant for adults, if a minor subscribes, how can it be detected.

Presently companies add a declaration "I am not a minor or I am above the age of 18 years and so on". But if such a declaration is simply accepted, the minor may anyway not be liable and hence the declaration is redundant. Except that it is a notice and perhaps a minor ignoring the notice may be accused of "Cheating", there is little value to the declaration.

If, however there is any payment involved in the subscription and the subscriber proposes a third party credit card, it could raise a suspicion that the data principal may not have a credit card since he may be a minor. Some additional verification in such cases may be in order.

There is a demand from some social media houses such as Meta that the age of providing independent consent should be reduced from 18 to a lesser age. In such cases people quote other country laws where the definition of a minor for data protection purpose is either 16 years or even 14 or 13 years.

Many cite the increased use of apps like Instagram or Face Book by minors. However, it is precisely for the reason that harm may be caused to the minors by many data fiduciaries, that there is a need for consent from the parent. This is a check against potential misuse. It is not clear if the Government will yield to the request of Meta in this case. Probably the laws in India under the Indian Contract Act invalidate the consents given by minors and hence Government may not be legally able to allow minors to give their own consent without diluting the status of "Consent" from a valid "agreement" to some thing lesser.

The provision of a minor by age is also extended to cases where a person is disabled and needs a guardian to represent him.

In the case of minors or disabled persons since the guardian is defined to be the "Data Principal" there is a possibility that after the minor attains the age of 18, there is no need to automatically consider the erstwhile parental consent as invalid and stop processing of the data.

Even when the personal data of a minor is processed with parental/ guardian consent,

There can be a reasonable period for handing over the property of the minor back to him on attaining majority.

The way this can be done is also a Jurisprudential issue which needs to be sorted out through a process. It is recommended that until the minor attains the majority the data principal continues to be the sole owner of the data and the consent given. On the minor attaining majority, the data may be considered as "Joint" with authority to operate being with "Either" of the joint holders. The processing may continue but within a reasonable time which the Government may define…say 3 months, the consent has to be renewed in the name of the erstwhile minor and the parental consent may be dropped. In the meantime, the erstwhile minor can be provided the authority to withdraw the earlier consent and issue his own consent.

The same procedure applies even if the consent is handled through a Consent Manager in which case the Consent manager can be more vigilant and ensure the switchover without much delay.

Even when the data of the minor is processed with consent of the parent o guardian, there are additional consents that apply to the processing.

Under Section 9(2) and 9(3), q Data Fiduciary shall not undertake such processing of personal data that is likely to cause any detrimental effect on the well-being of a child and shall not undertake tracking or behavioural monitoring of children or targeted advertising directed at children.

The Government retains right under Section 9(4) to exempt some class of data fiduciaries (e.g.: Counsellors against Child abuse) from some of these provisions including parental consent for which procedures may be notified separately.

As a contingency to reduction of the Consent age, Government has introduced section 9(5) which states:

The Central Government may, if satisfied that a Data Fiduciary has ensured that its processing of personal data of children is done in a manner that is verifiably safe, notify for such processing by such Data Fiduciary the age above which that Data Fiduciary shall be exempt from the applicability of all or any of the obligations in respect of processing by that Data Fiduciary as the notification may specify.

It is under this section that Meta is trying to persuade the Government to reduce the age of consent for some of the applications like Face Book or Instagram. We need to wait and see if the Government yields to the request of the industry.

Chapter X

Special obligations of Significant Data Fiduciary

Under Section 10(1) of the Act the criteria for declaring any Data Fiduciary as a "Significant Data Fiduciary (SDF) has been laid out. It can include any of the following 5 criteria namely.

a. the volume and sensitivity of personal data processed.

b. risk to the rights of Data Principal.

c. potential impact on the sovereignty and integrity of India.

d. risk to electoral democracy.

e. security of the State; and

f. public order.

The declaration of SDF can be for any single Data Fiduciary or a Class of Data Fiduciaries. At present there is no indication of what could be the kind of organizations that may be classified as SDF.

We are aware that Social Media Intermediaries, i.e., an intermediary which primarily or solely enables online interaction between two or more users and allows them to create, upload, share, disseminate, modify or access information using its services (e.g.: WhatsApp) is declared a "Significant Social Media Intermediary" if it has more than 50 lakh subscribers in India. This could be an indication of the volume levels that the Government may consider if Volume is the only criteria.

However, it is possible for the Government to consider "Sensitivity" and possibility of the activity having an impact on the national security or electoral democracy may also be considered as SDF. This could mean that not only the X (twitter) or Koo or Instagram could be considered as SDF but many You Tube Channels which have an impact on Electoral Democracy will also come under the SDF category.

Nothing prevents the Government to consider "All Listed Companies", "All RBI licensed Banks and NBFCs", " All Hospitals with more than X patients", "All Laboratories engaged in processing of genetic data", "All Data Fiduciaries processing biometrics and Aadhar/PAN cards", "All Data Fiduciaries engaged in services related to Defence Sector", "All Data Fiduciaries who process personal data of Indian data principals outside India", "All NGOs receiving foreign funds in excess of Rs X" etc as SDFs.

In a way since there is no definition of "Sensitive Data", the SDF criteria will be an indirect definition of "Sensitive Information" and indirect strategic tool to regulate any high-risk entities. While we may expect the first list of SDFs to be a small list of well-known Big Tech Companies, there could be frequent updating of the SDF list to expand it over a time.

Government may think of a threshold turnover size such as Rs 50 lakhs or threshold employee size of say 500 employees etc to further use this SDF classification as an instrument of regulating the Data Processing market.

It may be noted that if any Data Fiduciary is considered as an SDF, there is a higher level of risk to the Privacy of individuals arising out of the processing which will be captured in the Risk Assessment.

Accordingly, there will also be a need for higher level of security compared to other Data Fiduciaries. In terms of maturity of compliance, SDFs need a much higher level of Compliance than others.

Expectation therefore is that the organization would have a Certification of its Compliance under a comprehensive framework like the FDPPI's Data Governance and Protection Standard of India (DGPSI).

Significant Data Fiduciaries will have three specific obligations namely that.

1. The SDF shall appoint a Data Protection Officer
2. The SDF shall appoint an independent Data Auditor
3. .The SDF shall conduct periodic audit and DPIA.

The Data Protection officer (DPO) should be responsible to the Board of Directors (or similar governing body) indicating the seniority level of the position. He should be based in India and should be the point of contact for the grievance redressal mechanism. Additionally, DPO will represent the SDF under the Act with the Data Protection Board or the external world.

The Act at this time has not spoken of the credentials required and whether DPO needs to be registered with the regulator. It appears that DPO has to be an employee only though we need to wait if an individual who is a consultant can also be a DPO.

As regards the credentials it is clear that the DPO should have a good knowledge of the law, should have a good communication skill to manage the internal management of his responsibilities, have adequate skills in negotiating with individual data principals and resolving disputes. He needs to be technically competent enough to supervise "Compliance by Design" and "DPIA".

Hence the DPO should be an all-rounder with multiple skills not all of which can reflect in the form of Certifications. At present there are many professionals with qualifications in GDPR and Certifications such as CIPP-Europe etc. At present there is only one organisation in India namely Foundation of Data Protection Professionals in India (FDPPI) which conducts a focussed Certification program covering the Indian

Law, along with international laws such as GDPR and US laws besides a focussed Compliance framework titled DGPSI (Data Governance and Protection Standard of India). DGPSI incorporates the requirement of compliance to DPDPA besides ITA 2000 and the Data Privacy part of the Data Governance Standard of Bureau of Indian Standards (presently released as a Draft). The framework is discussed in greater detail in another part of the book.

Considering the need to be able to interact with the board an experience of around 10 plus years in the industrial environment would be ideal. In practice organization may place loyalty to the organization as a high priority since the DPO while needing to be firm should not destabilize the organization through immature handling of any crisis such as a data breach situation.

The position of DPO in a large organization is not simply a "Job" it requires "passion" and "commitment" apart from the knowledge and skills. He should be a born team leader and possess empathy to deal with the data principals in a grievance handling situation.

Another major requirement of an SDF is appointing an independent Data Auditor who would be auditing the compliance to the Act at least once a year but preferably on a concurrent basis. He is therefore not an employee of the SDF but an external specialist.

The Data Auditor needs all the skills of a Data Protection Officer and additionally an ability to conduct an audit and assessment. He can use a framework such as DGPSI and supplement it with an assessment methodology such as "Data Trust Score" developed by FDPPI as an extended use of DGPSI.

The Data Audit is not like a Financial Audit and hence it is not possible for statutory financial auditors to also conduct data audit. This would be a separate cadre of professionals who would come up now. The Data Protection Board which would be the regulatory authority is expected to define some accreditation criteria and allow only accredited persons to be able to register as Data Auditors. We need to wait and see how the Data Protection Board reacts since worldwide there is no such Data Auditor specification in other laws.

If we draw some inference from the previous versions of the law such as the PDPB 2019/DPA 2021, Government may suggest "Concurrent Audit" or "Continuous Audit" so that periodically at least at quarterly intervals the compliance activities are audited.

Lawyers can aspire to be Data Auditors provided they have a good exposure or experience in technology.

Alternatively experienced auditors who are today in ISO 27001/ISO 27701 should think of shifting to Data Audit.

Chapter XI

Cross Border Transfer of Personal Data

The most sensational part of GDPR as a data protection law is the control that the law tries to exercise on transfer of personal data from EU for processing outside EU. During discussions on earlier versions of the Indian law there was strong opposition from the industry supported by NASSCOM and DSCI not to have strict provisions of restricting transfer of personal data outside India. The current version can be considered as a highly diluted version in this respect which the Government seems to have adopted to avoid further delay in passing of the law.

The GDPR has a strict regulation of Data Localization by placing impossible conditions for transfer of personal data under Articles 44 fortified with the EUCJ (European Court of Justice) in the Schrems Cases striking down the arrangements between EU and US for personal data transfer repeatedly.

EU GDPR provides that personal data can be transferred freely within the EU since the EU-GDPR as a regulation is available in all these countries though individual countries are permitted to introduce some changes through local laws.

Additionally, EU in the spirit of assuming global leadership for Data Privacy grants "Adequacy Status" to few countries to whom personal data can be transferred freely under the assessment that processing of EU personal data in these countries affords adequate security to the EU residents whose personal data is the subject matter of the regulation.

The European Commission has so far recognised Andorra, Argentina, Canada (commercial organisations), Faroe Islands, Guernsey, Israel, Isle of Man, Japan, Jersey, New Zealand, Republic of Korea, Switzerland, the United Kingdom under the GDPR and the LED, (Law enforcement Directive), the United States (commercial organisations participating in the EU-US Data Privacy Framework) and Uruguay as providing adequate protection.

The decision to grant adequacy is often clouded with considerations and interpretation of the rule of law and human rights practices in the destination countries and therefore could have plenty of political issues involved.

Apart from the declaration of adequacy based on the decisions of the European Commission, GDPR recognizes "Contractual Binding" between the exporter of data in EU with the importer of data in a third country provided some standard contractual clauses (SCC) are incorporated and are binding. Similarly, when personal data is transferred within a multinational organization, adoption of a "Binding Corporate Rule" subjecting the processing of the transferred data to certain restrictions is also approved.

Though under Article 49 of GDPR, certain "Derogations" are provided for transfer of data in the absence of adequacy decision, they refer to specific situations such as explicit consent, medical emergency etc. these exceptions are not considered very useful since EUCJ has exhibited a high degree of intransigence in accommodating even the sovereign rights of other countries.

The striking down of the "Privacy Shield" arrangements between EU and US because of an objection of the powers of US law enforcement for investigation involving personal data and the US President's power to appoint an Ombudsman and the subsequent US agreement under the Data Protection Framework (DPF) has provided an exalted position for EU in dictating terms of data protection in third countries.

US has now signed an EU-US Data Protection Framework (DPF) and President Biden signed an executive order (14086) on 7th October 2022 which has now been ratified by EU.

Accordingly, US organizations who commit to a set of Privacy Principles namely the "EU-US Privacy Framework Principles " may be certified as an organization that meets the Adequacy criteria for personal data transfer from EU.

Apart from the general GDPR principles for processing of personal data which is a requirement under the EU-US DPF, the document also provides for a Recourse, Enforcement and Liability Principle which provides several measures of recourse to the data subjects to enforce their rights under GDPR. This was one of the contentions under Schrems II decision of EUCJ and the main reason for the invalidation of the Privacy Shield arrangement.

It appears that the US has effectively retained its powers of interception, surveillance and access to personal information for national security purposes subject to a due process of sanction from some of the designated authorities. The concession provided seems to be that the permissions are granted by some judicial authorities such as the "Foreign Intelligence Surveillance Court" (FISC) and based on the orders for seizure issued by such authorities.

Otherwise, in the EU-US DPF, the administrative powers for surveillance without Court order might have been restricted on paper. In India Section 69 of ITA 2000 has similar processes for ordering surveillance on an order of the executive committee whereas getting a warrant for search and seizure was always available and continues to be available.

The DPB is an independent body like an "Adjudicating body" and its decision is appealable to TDSAT and further to Supreme Court. Hence it appears that India already has a judicial structure similar to what has been proposed under EU-US DPF.

Whether India will surrender the administrative powers under Section 69 of ITA 2000 to try and get an adequacy approval is difficult to foresee. There is a possibility that once the new Digital India Act replaces ITA 2000, the Section 69-ITA 2000 may be quietly dropped.

The DPDPA 2023 has however found an alternative route to meet the EU demands halfway. DPDPA 2023 does not interfere with the processing of personal data of EU citizens in India. It allows the Indian processor to enter into a contract with the EU data controller and process the EU data in a separate technical environment which is outside the DPDPA 2023 regulation.

However, DPDPA 2023 does not provide under law any immunity to the processing from the powers of the law enforcement either under ITA 2000 or IPC or CrPC.

India therefore does not expect "Adequacy status" from EU. This may also reflect the current political dispensation which is strongly against colonization tendencies percolating through Data Processing regime again in India like the Portuguese, French and British colonies that took roots in India in the 15th to 20th century in our history.

As regards imposing our own restrictions on the transfer of personal data collected in India, Section 16 of DPDPA 2023 which addresses this issue has not indicated any restrictions for the time being.

The section 16 states

1. The Central Government may, by notification, restrict the transfer of personal data by a Data Fiduciary for processing to such country or territory outside India as may be so notified.
2. Nothing contained in this section shall restrict the applicability of any law for the time being in force in India that provides for

a higher degree of protection for or restriction on transfer of personal data by a Data Fiduciary outside India in relation to any personal data or Data Fiduciary or class thereof.

This section can be read with Section 38 of DPDPA 2023 which states.

1. The provisions of this Act shall be in addition to and not in derogation of any other law for the time being in force.

2. In the event of any conflict between a provision of this Act and a provision of any other law for the time being in force, the provision of this Act shall prevail to the extent of such conflict.

Effectively the Government has stated that it defers the decision about declaring any country "Adequate" or "Not Adequate" to a future day. It may also adopt an approach to give out a "Negative list" of countries to which data may not be transferred for processing rather than giving out a positive list of countries to which data can be transferred.

The negative list may be used sparingly and restricted to enemy countries. In the earlier drafts of the law Government had insisted on data localization which has been dropped from the law now.

However, under 16(2) the law has supported sectoral laws to provide a higher degree of protection for or restriction on transfer of personal data outside the country. This provision retains the flexibility of preventing data transfers of specific sectors such as Banking or Health sector where a list of "Adequate" countries or "Adequate sectors/Institutions" may be separately notified.

We may wait for further developments in this regard through notifications in due course.

Chapter XII

Exemptions from Applicability of DPDPA 2023

Section 17 of DPDPA 2023 is an important section that outlines the exemptions provided under the Act to certain categories of Data Fiduciaries in certain circumstances.

Though the exemptions have been an object of criticism for the benefits that the Government agencies may enjoy, such exemptions are also there in GDPR and are necessary.

Gdpr Provides "Exemptions" As Well As "Derogations":

Article 23 of GDPR states that Union or Member states can by law restrict the scope of the obligations or the Rights of data subjects to safeguard.

a. national security;

b. defence;

c. public security;

d. the prevention, investigation, detection or prosecution of criminal offences or the execution of criminal penalties, including the safeguarding against and the prevention of threats to public security;

e. other important objectives of general public interest of the Union or of a Member State, in particular an important economic or financial interest of the Union or of a Member State, including monetary, budgetary and taxation a matters, public health and social security;

f. the protection of judicial independence and judicial proceedings;

g. he prevention, investigation, detection and prosecution of breaches of ethics for regulated professions;

h. a monitoring, inspection or regulatory function connected, even occasionally, to the exercise of official authority in the cases referred to in points (a) to (e) and (g);

i. the protection of the data subject or the rights and freedoms of others;

j. the enforcement of civil law claims

Under article 49 of GDPR, derogations are provided for specific situations applicable to transfer of data in the absence of adequacy decisions which includes defence of legal claims, protection of vital interests of a data principal, under legitimate interest, public interest etc.

Also, under article 85 of GDPR, processing carried out for journalistic purpose or for the purpose of academic, artistic or literary expression.

Further, under articles 86 personal data in official documents held by public authority cay be processed in public interest, under article 87, member states may determine the conditions under which national identification number can be processed.

Member states can also by law or collective agreements provide more specific rules to process personal data in the context of employment.

Under Article 89, processing for public interest, scientific or historical research or statistical purpose may be provided some relief from regulation.

Member states can also adopt specific rules to address issues of professional secrecy and obligations.

Further the GDPR may not apply to churches and religious associations or communities (e.g., Vatican) which adopt a comprehensive self-regulatory practice.

Thus, GDPR also has a fair bit of exemptions built into the regulations and discretion to member states to alter the law. We need to view the exemptions provided under Section 17 of DPDPA 2023 under this context.

Exemptions under DPDPA:

The exemptions under Section 17 are contained under following 5 sub sections and all exemptions come with limitations and conditions.

17(1)	Circumstances Based on purpose of processing and type of organization
17(2)	To Government for National Security and for others for research
17(3)	To notified data fiduciaries or class of data fiduciaries
17(4)	To Government in other than National Security context
17(5)	Empowers Government to grant exemptions over the next 5-year period

Exemptions under Sec 17(1) are available in the following contexts of Processing.

a. the processing of personal data is necessary for **enforcing any legal right or claim.**

b. the processing of personal data by any **court or tribunal** or any other body in India which is entrusted by law with the performance of any judicial or quasi-judicial or regulatory or supervisory function, where such processing is necessary for the performance of such function.

c. personal data is processed in the interest of prevention, detection, investigation or **prosecution of any offence** or contravention of any law for the time being in force in India.

d. personal data of **Data Principals not within the territory** of India is processed pursuant to any contract entered into with any person outside the territory of India by any person based in India.

e. the processing is necessary for a **scheme of compromise** or arrangement or merger or amalgamation of two or more companies or a reconstruction by way of demerger or otherwise of a company, or transfer of undertaking of one or more company to another company, or involving division of one or more companies, **approved by a court** or tribunal or other authority competent to do so by any law for the time being in force; and

f. the processing is for the purpose of ascertaining the **financial information** and assets and liabilities of any person who has defaulted in payment due on account of a loan or advance taken from a **financial institution,** subject to such processing being in accordance with the provisions regarding disclosure of information or data in any other law for the time being in force.

Explanation.—For the purposes of this clause, the expressions "default" and "financial institution" shall have the meanings respectively assigned to them in sub-sections (12) and (14) of section 3 of the Insolvency and Bankruptcy Code, 2016.

The exemptions of processing under 17(1) **does not include**

a. Chapter II (Obligations of Data Fiduciaries) other than 8(1) and (5),

b. Chapter III (Rights) and

c. Section 16. (Transfer of data out of India)

Provisions of Section 8(1) and 8(5) are reproduced below.

What is not Exempted under Sec 17(1)

Sec 8(1) A Data Fiduciary shall, irrespective of any agreement to the contrary or failure of a Data Principal to carry out the duties provided under this Act, be responsible for complying with the provisions of this Act and the rules made thereunder in respect of any processing undertaken by it or on its behalf by a Data Processor.	Sec 8(5) A Data Fiduciary shall protect personal data in its possession or under its control, including in respect of any processing undertaken by it or on its behalf by a Data Processor, by taking reasonable security safeguards to prevent personal data breach

Since this 17(1) is a context-based exemption, excepting the above two sub sections of Section 8, other sections of prescribed obligations under section 8 such as

a. Responsibility for compliance of the Act
b. Responsibilities for Data Processors
c. Responsibilities for Data Quality
d. Technical and Organizational measures for compliance
e. Reasonable Security Safeguards
f. Data Breach Notification
g. Data Retention restrictions
h. Publishing of information about a Data Protection Officer
i. Grievance Redressal mechanism will all apply.

Under Section 17(2)(a), State and its instrumentalities notified in the interest of sovereignty and integrity of India, security of the State, friendly relations with foreign States, maintenance of public order or preventing incitement to any cognizable offence relating to any of these, as well as processing by the Central Government of data furnished by these instrumentalities will be exempt from the provisions of the Act.

This provision may apply to organizations like the ED or Income Tax etc.

Under Section 17(2)(b), personal data necessary for research, archiving or statistical purposes are exempted subject to the conditions that processing is carried out in accordance with specified standards and the personal data is not used for taking any decisions about the data principal.

In other words, the data may be used with the condition that it is in anonymized form and will be used only for creating reports for administrative purpose and not for taking any decision about the individual who has contributed the information.

Under Section 17(3) the Government may notify certain Data Fiduciaries or class of Data Fiduciaries, including startups, as Data Fiduciaries to whom the provisions of section 5, sub-sections (3) and (7) of section 8 and sections 10 and 11 shall not apply. The notification may be based on considerations of volume and nature of personal data.

Section 5 relates to the notice, Section 8(3) relates to the quality of data when processed for decision making about the data principal, section 8(7) relates to the limitation of retention and obligation for erasure on completion of the purpose both data with himself and with the downstream data processors. Section 10 relates to additional obligations of a Significant Data Fiduciary and Section 11 relates to the Right of access of the information by the data principal.

Further, under Section 17(4) all processing by the State or any instrumentalities of the State even if not related to national security reasons covered under 17(2), would be exempt from Sections 8(7), 12(3) and 12(2) when data is not used for decision making.

section 8(7) relates to the limitation of retention and obligation for erasure on completion of the purpose both data with himself and with the downstream data processors, 12(3) relates to the Right to erasure of data exercised by the data principal and 12(2) relates to the right for maintenance of accuracy, completeness and updating of the personal data when used for decision making or disclosure purpose.

Lastly, under Section 17(5) the Government has the power to notify exempted categories of data fiduciaries for a period of next 5 years. Hence organisations who will find it difficult to be compliant with the law or does not want to be compliant can keep lobbying with the Government for seeking exemption if not now any time in the next 5 years.

In summary we can observe that "Exemptions" are not restricted only for the Government and "Exemptions" are not absolute. Even the Government entities will be exempt only to part of the obligations or rights except when the processing is related to sovereignty and integrity of the state etc which are reasonable exemptions under Article 19(2) of the Constitution.

Chapter XIII

Data Protection Board of India

Chapter V (Sections 18-26) and Chapter VI (sections 27-28) of DPDPA 2023 describe the details of the regulatory authority namely the Data Protection Board of India (DPB) under DPDPA-2023 and its powers.

Constitution of the Board:

The DPB will be an independent body Corporate and will be governed by a Board with a Chairman and members. The exact number of members and the location of the headquarters have not been specified in the Act and should be indicated in the notification of constitution of the Board. It will have a common seal and be able to hold property in its name and will be a juridical entity that can sue and be sued.

According to Section 19(3), the Chairperson and other Members shall be persons of ability, integrity and standing. They shall possess special knowledge or practical experience in the fields of data governance, administration or implementation of laws related to social or consumer protection, dispute resolution, information and communication technology, digital economy, law, regulation or techno-regulation, or in any other field which in the opinion of the Central Government may be useful to the Board. At least one among them shall be an expert in the field of law.

The Board members will be appointed by the Government and there is no need that the Chairman shall himself be a legal or judicial persons nor the Government needs to consult either the Chief Justice of India or the leader of opposition etc.

Section 20 of the Act specifies that the members of the DPB will hold office for a term of two years and may be re-appointed. Their salary and allowances and other terms of service cannot be varied to their disadvantage during the term of their appointment to provide some independence in their operations.

However, under Section 21, a person may be disqualified for being appointed or continuing as a Chairman or a member if the person.

a. has been adjudged as an insolvent.

b. has been convicted of an offence, which in the opinion of the Central Government, involves moral turpitude.

c. has become physically or mentally incapable of acting as a member.

d. has acquired such financial or other interest, as is likely to affect prejudicially her functions as a member; or

e. has so abused her position as to render her continuance in office prejudicial to the public interest.

The Chairperson or Member shall also not be removed from her office by the Central Government unless she has been given an opportunity of being heard in the matter.

Under Section 22 of the Act, it is provided that a member may give notice and resign from the position and shall be effective from the date of acceptance. However, he shall cease to be in the office after 3 months or when the designated successor assumes office, or on expiry of the term of office whichever is earlier. The vacancy created by resignation, removal or death of a member shall be filled by a fresh appointment.

On relinquishing the office, the member shall not, for a period of one year from the date on which they cease to hold such office, accept any employment with any Data Fiduciary against whom proceedings were initiated by or before such Chairperson or other Member. Even after this period in case the member accepts such employment, the same shall be informed to the Government. The Government may however provide permission for such appointment if considered necessary.

Proceedings of the Board:

The Board may use digital means of conducting its transactions including authenticating the issue of its orders. Any proceedings will not be considered as invalid due to either any vacancy in the Board or any other irregularity in the procedure or defect in the appointment of the members, if it does not affect the merits of the case. When the Chairman is unable to discharge his functions owing to absence or illness etc., the senior most member shall discharge his functions.

The Board may with prior approval of the Central Government appoint other officers and employees as it may deem necessary. The Chairman, members, officers and employees of the Board shall be deemed, when acting or purporting to act in pursuance of provisions of this Act, to be public servants within the meaning of section 21 of the Indian Penal Code.

The Chairperson shall exercise the powers of general superintendence in respect of all administrative matters of the Board and also authorise any officer of the Board to scrutinise any intimation, complaint, reference or correspondence addressed to the Board.

The Chairman can also authorise performance of any of the functions of the Board and conduct any of its proceedings, by an individual Member or groups of embers and to allocate proceedings among them.

Powers and Functions of the Board:

Section 27 defines the powers and functions of the Board which is mainly focussed on responding to data breach and other complaints. Most of the general functions of regulation of the industry will be discharged by the Central Government/MeitY directly. The MeitY is likely to set up a division under the Secretary, IT to coordinate the regulatory requirements with the DPB.

On receipt of an intimation of personal data breach the Board may direct any urgent remedial or mitigation measures in the event of a personal data breach, and also proceed to inquire into such personal data breach and impose penalty as provided in this Act.

It is noted that this section does not designate the DPB as the sole authority for receiving the data breach notification and the authority of the CERT-In in this regard continues.

On a complaint made by a Data Principal in respect of a personal data breach or a breach observed by a Data Fiduciary of any of its obligations the Board may initiate the remedial actions.

The Board may also take note of a notice of breach on a reference made to it by the Central Government or a State Government, or in compliance of the directions of any court and decide to institute an inquiry. The use of the term "Inquiry" indicates that the Board may undertake an "Investigative enquiry" where it deems it necessary.

The DPB may also act on a complaint made by a Data Principal in respect of a breach in observance by a Consent Manager of its obligations in relation to the personal data and inquire into such breach and impose penalty as provided in this Act.

The DPB may also commence proceedings on receipt of an intimation of breach of any condition of registration of a Consent Manager, to inquire into such breach and impose penalty as provided in this Act; and

Under Section 37 of the Act, when a data fiduciary who is a data fiduciary under Information Technology Act 2000, (ITA 2000), has been imposed penalty in two or more instances and in the interest of public it is necessary to block access of a service of the data fiduciary by the public, the DPB may refer it to the Government following which such an intermediary shall comply with necessary directions.

If a reference is received that such a direction has not been complied with, the DPB may inquire into such breach and impose penalty as provided in this Act.

The Board may after giving the person on whom a complaint has been made an opportunity of being heard and issue such directions as it may consider necessary after recording reasons in writing.

The Board may, on a representation made to it by a person affected by a direction or on a reference made by the Central Government, modify, suspend, withdraw or cancel such direction and, while doing so, impose such conditions as it may deem fit, subject to which the modification, suspension, withdrawal or cancellation shall have effect.

Procedure for conducting its operations and Inquiry:

The Board is mandated to function as a digital office as far as practicable and receive complaints and conduct hearings and pronouncement of decisions through a digital process.

When taking a decision on the complaint, the Board shall first determine whether there are sufficient grounds to proceed with an inquiry and if the Board determines that there are insufficient grounds, it may, for reasons to be recorded in writing, close the proceedings.

In case the Board determines that there are sufficient grounds to proceed with inquiry, it may, record the reasons and institute an inquiry.

The inquiry shall follow the principles of natural justice and shall record reasons for its actions during the course of such inquiry.

For the purposes of discharging its functions under this Act, the Board shall have the same powers as are vested in a civil court under the Code of Civil Procedure, 1908, in respect of matters relating to—

a. summoning and enforcing the attendance of any person and examining her on oath;

b. receiving evidence of affidavit requiring the discovery and production of documents;

c. inspecting any data, book, document, register, books of account or any other document; and

d. such other matters as may be prescribed.

One of the limitations of the powers of the inquiry committee is that the Board or its officers shall not prevent access to any premises or take into custody any equipment or any item that may adversely affect the day-to-day functioning of a person.

The Board may however require the services of any police officer or any officer of the Central Government or a State Government to assist it for the purposes of this section and it shall be the duty of every such officer to comply with such requisition.

During the course of the inquiry, if the Board considers it necessary may issue interim orders after giving the person concerned an opportunity of being heard and on completion of the inquiry and again after giving the person concerned an opportunity of being heard, the Board may either close the proceedings or proceed in accordance to impose penalty with due recording of its reasons.

At any stage after receipt of a complaint, if the Board is of the opinion that the complaint is false or frivolous, it may issue a warning or impose costs on the complainant.

Appeal and Alternative Dispute Resolution:

An aggrieved data principal may approach the DPB with a complaint on which the Board may conduct an inquiry at the end of which may decide to either impose a penalty or consider that there has not been any violation of the act.

Complaints may also be made by a Consent Manger on a Data Fiduciary.

When a Data Fiduciary has a complaint against a Data Processor or vice versa, the dispute is based on the Data Processing contract and is not considered as a matter of dispute where the cause of action is entirely within this Act. Similarly, when a data principal has a demand for compensation, DPDPA 2023 does not specify that he is entitled to a compensation on the basis of complaint.

In both the above cases, it appears that the remedy lies with the Adjudicator of Information Technology Act 2000 under Section 43 or otherwise.

It is open for the MeitY to provide in its notification whether the DPB may consider disputes between the Data Processor and the Data Fiduciary or a request for compensation by the Data Principal as also a remedy that the DPB may consider for which we may need to wait for the notifications.

It is however expected that DPB will restrict itself to the disputes related to the compliance or noncompliance of DPDPA by a Data Fiduciary and let other data related disputes to be considered under ITA 2000.

Once a decision is provided by the DPB, if either of the parties are not satisfied, they may appeal to the appellate tribunal which in this case is the TDSAT (Telecom Disputes and Settlement Appellate Tribunal). The appeal shall be made within 60 days of receipt of the order and with such fees that may be prescribed with a discretion for the authority to condone the delay.

It is expected that the TDSAT should endeavour to dispose of the appeal within 6 months. Further appeal if required about the decision of the TDSAT lies with the Supreme Court.

It is interesting to note that under Section 29(10), even the TDSAT is mandated that as far as possible they should receive, hear and pronounce its decisions in a digital manner.

An order passed by the Appellate Tribunal under this Act shall be executable by it as a decree of civil court, and for this purpose, the Appellate Tribunal shall have all the powers of a civil court. However, if required the Appellate Tribunal may transmit any order made by it to a civil court having local jurisdiction and such civil court shall execute the order as if it were a decree made by that court.

Use of Alternate Dispute Resolution:

Under Section 31, DPDPA prescribes that if the Board is of the opinion that any complaint may be resolved by mediation, it may direct the parties concerned to attempt resolution of the dispute through such mediation by such mediator as the parties may mutually agree upon, or as provided for under any law for the time being in force in India.

It is possible that the Grievance redressal mechanism suggested as a Right of the data principal and an obligation of the data fiduciary under the Act itself may contain mediation in which case this remedy might have been already exhausted before the dispute is brought to the DPB.

Voluntary Undertaking:

In an interesting proposition, Section 32 of the Act prescribes that the Board may accept a voluntary undertaking in respect of any matter related to observance of the provisions of this Act from any person at any stage of a proceeding related to the imposition of the penalty.

The voluntary undertaking may include an undertaking to take such action within such time as may be determined by the Board, or refrain from taking such action, and or publicising such undertaking.

The Board may, after accepting the voluntary undertaking and with the consent of the person who gave the voluntary undertaking vary the terms included in the voluntary undertaking.

The acceptance of the voluntary undertaking by the Board shall constitute a bar on proceedings under the provisions of this Act as regards the contents of the voluntary undertaking and therefore becomes the final settlement of the penalty.

However, where a person fails to adhere to any term of the voluntary undertaking accepted by the Board, such breach shall be deemed to be breach of the provisions of this Act and the Board may, after giving such person an opportunity of being heard, proceed with the imposition of the penalty as if no such undertaking was accepted.

Chapter XIV

Penalties

Section 33 of DPDPA 2023 read along with Schedule I provides the details of the penalties prescribed under the DPDPA 2023.

S No	Subject Matter of Breach	Penalty
1	Breach in observing the obligation of Data Fiduciary to take reasonable security safeguards to prevent personal data breach, under sub-section (5) of section 8	May extend to two hundred and fifty crore rupees.
2	Breach in observing the obligation to give the Board or affected Data Principals notice of a personal data breach, under sub-section (6) of section 8	May extend to two hundred crore rupees.
3	Breach in observance of additional obligations in relation to children, under section 9	May extend to two hundred crore rupees.
4	Breach in observance of additional obligations of Significant Data Fiduciary, under section 10	May extend to one hundred and fifty crore rupees.
5	Breach in observance of the duties under section 15	May extend to ten thousand rupees.
6	Breach of any term of voluntary undertaking accepted by the Board under section 32	Up to the extent applicable for the breach in respect of which the proceedings under section 28 were instituted.
7	Breach of any other provisions of this Act, or rules made there under	May extend to fifty crore rupees.

According to the schedule, 7 different instances have been indicated for determining the penalty.

Unlike the GDPR which fixes the penalty based on the turnover of an organization, DPDPA 2023 has preferred to indicate a maximum amount for different types of noncompliance situations, if there is a breach in observing the obligations of data fiduciary to take reasonable security safeguards under section 8(5), penalty can extend up to Rs 250 crores.

If there is a breach in providing a data breach notification the penalty can be up to Rs 200 crores.

If there is a breach in observance of additional obligations related to personal data of minors, penalties up to Rs 250 crores can be levied.

If a Significant Data Fiduciary fails to appoint a DPO or a Data Auditor or conduct DPIA or periodical audit, penalties can go up to Rs 150 crores.

If a data fiduciary has provided a voluntary undertaking during an inquiry process and fails to fulfil the undertaking, then the penalty which could have been levied for the original noncompliance for which the undertaking was given would be applicable.

One of the exclusive provisions of DPDPA 2023 is the duties imposed on a data principal under section 15 of the DPDPA 2023. If there is a failure of a Data Principal to meet the duties prescribed, a penalty of up to Rs 10000/- can be imposed on the data principal.

Any other noncompliance can be penalized to the extent of Rs 50 crores.

The guidelines for determining the amount of penalty have been indicated under Section 33(2) and will consider the following factors:

a. the nature, gravity and duration of the breach.

b. the type and nature of the personal data affected by the breach.

c. repetitive nature of the breach.

d. whether the person, as a result of the breach, has realised a gain or avoided any loss.

e. whether the person took any action to mitigate the effects and consequences of the breach, and the timeliness and effectiveness of such action.

f. whether the monetary penalty to be imposed is proportionate and effective, having regard to the need to secure observance of and deter breach of the provisions of this Act; and

g. the likely impact of the imposition of the monetary penalty on the person.

The penalties as mentioned in the schedule are penalties up to the stated limit and could be less than the amount indicated. In case of multiple failures, the penalties for multiple types of breaches may be aggregated. It is also possible in cases of large data breaches; different instances of data breaches may be penalized independently, and the total penalty could be much higher than Rs 250 crores.

The amount collected as fine will be credited to the consolidated fund of India.

As already discussed, there is no provision for recovery of compensation by a data principal under DPDPA 2023. However, any data breach under DPDPA which creates some kind of harm to the data principal will also be one of the contraventions under Section 43 of ITA 2000 and hence Section 46 can be invoked, and adjudication can be initiated under ITA 2000.

Section 43A of ITA 2000 will be considered as withdrawn after DPDPA 2023 coming into effect but Section 43 remains. Contraventions that are recognized under Section 43 include.

1. Unauthorized access to a computer system
2. Unauthorized downloading from a computer system
3. Causing denial of access
4. Causing damage to any IT asset
5. Diminishing the value of information residing inside a computer or causing injury to the information (deletion, modification etc

In any personal data breach, one or more of the above contraventions of ITA 2000 will also occur. Hence Section 43 can be invoked in all cases of personal data breach.

Section 43 of the ITA 2000 is linked to Section 66 of ITA 2000 which recognizes that any contravention under section 43 is also a contravention of Section 66 if it has been caused with a malicious or fraudulent intentions. Section 66 is a cognizable offence which has 3 years of imprisonment associated with it.

Additionally, Section 43 has a sub section 43(f) which prescribes that "Assisting another person to commit a contravention" is also a contravention.

In the S.Umashankar Vs ICICI Bank case, TDSAT adjudged that "Negligence in securing IT transaction" could be considered as a "Passive Assistance" and "negligence" in implementing security safeguards which are considered as best/desired industry practices or compliance requirements under law, it could be considered as "43(f) contravention".

Hence data principals may have more than adequate means of recovering compensation for any personal data breach if not under DPDPA 2023, under ITA 2000.

Similarly, all the obligations under DPDPA 2023 and the penalties are directed at data fiduciaries and not data processors. If however the cause for data breach is negligence at the Data Processor's level, then either the data fiduciary can either use the contractual liabilities to claim damages or invoke ITA 2000. Similarly, if the damage is suffered by the data principal on account of the negligence of the data processor, data principal can invoke both claiming of damages and prosecution under ITA 2000.

Chapter XV

Miscellaneous

Chapter IX of the Act under Section 35 to 44 some miscellaneous issues have been covered.

Under Section 36 the Central Government retains the power to call for any information from either the DPB or a data fiduciary as it may consider necessary.

Under Section 37, based on a reference by the DPB, when penalties have been imposed on two or more occasions an appropriate authority of the Government may be asked to bloc access to any information generated, transmitted, received, stored or hosted in any computer resource that enables the data fiduciary to carry on any activity within the territory of India, after giving an opportunity for the data fiduciary to respond. This means that if DPB has fined say a you tube channel on two occasions, the DPB may refer it to the Government which may cause Google to block the channel.

Section 38 of the Act specifies that the provisions of this Act shall be in addition to and not in derogation of any other law for the time being in force.

In the event of any conflict between a provision of this Act and a provision of any other law for the time being in force, the provision of this Act shall prevail to the extent of such conflict.

Hence if there is any law at present either under RBI act or under SEBI act or ITA 2000, the provisions of DPDPA will continue to apply (Unless specifically modified under Section 44). If we consider the rules made by RBI regarding data localization as part of the RBI Act, then it would continue to be applicable though Section 16 of DPDPA 2023 is silent on cross border transfer of personal data.

Under Section 39, no civil court shall have the jurisdiction to entertain any suit or proceeding in respect of any matter for which the Board is empowered under the provisions of this Act and no injunction shall be granted by any court or other authority in respect of any action taken or to be taken in pursuance of any power under the provisions of this Act.

This section provides exclusive jurisdiction for any matters pertaining to this Act and no other civil court nor Consumer Forum can entertain any complaint.

Under Section 44 two other Acts have been amended. Firstly, in ITA 2000, Section 43A which addressed the responsibility of a body corporate handling sensitive personal data to follow "Reasonable Security Practice", failing which they would be liable to compensate any person who suffers a loss on account of their failure, has been removed.

However, Section 72A which imposes penalty of Rs 25 lakhs for contractual failure to process personal data remains. Similarly, Section 43, Section 67C, and several other sections that have an impact on processing of personal data either by a data fiduciary or a data processor remains in ITA 2000 and hence compliance of ITA 2000 remains a responsibility of all Data Fiduciaries.

Another Act which has been modified with the introduction of this Act is the "Right to Information Act" where under Section 8, "Information which relates to personal information" has been included as a type of data to which the right to information may not apply.

Other than this, some consequential amendments have been made in the Telecom Regulatory Authority Act 1997 to nominate TDSAT as the appellate Tribunal, and in Section 81 of ITA 2000 to include this Act under the acts on which ITA 2000 cannot have an overriding effect.

Central Government will have the powers to amend the Schedule of penalties for increasing the penalties only up to twice the current levels.

As would be necessary Government will have the power to make rules to give effect to different provisions of this Act under Section 40, power to remove difficulties under Section 43 of the Act. All such rules need to be placed before the Parliament for approval.

Under section 35, no suit, prosecution or other legal proceedings shall lie against the Central Government, the Board, its Chairperson and any Member, officer or employee thereof for anything which is done or intended to be done in good faith under the provisions of this Act or the rules made thereunder.

There are many rules that have been listed under Section 40 to be issued in due course. The issue of notifications is a continuous process which will go through for some time.

The industry is expecting the Government to set up the Board and indicate when the penalties will start being applied. The definition of Significant Data Fiduciaries is also an early requirement. The credentials of data auditors could also be an eagerly awaited issue.

The list of such rules currently listed under section 40 as due to be released are as follows.

Description
The manner of appointment of the Chairperson and other Members of the Board including salary and allowances, terms of appointment, the appointment of officers and employees of the DPB etc
The manner of authentication of orders, directions and instruments and techno legal measures to be adopted by the Board and any other matters related to the operation of DPB.

The manner in which the notice should be given by the Data Fiduciary to a Data Principal including publishing of the business contact information of the DPO
The time period after which the personal data given for a specified purpose needs to be no longer required
The other matters comprising the process of Data Protection Impact Assessment
Measures that the Significant Data Fiduciary shall undertake
The manner in which a Data Principal shall make a request to the Data Fiduciary to obtain information and any other information related to the personal data
The manner in which a Data Principal shall make a request to the Data Fiduciary for erasure of personal data
The manner of nomination of any other individual by the Data Principal
The period within which the Data Fiduciary shall respond to any grievances
The form, manner and fee for filing an appeal
The procedure for dealing an appeal
The manner of accountability and the obligations of Consent Manager
The manner of registration of Consent Manager and the conditions relating thereto,
The subsidy, benefit, service, certificate, licence or permit for the provision or issuance of which, personal data may be processed without consent
The form and manner of intimation of personal data breach to the Board
The manner of obtaining verifiable consent in case of minor's data
The classes of Data Fiduciaries, the purposes of processing of personal data of a child and the conditions relating thereto.
The standards for processing the personal data for exemption
Any other matter which is to be or may be prescribed or in respect of which provision is to be, or may be, made by rules…including who is a Significant Data Fiduciary

In summary we can say that DPDPA 2023 has been designed to be different from GDPR but as simple as it can be. It is expected that the Government will constitute a Data Protection Board shortly and release some of the notifications such as the classification of Significant data fiduciaries and the data breach notification requirements. We can expect more notifications in the next six months.

Government is also considering replacing ITA 2000 with a new version of Digital India Act and work is in progress. This may also impact some provisions of DPDPA 2023.

It is expected that once the DPB comes into existence any data breaches that are reported after August 11, 2023 may be considered for inquiry though in the initial few months, the DPB may make use of the provisions of "Voluntary undertaking" and focus on correcting unintentional mistakes. Imposition of high penalties may be deferred for some time. Also some of the classes of Data Fiduciaries such as SMEs and MSMEs may be given some time for implementation while large IT companies particularly the social media companies may be expected to achieve compliance within a shorter time.

Buyers of this book can claim at least one E-Book supplement in the next 6 months if they provide evidence of purchase and contact the author/publisher so that they will be appraised of the developments.

Chapter XVI

Compliance of ITA 2000

In this chapter, we shall briefly discuss how Compliance to ITA 2000 is related to compliance of DPDPA 2023. A detailed discussion on ITA 2000 is out of scope of this book.

Information Technology Act 2000 (ITA 2000) has been in existence in India as a law that applies to handling of Electronic documents by individuals and organizations.

It provides legal recognition to electronic documents, defines the method of authentication of electronic documents through electronic signatures. It defines contraventions that create liabilities for a person to pay financial compensation to another person in certain circumstances and imposes punishments for certain other violations. It also provides for a grievance redressal system through a system of an "Adjudicator" who is the regulatory authority for adjudging contraventions and awarding compensation.

The offences which may be prosecuted for imprisonment and fine are handled through the criminal justice system and have a component of imposing vicarious liabilities on organizations that might have directly or indirectly contributed to the commission of offences. The criminal liabilities arising our of such offences can be escalated onto the executives of an organization in case adequate measures are not taken by them to prevent occurrence of such contraventions or offences. This is the concept of "Due Diligence" as a requirement to incidence of criminal liabilities on executives of an organization.

The "Reasonable Security Practices" that data protection regulations refer are part of the "Due Diligence" which ITA 2000 makes a reference to. Further, while data protection laws recognize the two types of data handling companies namely "Data Fiduciaries" and "Data Processors", ITA 2000 distinguishes organizations from the point of view of whether they handle data for there own use or provide a platform for passage of third party information through their services. Such companies are defined as "Intermediaries" and this corresponds to the concept of "Data Processors" in data protection regulations where the organization does not take independent decision about the purpose and means of collection of personal data.

An intermediary handles third party information such as hosting it on its systems or transmitting it as an email service provider or mobile service provider or as a platform like Amazon on which users can sell and buy products or platforms like FaceBook (Meta) or Twitter (now known as X) or YouTube which act as digital media on which information contributed by third parties are hosted. The intermediaries distinguish themselves from "Non-Intermediaries" in the fact that they act as only conduits of information without on their own consuming the information and converting it into a form of their own with value addition. Such "Non-Intermediaries" are "Consumers of third party data" who convert them to information products and services of their own and take responsibility for such services.

In terms of legal liabilities, an intermediary handling only third party information for hosting or transmission without actively involving itself in determining how the third party information on its platform is distributed is provided a safe harbor protection. Under this provision, if the information hosted by the intermediary results in any contravention of law, the liability will not be borne by the platform but by the person who hosted the information. This protection is conditional to certain "Due Diligence" requirements such as informing the users about their obligations such as not to infringe on the privacy of others etc. As a result expression of "Privacy Policies" on the service platforms is a prominent action taken by any intermediary. Such Privacy policy is like a "Privacy Notice" that data protection regulations speak about.

A Data Fiduciary under a data protection regulation issues a notice to persons from whom personal information is collected indicating the purpose of collection and how the information is used etc and obtains a consent for processing.

An intermediary on the other hand expresses its privacy policies to the users of its services so that they are aware of what happens to the personal data or non personal data that is transmitted by the user through the platform. These "Privacy Policies" are also related to the terms of use of the service where information security process used by the intermediary to protect the information handled by it through the service or otherwise may be provided as information to the users.

When information is hosted on a website by an organization, the website hosting company is an intermediary providing hosting service to the person who creates the website. But the company whose website is hosted is the owner of the content and also the consumer of any information collected by the website (other than technical information required for delivery of content by the hosting service provider). Hence the website owner presents his "Notice for collection of information" to the visitors of website which is normally titled as "Privacy Policy". The technical information that is collected by the hosting company may be partly required for its own service delivery but may also be shared with the website owner.

For this purpose the website owner also designs his own means of collection of additional information of visitors through a system referred to as "Cookies". Cookies are pieces of information associated with a visitor of a website which some times are used as "Session Cookies" temporarily during a browsing session and discarded or as "Persistent Cookies" that are stored and used for reference for returning visitors. Some cookies are considered necessary for the efficient delivery of the service. An example could be a cookie that identifies whether the user is browsing through a mobile or a computer so that content can be presented appropriately. A cookie that identifies the IP address and the country from which the visitor is coming may also be a necessary cookie in some cases. On the other hand, advertisers try to use cookies to create a profile of the visitor which is not necessary for the delivery of the content service but may be used subsequently for displaying relevant advertisements etc. Such services are considered as supplementary purpose and hence any information collected is considered as not related to the main purpose of browsing the website.

In this context of a website therefore if any personal information is collected by a cookie the collection comes under the provisions of data protection laws. Hence there is a need to give a notice to the visitor about what types of cookies are used by the website and what types of information is collected by them and how they are used etc. Hence Cookie management is an important aspect of website privacy management.

It must however be recognized that the cookies can only collect certain "Identifiers" and they can identify an individual only if it is associated with some other information with the website owner or the hosting company. For example, a cookie can collect IP address or type of operating system used by the user but it cannot identify who is the person actually visiting the website. Hence cookie information may be considered an "Identifier not amounting to Identity".

In case the website has a membership scheme and has collected the personal details of the member and the cookie is a persistent cookie that identifies the visitor with his membership then the cookie becomes an identity since it can be used to identify an individual who has the rights of privacy.

A website owner who runs a service where identities are used to deliver any service is not a simple third party information transmitter and hence may not be considered as an "Intermediary". If a subscription service is hosted on a GoDaddy platform, the website owner is not an intermediary since his collection of personal data is as a consumer for providing services. But GoDaddy can be considered as an intermediary in case it uses only cookies not identifiable with any individual and does not exercise visibility to the content indicating the identity of the visitor. In case GoDaddy wants to view the content, develop any insights into who are all subscribing to the service hosted by the website etc., then they also lose the status of an "Intermediary". To the extent the information is generated by the website owner and used by both the hosting company and the website owner, both of them become joint data fiduciaries for the personal information contained in the content. If however GoDaddy strictly restricts its activities to hosting and does not know who is actually subscribing to a service etc (though the IP address may be known) but goes through the processing as requested by the website owner, then the processing of data by GoDaddy is like that of a "Data Processor" under DPDPA and also an "Intermediary" under ITA 2000.

A Data Fiduciary by virtue of his role determining how the data is processed does not become an intermediary eligible for safe harbor protection under ITA 2000 (Please refer to Section 79 of ITA 2000). It would therefore be appropriate to say that a "Data Fiduciary" under DPDPA cannot be an "Intermediary" under ITA 2000. He is a consumer of data and is responsible for the consequences arising out of the data. He is expected to follow the obligations under DPDPA and liable for penalties under DPDPA.

A Data Processor under DPDPA can in certain circumstances be also an "Intermediary" under ITA 2000 and can be eligible for safeharbor protection under ITA 2000 besides not being directly responsible for the obligations prescribed under DPDPA 2023.

However, if a Data Processor under DPDPA 2023 is an intermediary under ITA 2000 and does not meet the due diligence obligations under ITA 2000, he may be responsible for any contraventions of ITA 2000 arising out of the information hosted by the intermediary. Under the DPDPA

2023, his liability is determined by the contract with the data fiduciary. The DPDPA liability is only civil liabilities but ITA 2000 liabilities could be criminal liabilities too.

In any instance of a data breach at the data processor, negligence can be attributed to the data processor and a failure of "Due Diligence" can be flagged under ITA 2000 besides the failure under the contractual clauses. Hence in such cases, the data processor besides being liable under the contract to the data fiduciary may be open for prosecution for offences under ITA 2000.

Further, DPDPA 2023 may not provide compensation to a data principal in case of data breaches though penalties may be levied on the data fiduciary. However the data principal can claim compensation under ITA 2000 available to any person who suffers a wrongful loss due to any contravention of ITA 2000.

Since DPDPA 2023 has removed Section 43A of ITA 2000, the responsibility of a body corporate to implement "Reasonable Security Practice" to protect "Sensitive personal information", failing which a compensation to be paid to a victim, is no longer available under ITA 2000. However under Section 43, wrongful loss caused to a person by any contravention of ITA 2000 is subject to payment of compensation which may be awarded by the Adjudicator under ITA 2000 or by a competent Court. Such compensation is payable in cases of "Unauthorized Access", "Unauthorized damage to information", "Unauthorized denial of access", "Diminishing the value of information residing inside a computer" etc any one of which will certainly be recognized in any data breach recognized under DPDPA 2023.

Hence any "Personal Data Breach" as defined under DPDPA 2023 is also a contravention of Section 43 of ITA 2000 and hence the cause of action to claim compensation arises under ITA 2000. Further Section 43 of ITA 2000 is linked to Section 66 of ITA 2000 and if the data breach can be attributed to malicious intentions, the criminal liability under ITA

2000 can be invoked along with the vicarious liabilities of the executives of a company under Section 85 of the Act.

More over there is Section 72A where the breach of any contractual obligations of a Data Processor can be considered as a cognizable offence.

There are several provisions related to data retention, data archival, data disclosure, data updating etc in ITA 2000 which are relevant for personal data protection.

In view of this, ITA 2000 compliance is considered integrated with DPDPA 2023 compliance. Whether we consider DPDPA 2023 as an extension of ITA 2000 or Vice Versa, the compliances of both acts are integrated. We may consider DPDPA 2023 compliance as "Due Diligence" under ITA 2000 and "ITA 2000" as a reasonable security safeguard under DPDPA 2023.

While ITA 2000 applies both to Personal Data and Non Personal Data, DPDPA 2023 may apply only to Personal Data. Further ITA 2000 applies to all Data whether it is data of Indians or foreign nationals while DPDPA 2023 is limited to data collected in India in digital form.

A Data Breach notification whether of Personal data or non personal data needs to be reported to the CERT-IN. Several guidelines of CERT IN or the "Intermediary Guidelines" under ITA 2000 (Latest notification dated April 6, 2023) are applicable for personal data handled by data fiduciaries and data processors under DPDPA 2023.

We therefore consider the following ITA 2000 risks as also risks to be taken care of by any DPO under DPDPA 2023.

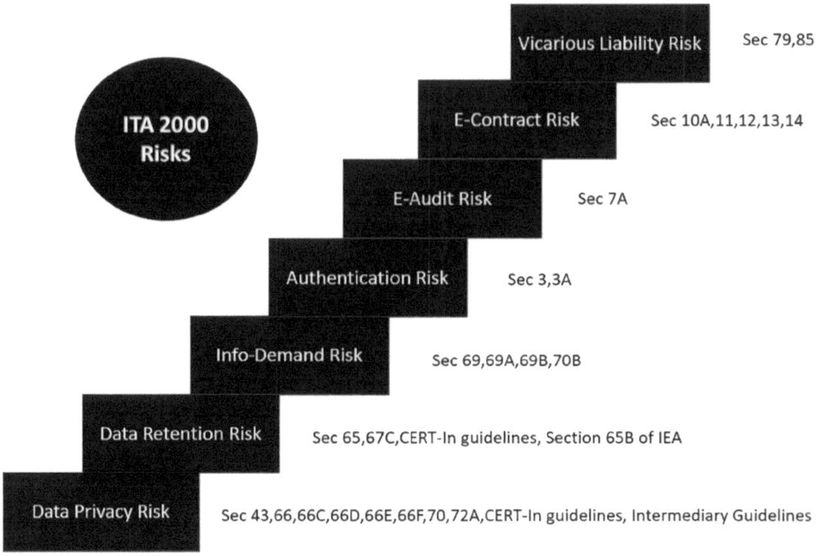

The impact of some of these risks can be indicated as follows

Section 43: Different Unauthorized activities	Civil penalty as compensation: No limit
Section 66, (unauthorized acts), 66C,(identity theft), 66D (impersonation), 66E (Obscene picture taking):	3 years imprisonment plus fines
66F: (unauthorised access/attempt to access, restricted information)	Life imprisonment
67,67A,67B, (violation of privacy by publishing or transmitting obscene information)	3 to 7 years imprisonment with fine
67C and 65: Retention of Information	3 years imprisonment, fine and civil penalty
69,69A,69B and 70B: Powers of different authorities for blocking or demanding information etc. Failure to cooperate	1 to 7 years imprisonment, fine and civil penalty
72A: Violation of Personal Data processing contract leading to unauthorized disclosure	3 years imprisonment and fine
Any Chapter XI crimes read with Section 85/ Section 79 (Vicarious liability) and Section 84B(abetment) and 84 C (attempt):	Imprisonment from 1 year to 3/5/7/10 years or life as well as fine and civil penalty

The author had created a framework for compliance of ITA 2000 called the Indian Information Security Framework (IISF 309) in March 2009 which currently was being used 33 controls for compliance of ITA 2000 indicated below.

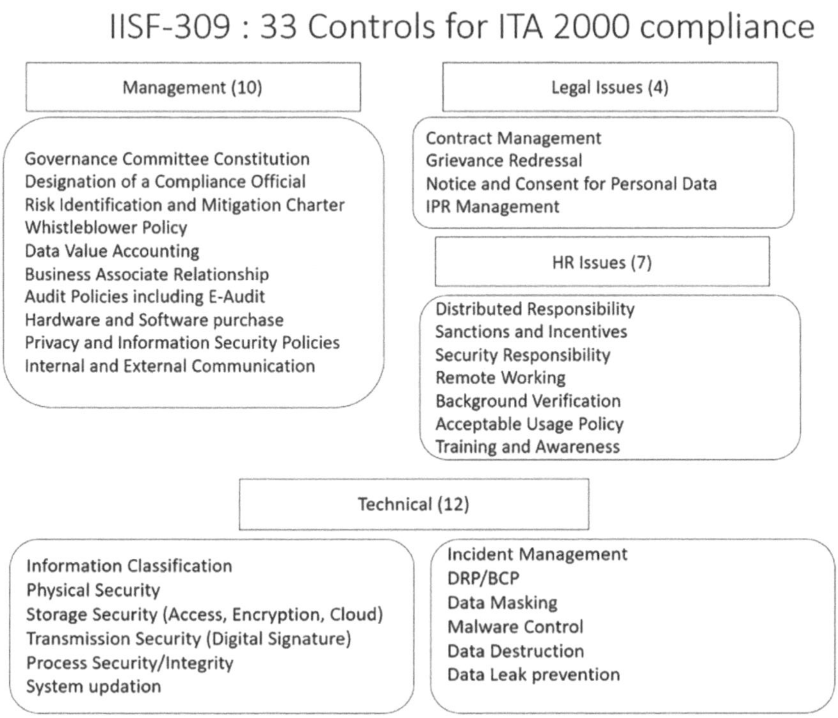

Now if ITA 2000 compliance is considered part of DPDPA compliance, it is essential to cover these requirements for compliance and merge it with the DPDPA 2023 compliance framework.

Chapter XVII

Compliance of GDPR

In this chapter, we shall briefly discuss the salient features of Compliance to GDPR (EU-General Data Protection Law) and so that readers are able to understand the salient differences. A detailed discussion on ITA 2000 is out of scope of this book.

Any company present on the web automatically receives visitors from all over the globe. If the website offers any additional services such as subscription or any white paper to be downloaded, the visitors may request for the same providing further personal information such as the email address and the mobile number. In such cases the website owner receives personal information of persons outside India who may have an expectation of protection of their rights under laws applicable to them. For example a EU visitor may expect that the website is GDPR compliant while a Californian may expect it to CRPA compliant or a Singaporean may expect that it is Singapore PDPA compliant.

Unless the website provides appropriate disclaimers wrong expectations may be created in the visitors which should be taken care of during compliance management.

Also, India being a data processing hub, many Indian companies have service level agreements which may have exposure to GDPR. Some clients without understanding the principles of data protection may demand their Indian clients to be GDPR compliant whether it is relevant or not.

Hence many companies in India may be exposed to GDPR as well as some US laws. Considering that GDPR is considered as one of the prominent laws, let us briefly discuss the compliance requirements under GDPR.

It is understood that GDPR is applicable if an organization processes personal data (as defined under GDPR) under an activity which falls within the scope of the European Union law. It will apply if data is processed within the Union or when processed outside, it relates to offering of goods and services in EU or monitoring of the behaviour of people within EU.

Most data protection laws use similar description to fix the applicability of their laws. The organization that is collecting personal data needs to be able to segregate the personal data in their hands according to whether GDPR is applicable to them or not and create different data buckets based on different jurisdictions.

Having segregated data for which GDPR is applicable, the compliance needs to be worked on. since the penalties under GDPR could be up to 4% of the global turnover of a company and fines up to US$1.2 billion has been imposed on a single client in the past, the non compliance issues of GDPR are considered serious. If an organization does not have an establishment in EU nor directly offers goods and services to EU location involving collection of personal data from EU, GDPR application can only arise through a contractual agreement between a foreign Data Controller and an Indian Data Processor. Penalties under such contracts are normally defined in the contract with some reasonable limitations.

For the purpose of GDPR, organizations need to determine their roles as Data Controllers who determine the purpose and means of processing of personal data from that of Data Processors who process data on behalf of data controllers. In certain cases there could be joint data controllers also where more than one organization determines the purpose and means of processing of personal data.

Once the status of an organization and the applicability of GDPR is determined, the organization needs to apply "Privacy By Design" concepts to meet the obligations of compliance as per the GDPR.

The different instances of enforcement of fines indicate the compliance requirements.

1. Sufficient Legal Basis for data processing
2. Sufficient technical and organizational measures to ensure information security.
3. Compliance with general data processing principles
4. Sufficient fulfilment of data subject/s rights
5. Sufficient fulfilment of information obligations
6. Sufficient cooperation with supervisory authority
7. Sufficient fulfilment of data breach notification obligations
8. Appointment of data protection officer
9. Sufficient data processing agreement

Organizations needing to be compliant with GDPR may ensure that they are able to prove the existence of at least one of the following legal bases.

a. the data subject has given consent to the processing of his or her personal data for one or more specific purposes;
b. processing is necessary for the performance of a contract to which the data subject is party or in order to take steps at the request of the data subject prior to entering into a contract;
c. processing is necessary for compliance with a legal obligation to which the controller is subject;

d. processing is necessary in order to protect the vital interests of the data subject or of another natural person;

e. processing is necessary for the performance of a task carried out in the public interest or in the exercise of official authority vested in the controller;

f. processing is necessary for the purposes of the legitimate interests pursued by the controller or by a third party, except where such interests are overridden by the interests or fundamental rights and freedoms of the data subject which require protection of personal data, in particular where the data subject is a child.

GDPR recognizes special category of personal data where "Explicit Consent" is required as the legal basis for processing. The special categories are personal data revealing racial or ethnic origin, political opinions, religious or philosophical beliefs, trade union membership, genetic data, biometric data, data related to health, sex life, sex orientation etc. In certain cases exemptions from explicit consent is also available.

GDPR recognizes certain principles related to processing of personal data which shall be the responsibility of the data controller to demonstrate. Such principles include lawfulness, fairness, transparency, purpose oriented collection, data minimisation, data retention minimisation, data accuracy, securing against unauthorized access or modification etc. These obligations along with measures required to protect the rights provided to Data Subjects under the Act are required to be implemented by the Data Controllers and enforced with the Data Processors. The rights protected under GDPR include Right to information, Right to rectification, right to be forgotten, right to withdraw consent or restrict processing, right to data portability, etc.

Under other compliance obligations, keeping a record of processing activities, risk based security management, data breach notification, conduct of Data Protection Impact assessment in high risk processing are also included.

In instances involving large scale processing of sensitive data, a Data Protection Officer need to be appointed.

GDPR also restricts transfer of personal data outside the EU. EU Council has declared certain countries as having adequate security to which these restrictions are not applicable. Excepting such "Adequacy countries", in other cases, transfers are permitted on the basis of appropriate contractual obligations or approved Binding corporate rules.

Between EU and US a separate agreement called EU-US data protection framework has been developed under which data transfers can take place without restrictions.

The ISO had come out with a framework for compliance of GDPR in the form of a guideline ISO 27701 which if implemented along with ISO 27001 is also certifiable. ISO 27701 has 28 requirements for PII Controllers and 21 requirements for Data Processors directed towards Privacy management which has been separately discussed.

For Indian Companies, GDPR compliance is in addition to DPDPA 2023, if it is applicable and for only the GDPR data set. Additionally there are exemptions available under DPDPA 2023 from DPDPA 2023 obligations if data is processed in India but consists of data of foreign nationals under a contract with an external data controller.

The framework of DGPSI (Data Governance and Protection Standard of India) of FDPPI covers all the requirements of DPDPA 2023 and provides that through data classification organizations may segregate the GDPR related personal data so that special compliance measures can be applied to them.

For understanding the difference between DPDPA 2023 and GDPR, a brief comparative table is given below.

GDPR Vs DPDPA 2023

GDPR	DPDPA
Territorial Scope	
The GDPR applies to: 1. Organizations that have an establishment in the European Union ("EU") and process personal data "in the context of" the EU establishment 2. Organizations that are not established in the EU, but process personal data in relation to either (a) offering goods or services in the EU, or (b) monitoring the behaviour of individuals in the EU.	DPDPA applies to personal data collected in digital form in India or collected manually and converted to digital form. It applies also to digital data processed outside India if it is related to offering goods or services in India Similar.
Subject Matter Scope	
Applies to Personal data excluding anonymous data. Also applies to automated processing or nonautomated processing where personal data forms part of a filing system. Does not apply to: Personal data processed by natural persons for purely personal or household purposes. Processing by law enforcement and national security agencies.	Applicability is to "Digital Personal Data". Hence non automated processing is automatically excluded. Digital personal data processed by individuals for domestic purpose also excluded. Anonymous data can be considered as not personal data if it cannot be identified with any individual. Other exemptions are separately provided and includes law enforcement requirements.
Definition of personal data	
Personal data is any information relating to an identified or identifiable natural person (data subject); an identifiable natural person is one who can be identified, directly or indirectly, taking into account "all of the means reasonably likely to be used.	"personal data" means any data about an individual who is identifiable by or in relation to such data;

Definition of sensitive personal data	
"Special categories of personal data" is defined as personal data revealing: Racial or ethnic origin; Political opinions, religious or philosophical beliefs; Trade union membership; Genetic data; Biometric data (for the purpose of uniquely identifying a natural person); Health; or Sex life or sexual orientation. Personal data relating to criminal convictions and offenses, while not special category data, is subject to distinct rules defined by EU or Member State law.	There is No definition of sensitive personal data in DPDPA 2023. The Data fiduciaries are classified into Significant Data Fiduciaries where processing of different kinds of personal data and their sensitivity is taken into account.
Relevant parties	
Controller: the natural or legal person, public authority, agency or other body which, alone or jointly with others, determines the purposes and means of the processing of personal data. Processor: a natural or legal person, public authority, agency or other body which processes personal data on behalf of the controller. Data subject: an identified or identifiable natural person.	Data Fiduciary ...includes all types of persons including individuals, Companies, Government etc Government reserves the right to exclude any class of data fiduciaries including Start Ups for limited period from certain provisions such as consent but not from "Security", "Rights" etc Even Charitable and Religious institutions are not presently excluded

<table>
<tr><th colspan="2">General principles</th></tr>
<tr><td>GDPR sets out seven principles in Article 5:
1. Lawfulness, fairness and transparency;
2. Purpose limitation;
3. Data minimisation;
4. Accuracy;
5. Storage limitation;
6. Integrity and confidentiality; and
7. Accountability</td><td>Though not explicitly specified, lawful basis and purpose oriented consent covers all these aspects under obligation</td></tr>
<tr><th colspan="2">Legal Basis for Processing of Personal Data</th></tr>
<tr><td>There are six lawful bases for processing personal data, subject to Member States adding more:
1. Consent;
2. Performance of a contract;
3. Legal obligation;
4. Legitimate interests;
5. Life protection and vital interests; and
6. Public interest.</td><td>Consent is the main basis. Legitimate uses cover other aspects including employment data</td></tr>
</table>

Consent	
GDPR imposes a number of requirements for obtaining valid consent: Consent must be freely-given, specific and informed; It must be granted by an unambiguous affirmative action; Generally, provision of a service cannot be made conditional on obtaining consent for processing that is not necessary for the service; A request for consent must be distinct from any other terms and conditions; Consent for separate processing purposes must be provided separately; and Individuals have the right to withdraw consent at any time "without detriment" and it should be as easy to withdraw consent as it was to give it.	Similar requirements are there including the provision of a Consent Manager who can provide and withdraw consent on behalf of the data principal.
Legitimate interests	
Processing is permitted, without consent, where it is necessary for the controller's (or a third party's) legitimate interests and provided such interests are not overridden by the rights and interests of the data subject. It is the controller's responsibility to determine whether the interests it pursues under this basis are legitimate and proportionate, and controllers are expected to document their assessments.	Legitimate uses separately indicated and include Employment purpose, securing the employer's interest on trade secrets, IPR besides medical emergency and public order emergencies

<table>
<tr><th colspan="2">Conditions for Processing of Sensitive Data</th></tr>
<tr><td>There are ten lawful bases for processing sensitive data, subject to Member States adding more:

1. Explicit consent;

2. Comply with obligations and exercising rights in the employment and social security context;

3. Life protection and vital interests;

4. Legitimate activities (by a foundation, association or other not-for-profit body with a political, philosophical, religious, or trade union aim, processing data about its members);

5. Establishment, exercise or defence in legal claims;

6. Manifestly made public by the individual;

7. Substantial public interest defined by law;

8. Preventive or occupational medicine, assessment of the working capacity of the employee, medical diagnosis, the provision of health or social care or treatment;

9. Substantial public interest in health; and

10. Archiving, scientific, or historical research purposes.</td><td>Will be covered in the Significant Data Fiduciary notifications for different categories.

DPIA, Data Auditor and DPO appointment is currently indicated.</td></tr>
</table>

Children	
GDPR imposes additional obligations when collecting consent from children under the age of 16 (or, at an age set between 13 and 16 by Member State law). Where providing certain electronic services at a distance (i.e. "information society services") directly to a child, and where the processing is based on consent, consent must be provided by a parent or guardian. Processing personal data of children is pertinent to other GDPR requirements (e.g. notices must be tailored to children; the fact that data subjects are children could tip the balance of the legitimate interests test or trigger a data protection impact assessment). One recital states that significant automated decisions should not be taken concerning children.	The age criteria is 18 years. There is a provision for reduction in specific cases through notification. Provisions applicable to minor is also applicable to other cases where legal guardian is appointed. Behavioural monitoring and targeted advertising to minors is not allowed.
Transparency requirements	
Information must be provided in a concise, transparent, intelligible and easily accessible form, using clear and plain language. Where personal data is collected directly from the individual, notice must be provided at of before the time of collection. For personal data collected indirectly (i.e. from another source), notice must be provided within one month (or upon first contact with the individual, if earlier), unless providing notice would be impossible or would require disproportionate effort. Detailed requirements for the content that must be included in notices.	Similar requirements through Notice which should also be available in multiple languages. It can be handled through the Consent Manager system also.

Right of access	
Individuals have the right to receive information about how their personal data is processed and a copy of their personal data. Personal data must be provided: Free of charge (except where requests are manifestly unfounded or excessive, or for additional copies); In electronic form (when so requested); and o Within one month (unless an extension applies). Exceptions apply where providing the information above would adversely affect the rights and freedoms of others (including intellectual property rights).	Similar right available
Right of Portability	
The right to portability applies only to: Processing based on consent or a performance of a contract; Where the data is provided to the controller by the data subject (which includes information observed about the data subject, but not inferences); and The processing is carried out by automated means. Where the right applies, personal data must be provided in a structured, commonly-used and machine-readable format, with the right to transmit such data to others without hindrance. Where technically feasible, an individual may ask for the data to be transmitted directly to another controller. As with the right of access, there is an exception to protect the rights and freedoms of third parties.	Not available

<table>
<tr><td colspan="2">Right of Correction</td></tr>
<tr><td>Grants data subjects the right to: Correct inaccurate personal data; and to Complete incomplete personal data.

Where personal data is updated, it must be communicated to each recipient to which it was disclosed, unless this would involve disproportionate effort.

The controller must restrict processing where the accuracy of the data is disputed for the time needed to verify the request.</td><td>Available</td></tr>
<tr><td colspan="2">Right to be Forgotten</td></tr>
<tr><td>GDPR grants data subjects the right to request the deletion of personal data processed by the controller, where the data is no longer needed for the purpose for which it is processed, where the data subject withdraws consent or objects, and where processing is unlawful or deletion is required by law.

If the controller grants a request for the deletion of data that was previously made public, the controller would need to "take reasonable steps" to inform any third-parties that may be processing the data of the data subject's request. There is also an obligation to communicate the request directly to any known recipients of the data, unless it would be impossible or would require disproportionate effort.

Controllers may rely on a number of exceptions, including establishing, exercising or defending legal claims, conducting research meeting certain conditions, and other compelling legitimate interests to override a request.</td><td>Not specifically mentioned though Right to withdraw consent, and Right to erasure does exist subject to the rights of the data fiduciary and legal compulsions to retain the data.

It may be correct to say that Right to Forget in the sense GDPR promotes is not available and it is better to escalate such requests to the DPB.

However stopping of processing and secure archiving of data may be required.</td></tr>
</table>

Rights relating to Profiling	
Data subjects have a right not to be subject to solely automated decisions, including profiling, that produce legal or significant effects, unless certain conditions are met. Where such decisions are permitted, data subjects have a right to obtain human intervention and to contest the decision. Controllers must also provide meaningful information about the logic of decisions and take reasonable steps to prevent bias, error or discrimination.	Consent based profiling is feasible though restrictions apply in cases of Children
Appointment of a Representative	
Controllers and processors not established in the EU (which are subject to the GDPR) must appoint a representative in the EU, except if processing is occasional and does not involve large scale processing of sensitive data.	Significant Data Fiduciaries need to have a DPO based in India
Appointment of DPO	
Required (for private entities) only where a "core activity" of the controller or processor involves either (a) the regular and systematic monitoring of data subjects on a large scale, or (b) the large scale processing of sensitive data. The DPO must have sufficient independence and skill to carry out its functions, and must be able to report to the highest levels of management within the organization. DPOs may be outsourced. Guidance from EU regulators recommends that the DPO should be based in the EU.	Necessary for Significant Data Fiduciaries...should be based in India

<table>
<tr><td colspan="2">Record of Processing</td></tr>
<tr><td>Controllers and processors must retain detailed records of their processing activities unless very narrow exceptions apply</td><td>Necessary as part of the compliance but not specifically indicated</td></tr>
<tr><td colspan="2">Data Protection Impact Assessment (DPIA)</td></tr>
<tr><td>The GDPR requires controllers to conduct a DPIA for certain “high risk” activities, including (a) systematic and extensive profiling, (b) processing sensitive data on a large scale, and (c) systematic monitoring of a publicly accessible area on a large scale.

In cases where the risks cannot be mitigated, the controller must consult with the DPA before engaging in the processing.</td><td>Necessary for Significant Dat Fiduciaries</td></tr>
<tr><td colspan="2">Privacy by Design</td></tr>
<tr><td>Requirement to implement appropriate compliance processes through the lifecycle of any product, service or activity.

By default, only the personal data necessary for a purpose should be processed and personal data should not be publicly disclosed without an individual’s affirmative action.</td><td>Not specifically mentioned but would be necessary for compliance.</td></tr>
<tr><td colspan="2">Appointment of Processors</td></tr>
<tr><td>Processing by processors must be subject to detailed contracts, with requirements set out in Article 28 of the GDPR.</td><td>Similar contractual binding required. All compliance responsibilities on the Data Fiduciary.

Withdrawal of consent or erasure has to be carried out even at the Processor</td></tr>
<tr><td colspan="2">Information Security</td></tr>
<tr><td>Controllers are processors are required to implement appropriate technical and organizational measures to protect the security of personal data.</td><td>Required in DPDPA also</td></tr>
</table>

Breach Notification	
Controllers must notify the DPA of a breach within 72 hours, unless the breach is unlikely to result in a risk to individuals. Notification may be made in stages as information becomes available. Controllers must notify individuals of a breach without undue delay only if it is likely to result in a "high risk" to individuals. Processors must notify a controller of a breach without undue delay.	Required. details to be notified. Reporting to CERT- In within 6 hours may also apply
Data Localization Requirements	
Localization is not required (unless international data transfer requirements are not met).	No restrictions at present. Countries to which restrictions may apply may be notified.
International Data Transfer	
The transfer of personal data outside the European Economic Area is permitted only where: The recipient is in a territory considered by the European Commission to offer an adequate level of protection for personal data (after an assessment of its privacy laws and law enforcement access regime); Appropriate safeguards are put in place, such as European Commission-approved standard contractual clauses or Binding Corporate Rules approved by DPAs; or A derogation applies, such as where data subjects provide explicit consent, the transfer is necessary to fulfil a contract (and occasional), or there is an public interest founded in EU or member state law, among others	No Restrictions at present

Penalties	
Administrative fines up to the higher of 20 million Euros or a 4% of a group of undertakings' annual global revenue. DPAs may also issue injunctive penalties, which include the ability to block processing, restrict international transfers, and require the deletion of personal data Individuals may bring claims in court for compensation and mechanisms exist for representative actions on behalf of a class of individuals.	Could go up to Rs 250 crores for different types of breaches but different types of breaches may be aggregated and also multiple affected persons may be considered as different breaches. Penalties may therefore may be much higher than Rs 250 crores
Anonymized Data	
Although not defined by the GDPR, anonymous data (which cannot identify an individual by means reasonably likely to be used) falls outside of the scope of the law (reasonable steps to reidentify). In practice, anonymization is a high standard to meet.	No mention in the Act
Social Media Intermediaries	
N/A	May be designated as Significant Data Fiduciaries and regulations applied along with ITA 2000

<table>
<tr><td colspan="2">Exemptions for Research</td></tr>
<tr><td>The GDPR permits a number of exemptions for scientific or historical research, archiving in the public interest, and statistical purposes, including:

Further processing for such purposes may be considered "compatible";

EU or Member State law may permit controllers to process sensitive data for such purposes; and o EU or Member State law may provide derogations from certain individual rights

In order for the research exemptions to apply, controllers must implement appropriate safeguards, which may be specified by law, such as pseudonymization</td><td>Similar provisions available. Details need to be notified</td></tr>
<tr><td colspan="2">Rulemaking Authority</td></tr>
<tr><td>National DPAs (and the EDPB) are may issue guidance clarifying the application of provisions of the GDPR, but the guidance is non-binding.

Some limited areas of the GDPR are left to national law, such as clarifying the conditions for processing criminal record data or adopting additional derogations from certain provisions.</td><td>Ministry may directly oversee the further rule making.

Data Protection Board will handle the complaints.</td></tr>
</table>

Application to Public Authorities	
The GDPR applies to public entities, subject to narrow exemptions: To Law enforcement and other "competent authorities" are subject to a separate, but similar framework where they are processing personal data for law enforcement purposes. o EU institutions are subject to a separate but similar framework. Activities that fall outside the scope of EU law, such as national security and intelligence services, are subject only to national law.	Applies to Government agencies. Powers to exempt any agency of the Government for National Security reasons exist.

Chapter: XVIII

Managerial Perspective of Data

In the earlier part of this book we discussed DPDPA 2023 as a law and for that purpose we looked at Data from the Techno legal perspective. We discussed that Data is created by technology as a sequence of binaries but law recognizes it as a human interpretation of a set of software and hardware which converts the binaries into human experience which can be seen, heard etc.

We observed that DPDPA 2023 recognizes Data as a property that can be nominated. Law does not discuss the value of the property but only addresses how it needs to be classified into Personal Data and Non Personal Data and how permissions can be given for collection, processing, disclosure and usage of personal data.

The Kris Gopalakrishnan Committee set up by the Government earlier in 2019 for recommending the regulations of non personal data had submitted a recommendation in 2020 which included how non personal data in a business entity can be monetized and exchanged through a Data Exchange System.

This report has not been implemented as the Government was bogged down with the legislation related to personal data.

But the industry has always recognized that "Data" is a key asset for an organization that has the potential for generating revenue.

Data is no longer just a decision making tool for the management but is the operating asset by itself. Data driven organizations not only use "Data" for decision making but for production management because the machines are mostly CNC machines with sensors reading the production status and sending it to the central server which instructs whether the machining head has to be moved here or there.

3D printing is another area where data becomes the end product by itself.

Additionally there are AI driven robots, some of them are humanoid robots. They are today receptionists, Journalists, News Readers etc. There is at least one company which has appointed a humanoid robot as its CEO.

We often hear the statements like "Data is the new Oil" from the perspective of the tremendous unexplored financial benefits that an organization can derive from the processing of data.

Essentially there is an agreement that "Data" has financial value and hence is a business asset. This is the difference in the perception of Data by a Business Manager compared to a Lawyer or a Technology person.

For a Business Manager "Data" is an asset that needs to be managed so that the Company gets a return.

Chapter XIX

Data Monetization, Valuation and Insurance

The Concept "Data is oil" was initially floated considering the virgin potential of Data to create wealth for a company. Subsequently some industry observers also saw data like a wet sponge from which value could be squeezed out.

In the industry, the more appropriate way of looking at "Data" is as an "Asset". All assets need to be either bought or created from within the organization and will have a "Cost of Acquisition". Sometimes Data is the raw material from which value-added products can be developed and the concept of raw material, work in progress and finished goods are relevant for valuation of the asset.

In some contexts, "Data" is not the finished goods but is generated in a business just as "Scrap" gets developed in a manufacturing process. It has to be either harnessed for profit or handled as a hazardous waste with safe disposal practice.

Some "Data" churns out valued sub products and remains like a fixed asset depreciating over time but having a long-term utility.

Some "data" is like "Consumables" and gets absorbed in the service.

Data Valuation:

An organization which has spent money on an asset and holding it for further use must look at it as an asset of value, a part of its asset inventory and protect it from loss or damage. Some of these assets like the "Personal Data" can be considered "Hazardous" because law prescribes that they shall be handled in a particular manner and in case of failure there can be penalties both civil and criminal.

When a hacker steals some data, he is able to offer it for re-sale at a price. This indicates that he knows the value of data. Sometimes he uses a ransomware just to deny access to the owner to extract a ransom payment. The Organization pays because it realizes that the data has a value, and it has to get the access back.

But if we ask a CEO about how much you would like to invest in data security or ask the CFO how much of Cyber Insurance Premium you would budget for this year, or ask a marketing manager, how much of data security premium you want to add in your quote, they will find it difficult to answer. The CISO or the DPO or the Privacy Officer on the other hand will struggle to get budget for hiring new talent or conduct audits or buy security products.

This situation arises because the top management of an organization may not have "Visibility" to the value of data in the hands of the organization. They may have a vague understanding that they have valuable assets but are not able to quantify if they have Rs 1000 crore worth of data or Rs 10,000 crore worth of data.

Meta was recently fined US$ 1.2 billion, and Amazon was recently fined US $ 887 million as penalties for not protecting their personal data assets as required under the law. Obviously, the assets themselves were worth perhaps hundreds of time the penalties. A few years back Air India suffered a data breach in which the hackers priced the data at around Rs 6000 crores in the dark web. The exact price is not an issue but the fact that the organization had not recognized this value in their balance sheets before some hacker said your data is valued at Rs 6000 crores is a matter of concern.

The dark web has a price list for different types of data such as Health Data, Credit Card data etc. Same way if the data is current there is a value and if it is old there may be a different value. If the data set consists of detailed information including say PAN card or Aadhaar Number or genetic data etc, the depth of the data commands a premium.

This is the concept of "Data Valuation" where data value depends on the type of data, the depth of data, the age of the data, the reliability of the data etc. The Data Valuation Standard of India developed by Naavi tries to provide a guidance to the valuation of data by a management on the basis of these parameters.

Alternatively, organizations may consider valuation of data by any other means such as the "Marketability" or "Cost of acquisition" etc or a combination of these.

At present the accounting community has some idea of valuing intangible assets like trademark as well as IPR like Copyright and Patent which can all be licensed for profit or consumed within the organization. But the accounting community is yet to develop an acceptable standard for valuing Data and bringing it to the Balance sheets.

Until the accounting standards are developed, we may have to consider the value of data to be brought in either like a foot note or as a contra entry.

Monetization:

Data Monetization is a term used in the Privacy industry for realizing value out of data. Privacy does not look favourably at personal data being sold for profit by an organization. But principle of business management has to take into account every possibility of earning revenue and cannot ignore earning revenue out of data.

The Privacy laws cannot take away this fundamental right to monetize data but place many controls so that the data subject's right on the personal data is not misused.

As a result, "Profiling" of a data subject or "Monetizing" of personal data are considered activities for which explicit consent of the data subject must be obtained by the data processing organization (Data Controller or Data Fiduciary).

Data Analytic industry always looks at how to extract value of available data and the whole Big Data Industry is dependent on such technology.

Hence organizations need to device legally permissible ways of using personal data for monetizing as well as for profiling which may lead to advertising revenue.

Law therefore sees a conflict of interest between the Data Protection responsibility of a Data Protection Officer and the Data harnessing responsibility of the IT industry. Hence law expects DPO to be an independent official to advice an organization on Privacy.

DPO is normally considered as a "Trustee" of the data principals and hence has to be a single point contact for grievance redressal and work independent of the CISO.

All these are consistent with the nature of personal data as a "Hazardous Asset" and the protector of this hazardous asset is as much responsible for the environment and the neighbourhood as the company which pays his salary.

This sort of fiduciary responsibility is not new in the industry since a Company secretary, or a statutory auditor also have similar responsibilities.

If an organization has to appreciate the importance of the role of a DPO, there must be an appreciation of the value of data that this role is trying to protect. His role is not only important for ensuring that data is not lost, but also ensure that regulatory authorities do not find reasons to impose penalties on the organization.

It is for this reason that the DGPSI framework of Compliance recommends that an organization must endeavour to bring the value of data assets into the balance sheet. It is not necessary to bring it as an above the line asset but at least as a contra entry/foot note.

There have been instances in USA where the personal data assets have been valued and taken into account to bring the organization out of a bankruptcy situation. Such things are possible of Data Valuation is an accepted accounting practice in an organization.

Additionally, data valuation will provide an opportunity to take budgetary decisions and calculate the ROI on security related investments.

Cyber Insurance:

After a risk assessment throws up certain risks, the technology department will try to mitigate those risks to the extent possible. However, some risks have to be accepted because they are required for the business. Such risks if possible, should be insured.

Insurance related to Data Security is a "Liability Insurance" that covers the liability of any compensation payable to the data principal or penalties payable to a regulatory agency.

Insurance can also cover the cost of regeneration of lost data in which case valuation of data lost need to be agreed with the Insurance company. Even while undertaking the Insurance the Insurance organization needs a valuation of data that it is insuring. At the time of claim it is required to assess the loss.

In practice however insurance is normally done as "Co-Insurance" with the insurance agency covering only part of the data assets and with several sub limits for settlement of claims.

Without an established policy for valuation of data and using it for determining the premium or for claims, it is difficult to resolve the insurance disputes.

Hence managers need to insist on valuation of data assets and preferably bringing it into the balance sheet in some form.

The Data Protection industry through various certifications can bring down the cost of Insurance since an insured with "Certification of Adequate Data Security practices" commands a premium reduction compared to another without such assurance. Hence ISO 27701 certification or DGPSI certification is a means for the Insured as well as the Insurer as a tool of arriving at the cost of insurance or determining the claims.

Data Valuation Standard of India (DVSI):

Naavi has attempted to develop a methodology for valuing Data and bringing it to the balance sheet for discussion with the industry and accounting specialists. The concept of data valuation is gradually gaining acceptance and in the coming few years, it may become common for organizations to provide an idea of the value of data assets they possess.

In recent days, following incidents in India have highlighted the need for a proper data valuation system to be developed.

1. Zomato made a successful public issue and sold its shares at a premium of Rs 7500% to raise Rs 9750 crores from the IPO market, despite incurring substantial continuous losses in the previous three financial years. The shares were subsequently listed at double the issue price and are still traded at Rs 137 per share (of face value Re 1) providing a market valuation of nearly Rs 1 lakh crore to the company, baffling the traditional investment community.

2. CIBIL (now known as TransUnion Cibil), which started as a company owned by Indian banks and holding sensitive personal data of over 100 crore Indians potentially valued at Rs 7 lakh crores was acquired by a US Company. Indian Banks transferred

82% shareholding in CIBIL but without realizing the full value of the data transferred in the process from CIBIL to TransUnion CIBIL.

3. Net4India a company with data roughly valued at more than Rs 100 crores was declared insolvent without taking into account the value of the data as an asset and the bankruptcy proposal was approved by NCLT.

At the same time, in US, at least three major data valuations were reported indicating the huge potential of personal data assets held by companies.

Firstly, American Airlines got its "Customer Loyalty Program" valued at $ 19.5 billion to $31.5 billion.

Secondly, United Airlines got its customer loyalty program valued at $ 20 billion.

At the time of these valuations, the market capitalization of American Airlines was $8 billion and market capitalization of United Airlines was $9 billion.

Thirdly, in an insolvency proceeding of Caesar Entertainment, creditors in US encashed the customer loyalty data base for over $1 billion establishing the potential of data to be valued and collateralized for loans.

Above incidents show how the inability of our current accounting practices to bring a fair value of data into the financial statements is preventing the Indian investors from realizing the true value of the corporate assets.

These incidents also point out that lack of proper valuation of data as an asset and a Data company as an enterprise is a potential risk to the capital markets and could trigger the next huge recession.

By adopting a proper data valuation system, we can ensure that investors can manage the risks with confidence, and we will have a healthy capital market system.

In the process, we may be also providing a global leadership for this new area of valuation of industries who are furiously working on digital transformation in every sphere of our activity.

It must however be recognized that "Valuation of Data as an Asset", "Valuation of a Data Enterprise" and valuation of a Company in the perspective of "Market Capitalization" of shares are different aspects. While the enterprise value could be an aggregation of its asset base, stock market valuation may be based on the estimated future cash flows. The balance sheet valuation is however on the historical cost or realizable market price (whichever is less if we are using a conservative valuation principle).

Naavi's Data Valuation methodology:

Naavi's data valuation method takes into account the current asset valuation principles such as "Cost of Acquisition", "Market Price", "Capitalization of Net present value of future earnings", "Periodical revaluation by an expert appraiser" etc. It also factors in "Going Concern" and "Gone Concern Concepts", "Conservative" or "Pragmatic" approach, concept of "depreciation", "revaluation", "intangible assets", "Actionable claims" etc.

The method also takes into account classification of data as "Personal" and "Non-Personal" and factors in "Sensitivity", "Quality", "Age" and "Depth" of data elements to augment the intrinsic value of data computed on the basis of Cost, Market price etc with additional weightage essential to arrive at a more realistic value of data for business purpose.

Data Valuation is a complex exercise since "Data" is an asset class which is unlike the other known assets such as Fixed Assets, Current Assets, Intangible assets etc.

Data can generate revenue over a long run like a fixed asset either not depreciating or depreciating very slowly. Data can also convert itself during the process like a current asset converting itself from raw material to finished goods. Data can replicate itself at zero cost and can be sold many times over some times at constant prices and sometimes at different prices. It is intangible but its value is not created by law like the Intellectual property law etc. The replicability of data, the reversible life cycle it goes through and the value additions and deletions occurring through processes such as aggregation, filtering, profiling, de-identification, pseudonymisation and anonymization, create their own complications in developing a system of valuation of data.

Category of Data:

Data to be valued may belong to two main categories namely "Personal Data" and "Non Personal Data". Personal data is by law regulated to be used only for specified purposes and hence the flexibility for monetization of the personal data is low. Personal data collected for one purpose cannot be used for any other purpose and hence it depreciates on the basis of the restrictions placed in the consent provided by the data principal.

Personal data can be converted to non-personal data through the process of "Anonymization" and non personal data can be used by data analysts to build value through intelligent analytics. The valuation of personal data (PD) and Non Personal data (NPD) need to be therefore addressed differently.

Naavi's method adopts a two stage process for data valuation. In the first stage, the intrinsic value of data is determined based on "Cost" or "market Value". In the second stage, the intrinsic value is adjusted with appropriate weightages for different aspects such as "Sensitivity", "Quality" and "Depth".

Valuation of Data as an Asset and the Valuation of an Enterprise:

Naavi's method recognizes that "Valuation of Data as an Asset" must be considered different from "Valuation of an Enterprise which uses data".

Some times there is a confusion in the market place when significantly data dependent companies are valued as an enterprise. Since a significant part of the business assets of the organization (e.g. Twitter or Face Book) is in data form, the valuation of the enterprise appears as if is also the valuation of the data.

Conceptually whether the assets have an inherent value of their own or their derived value arises out of the revenue generating potential needs to be sorted out.

If there is a fixed asset such as "Land" it may have a cost and it may have a general market value. These are normally considered for valuation. If a user puts up a Car factory or a steel factory in the same land, then the revenue earning potential may be different in the two projects. We cannot therefore assign the revenue potential of an imaginary project to be the derived value of the land.

This is the fallacy behind the valuation of Zomato shares as well as the American Airlines and United Airlines customer loyalty programs.

Such methods based on the projected cash flows of an imaginary method of use of data in future may however be continued to be used for valuation of the enterprise on the basis of "Market Perception".

Value Multiplication Matrix (VMM):

While Naavi's method uses the familiar system of cost or market value for valuation of asset, the resultant value is considered as the "Intrinsic value" requiring further adjustments. This method has suggested a "Value Multiplier Matrix" where the intrinsic value is multiplied by a factor.

This Value multiplication factor is set in a matrix taking into consideration,

a. Weightage for depth of information
b. Weightage for quality of information

c. Weightage for Age of information

d. Weightage for sensitivity of information.

There is a logic for including each of these parameters for value adjustment. Naavi's valuation multiple matrix (VMM) uses certain multipliers as an indicative principle. There can be debates on whether these factors need to be refined through appropriate research.

The VMM is different for Personal Data and Non personal data.

For personal data the accompanying VMM is used.

The multiplication factors used here may be considered as indicative and may be refined. Also there are more dimensions to the data that may be considered as part of a multi dimensional matrix which can be represented in a algorithmic computer modelling.

Valuation of Personal Data : Value Multiplier Matrix

(Intrinsic value to be multiplied by this factor to arrive at the value)

Quality of Data (Horizontal Type of Data (Down)	As collected. (unverified and unconfirmed)	Confirmed by Data Principal	Verified by User	Verified and confirmed
No Personal Identity Parameter (Non-Personal Data)	1	1.2	1.5	2
One simple Identity parameter (eg: Name or E Mail)	1	1.2	1.5	2
Two Simple Identity Parameters	1.5	2	2.5	3
Three or more simple identity parameters	2	2.5	3	4
Unique ID such as PAN or Aadhaar	2.5	3	4	5
Sensitive Personal Data other than Identity)	3	3.5	4.5	6
Health or Financial Data	4	4.5	5.5	7
Biometric Data	5	6	6.5	8

Keeping the limitation of presentation of the model on paper, we have retained few parameters on the VMM and a few have been incorporated in the computation of the intrinsic value of the data.

These are subject to discussion with professionals from other disciplines such as Professional asset Valuers.

We will take the example of one Company which collects personal data under a proper consent, uses it for its activities and runs a business.

In the context of Zomato or Amazon, it is like collecting customer data and delivering a service. The collection of personal data is for the specific purpose of providing the service and by consent a data principal may agree that the data may be retained for future use for the same or incidental purpose. Normally such consents are not applicable for "Discovered" new uses which are the basis for the fancy valuations of such companies.

Also, as per law the customer always has a right to withdraw consent after which the personal data needs to be either archived for legitimate interests or deleted.

In such companies, we can compute the total number of data of different categories, list them as an inventory of personal data and then assign the classification tag for "Depth", "Quality", "Sensitivity" or "Age". Accordingly the VMM will be determined as indicated in the table.

As an example, for a personal information data set that contains three levels of information namely name and contact information in the first level, Unique IDs such as PAN card or Aadhaar number or Biometrics, at the second level, and additional associated data such as health data or financial data at the third level depending on the quality of data such as whether verified or not etc., the multiplier can vary from 1 to 10. The multiplier means that the intrinsic value computed on the basis of acquisition cost or market value may have to be multiplied by the VMM. In case the market value is used as a parameter for determining the intrinsic value, care needs to be taken to ensure that there is no "Duplication" since the market value may be available on the full data set which may incorporate the depth, sensitivity etc. When dark web places a market value of US$6000 for

French passport data, such market value already incorporates the complete set of data elements contained in the data and hence using the VMM again may distort the value.

Since the above table is for Personal Data (PD), the multiplier for Non Personal Data (NPD) is indicated as zero. Further the "Age" factor is integrated with the intrinsic value calculation since under Indian law, a "Renewal of Consent" is required at annual intervals and if such renewal is not obtained, the data will have to be depreciated to the extent of 100%. This is like a licensed asset where after the license period the asset has to be decommissioned. Hence a personal data older than 1 year may have to be valued at zero. This is considered as "Depreciation" and not figuring in the above VMM table.

In the case of NPD, the depreciation may be placed at around 50% since the drop in value is not legally directed but is determined by the obsolescence of the data value with the efflux of time. The intrinsic value of NPD may still be computed on the basis of cost of acquisition. If a company already has PD which is then anonymized, then it will lose value as a PD by depreciation but regain value as an NPD for which cost of acquisition would be cost of anonymization.

Computing the cost of acquisition where data is built within the organization is a "Costing exercise" where different expense elements have to be identified and loaded as cost elements.

In determining the market value of personal data or non personal data, as has been already mentioned, the perceived market value of personal data may vary according to the capabilities of the user. This will be reflected as a further value added product which we normally refer to as "Profile" which may be an identified profile in the case of Personal data and anonymous "Big Data" in the case of non personal data. Once a PD is converted into a profile, it can be considered as a data product and valued. But "Speculative consideration that a set of PD may be converted into a profile and used productively" is not considered for valuation.

In the case of Zomato valuation, some valuers have argued that the personal data resulting from food delivery may be used to create a profile of the eating habits, can enable Zomato to set up cloud kitchens, develop its own brand of food products etc and thereby earn income. The speculative part of such future plans are not considered under the above model.

The data valuer needs to be aware that there is a dark web market where every data is sold at specified values and could be an indicator of the perceived market value to some extent. In the case of mergers and acquisitions, the acquirer knows how he can use the data and hence may assign a value that the seller may not be aware of.

A classic example in India was the case of the shares of CIBIL that were transferred to TransUnion, at a price which was like selling diamond as glass beads. TransUnion knew the real value, but the Indian Banks did not.

Another example we can consider examining the working of the above model is the reported Data Breach of Air India. In this incident 45 lakh data sets were breached. The depth of the data set was more than 3 levels since it included Name, Date of Birth, Contact Information, passport information, ticket information, frequent flyer status and credit data. This is a complete set and in the dark web the value of such sets is more than US$250/-.

We therefore know the number of data sets, the depth, as well as their market value. The quality is high since it is integrated with credit card data and is therefore verified. The age factor is not known. As the age of this data increases, some credit cards could have expired, some addresses could have changed and therefore the value would have depreciated. From the public information we are not aware of the age of the data but in an actual data valuation exercise, the age would be easily computed.

Hence a data valuer who today examines the Air India portfolio may assign a value of around Rs 78,750 crores for the leaked 45 lakh data.

Despite the leak, the data still remains with Air India as an asset and can be cleaned up by

a. Updating the information

b. Re issue of Credit cards (for which the cost may be borne by Air India as part of its data breach penalty)

After such clean-up the value of the data will remain at Rs 78,750 crores less the cost of data breach related penalty. Perhaps the data breach has enabled the market to discover that Air India also has data similar to American and United Airlines of America though the probability of conversion of mileage points into actual sales may be lower. But by tying up with other airlines if the mileage points can be encashed more easily the value of the data will be restored to the levels used in American/ United Airlines valuations.

In all future public sector disinvestments, if the Government of India does a data valuation and brings it into the balance sheet in some form of visibility, then the Government disinvestment plan would get a new boost.

Valuation of Data held in Platforms like Twitter:

Intermediaries like Twitter, Facebook etc., are to be considered as different from companies who process data for their own business and convert the raw data to value added data and use it themselves or sell it.

The intermediary platforms basically are like reservoirs of third-party data on which they create advertising revenue. They may not like to make changes to the data but let visitors view the data and in the process create opportunities for advertisers.

In such companies' valuation of data which is under their control could be done on the basis of number of data elements held (say number of tweets) or number of active users. But this data should be considered as not available for value added conversion and if they resort to such manipulation of data, they will lose their intermediary status. They do not therefore have the status of "Current Data Assets".

Assuming that intermediaries remain purely as intermediaries, and Twitter is one such intermediary, then we can value such companies on the basis of the advertising potential of the reservoir of data.

For example, Twitter gets about 500 million tweets per day and most of such data never get deleted. The stock therefore keeps on widening though from advertising potential the value of old data is less than current data and lesser than "Breaking Data". The depreciation should be high in the first one month and first year. This need to be factored into the valuation.

The valuation of Twitter's data stock has to be done on the basis of identifying the total number of place holders for advertisements which is reflected by the number of tweets. Then the age of the tweet may be factored in, and value assigned. Conversion of this value into actual potential is to be put on a probabilistic estimate based on the historical information.

In assigning a weightage to such tweets, the fact whether the account holder is a "Verified account holder", whether he is having the status of a "Celebrity", the number of "Retweets" and "followers" are also to be considered. Essentially such characteristics determine the estimated "Viewing prospect".

In Facebook the same weightage could take the shape of "Number of Likes", "Number of Friends" etc.

While we may develop a VMM table for such valuation similar to the one developed for personal data, since different platforms have different business models, there is a need for customization of valuation methods.

Just as a precious stone valuer may look at the value from the point of view of purity, size and nature of the stone and adopt different yard sticks for different types of stones, data valuer of a platform may also have to adopt customized methods for valuation of the platforms.

Platforms like WhatsApp are intermediaries, but they may not have access to the content of messages. The data they may collect, and exploit are the meta data of a message and the personal data of the account holders. Hence the value of data of such platforms will depend on the number of active users and the frequency of usage just like the Twitter.

WhatsApp may not use advertising on the content but only let the profiling be passed onto Face Book which may use it for advertising.

Representation of data on Financial Statements:

After a valuation of data is undertaken by a data valuer the next question to be addressed is whether the valuation has to be disclosed to the shareholders and the larger public.

In order that the management has a visibility of its own assets so as to provide necessary resources for their management and to let their financiers/ lenders/prospective buyers be aware of the real wealth of the company, it is essential that the value of data is reflected in the balance sheets.

However, since accounting professionals are bound by the internationally accepted accounting principles, it would take some time for the data asset value to be reflected as part of the other assets like the intangible asset.

However, until such time, the value of data may be reflected in the balance sheets as a "Contra Entry" both on the asset side and the liability side or added as a comment in the shareholders report.

Since data valuation is done by a data valuer and not by the statutory financial auditor, the report of the data valuer is submitted to the management and the management may make it available to the statutory financial auditor. Then it may be added in the notes to the account "as per the valuation of a qualified data valuer and accepted by the management".

The Indian law on the personal data protection has suggested a mandatory data audit which can cover the valuation of personal data on an annual basis as part of the computation of Data Trust Score (DTS).

The valuation of NPD however is not required to be done under the Personal Data Protection law and hence it may have to be commissioned and carried out separately. Such a valuation of NPD will also become necessary when the Government comes with the Non-Personal Data Governance Act which is under discussion now.

Chapter XX

Managerial View of Data Security

The terminology of "Data Security" has to be understood along with the related terms such as "Information Security", "Cyber Security", "Personal Data Protection", "Data Privacy" etc.

"Data" is typically information that is in binary form expressed as a sequence of zeros and ones arranged in a sequence and capable of being processed by devices which are designed to respond to binary information in specific form using a standard protocol.

If we take the literal meaning of "Data Security" as securing "Data", it is same as "Information Security". "Cyber Security" is also a term which can be equated to "Information Security" though "Information Security" is often inward looking at securing the information residing inside a network where as "Cyber Security" is more often focussed at securing the data from attacks from outside the network. "Cyber Security" is an attack centric perspective where as "Information Security" is an effect centric perspective of what happens to data because of an attack.

In the context of "Protection of Right to Privacy" of an individual, "Data Protection" or "Data Privacy" are terms used to mean securing the "Personal Data" in such a manner that the "Right to Privacy" is preserved when personal data is processed by an organisation. "Personal Data" is itself data that is identifiable to an individual and consists of a combination of elements called "identifiers" that together contribute to identifying an individual by a human observer.

In the Privacy related Data Protection domain, we often refer to General Data Protection Regulation or GDPR (The term EU-GDPR is used to represent the original European Union version which became effective on 25th May 2018 whereas UK-GDPR is a version adopted by UK after it exited from the EU. We use the term GDPR in this book to represent EU-GDPR unless the context refers it to any other law) or the DPDPA (Digital Personal Data Protection Act 2023 which is the Act passed in India with a Presidential asset and gazette notification on 11th August 2023). These and similar laws of other countries speak of "Appropriate Safeguards" or "Reasonable Security". These terms normally mean, "Preserving the Confidentiality, Integrity and Availability of Information". This is called the CIA triad and is the foundation of Information Security. The word "Appropriate" normally means a commensurate to the "Risk".

In the managerial perspective of Information Security, the concept of "Information Assurance" overtakes the concept of Information Security and includes two more parameters namely "Accountability or Authentication" and "Non-Repudiation".

Achieving the information security objective is a "Journey" and hence some kind of prioritization is inevitable.

In this context the "Pyramid" model of representing the Information Security journey indicates the hierarchical prioritization that may be followed by the management.

In other words, while Confidentiality, Integrity, Availability, Authentication as well as Non Repudiation are all necessary for meeting the objective of Information Security, the journey starts with availability and goes up to Non Repudiation.

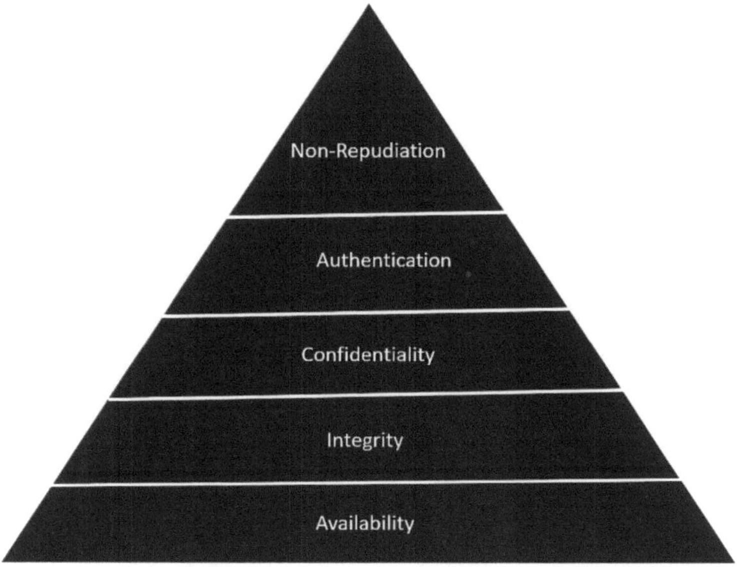

We often say that "Security is as weak as its weakest link". Hence when speak of achieving our Information Security objective, all aspects of Information Security have to be covered.

One way of representing this approach is used by the author in representing the Cyber/Information/Data Security as a polygon where different parameters are the walls of Security and together guard the information by closely integrating with each other. This polygon model of Information security consisting of the five elements above can be depicted as indicated in the Naavi's Information Security Pentagon. In this model, the Confidentiality, Integrity and Availability as well as Authentication and Non-Repudiation refers to the which is the subject matter of Information Protection. It could be personal data or non-personal data.

When we get into the domain of "Data Privacy" or "Personal Data Protection", we need to further expand our model from a pentagon to a septagon (or Heptagon) by adding two more parameters of focus namely "Consent" and "Law". Additionally, we have merged the Non repudiation with Authentication and added "Governance" as an additional factor.

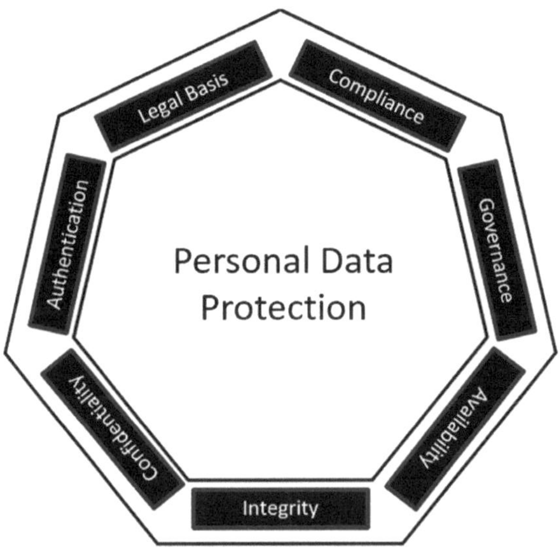

At the same time, in the context of Personal Data Protection, the factors of Confidentiality, Integrity, Availability, Authentication and Non-Repudiation apply to "Personal Data" which is the subject matter of protection of Privacy of an individual whose personal data is being protected by an organization.

This Naavi's Septagon (Heptagon) model of Data Protection represents the requirement for Personal data protection whether it is in India or elsewhere and whether the law is DPDPA or GDPR.

The idea of presenting the model as a polygon is that unless all the elements combine together there could be a leakage of security. Hence an organization needs to have a comprehensive and coordinated approach to meet all the parameters to achieve the objective. Achieving one to the exclusion of another does not fit into this model.

Concept of Data Security in the Data Privacy domain is conceptually different from the concept of data security under the Information Security domain because it brings in the element of a human choice in the form of "Consent" and the obligation to be compliant with a "Law".

"Consent" establishes the "Right of Choice" of an individual about how his/her personal data is processed by a third party while "Law" expands the concept to several other aspects of security including establishing other legal bases for processing, legitimate uses, restrictions on cross border transfer etc.

Governance in this context may be restricted to Personal Data or extended to all Data as an Asset since personal data is often carved out of the "Total universe of data at the disposal of an organisation" and there may be convertibility of personal data to non-personal data and vice versa.

States of Data:

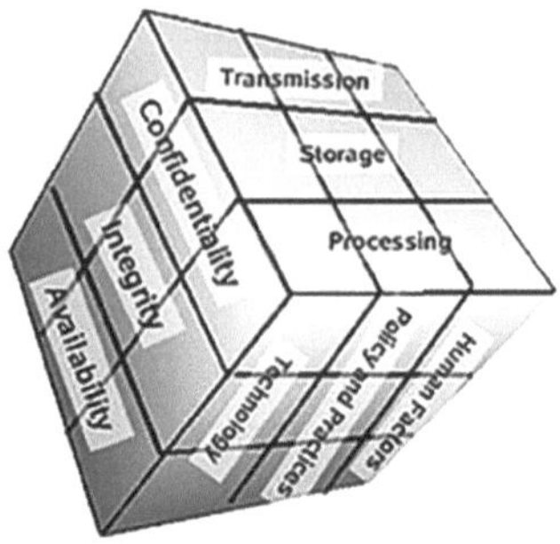

Additionally, "Data" remains in an organization "At Rest" or "Under transmission" or "Under Process". The adjoining Mcumber Cube represents the interaction between the CIA triad and the state of data.

Data when born is in a state of a chaotic distribution of zeros and ones in a data storage device (E.g.: black hard disk). When the binaries get oriented in bits of 8, they are ready to represent bytes of data. A reading device following a certain protocol reads the bytes as text or number and it leads to further actions being triggered by the system.

Processing further continues to aggregation of different sets of data and create a meaning to the binary stream.

This Processing of data takes it through a life cycle when raw meaningless data becomes meaningful bytes and groups of bytes become a word and thereafter sentence etc.

Some streams of bytes trigger specific software, and the content gets interpreted and displayed as picture or other forms.

In this entire process, some data assumes forms of "Identifiable" to an individual and hence personal data. Then the depth of such data increases as more and more elements of data are added until it matures into "Information" that gets a marketable value. At that time, it may be disclosed to an outsider as if it is "Sold". But the nature of data is such that even when it is "Sold" a copy remains with the seller. Hence the data has to be finally "Destroyed" and converted back into its chaotic distribution state to make it end the life cycle.

It is also understood that this lifecycle is reversible since data elements can be removed as easily as they are added. Hence a data which becomes personal data with addition of data elements can also become non personal data with the removal of the data elements.

The technological process of data analysis therefore involves changing of the state of data from one state to another till it is destroyed through a process from which it cannot be recovered.

Forensics suggest that data which is deleted remains in some part of the data storage though not discovered by the applications. Such data may be recoverable partly or fully through a forensic recovery process. To completely remove the data, it has to be "Forensically destroyed" like "Shredding" which may involve multiple deletions and over writings. The "Deleted" state is again as good as the deletion technology used.

When we speak of "Information Security" therefore, we need to take into account security in each of the different states of data in the life cycle.

"Data Protection" for the purpose of "Privacy Protection" is relevant only for data which is identified as "Personal Data". Personal Data or Personally identifiable Information (PII)is such data which can be identified as related to an individual. Information related to an organization is non personal data which can be called "Corporate Data". Information related to the environment or the economy etc is neither personal or Corporate and could still be considered as "Non-Personal Data". If an organization has paid value for acquiring such data, then it may be considered as "Corporate Asset" and we may consider them also as "Corporate Data" recognizing the ownership of the company over such data.

Similarly, software applications either created by a company for its own use or bought or licensed from outside are "Corporate Assets of Value" and hence can be considered as "Corporate Data" and is "Non Personal Data".

Thus, the objectives of "Data Protection" has to recognize that there are different types of data and they require different security objectives to be set before going into the technology of data protection.

Distinction of Personal and Non-Personal Data:

One of the important things to realise in understanding the life cycle of data is that "Data" which is "Non-Personal" may transition to "Personal Data" if identity parameters are added to the data so that it becomes identifiable.

For example, a video of a person walking in the street is non personal data related to the activity in the street. But if we identify the person through face recognition or the video has another person calling out the name of the individual, then the same video becomes "Personal Data".

Similarly, a personally identifiable data can be converted into non personal data if we can mask the identity parameters associated with it. This process is called "De-Identification". When personal data in the custody of an organization is "De-identified", the company may retain a mapping of what was the identity before it's dis-association with the subject data. Such de-identification is reversible. If, however the identity parameters are removed and destroyed irrevocably, then the resulting information is called "Anonymized Information". Anonymized information is normally considered as impossible to be re-identified.

In between these two categories of "De-Identified" and "Anonymous" information both of which could be transformations from a personal information state, we can identify another category of de-identified information called "Pseudonymised information". Pseudonymisation is a process where different identity parameters associated with a personal information are replaced and substituted by similar information so that the entire data set looks as realistic as the original but the identity parameters don't lead to the identity of the real person to whom the data belongs. In comparison "De-Identification" removes all identity parameters and bundles them into a single "Proxy ID" such as "Customer ID" and keeps the mapping of all identity parameters tagged to the single proxy ID.

In Pseudonymisation, each parameter is mapped to a pseudo parameter and hence if 5 identity parameters are associated with a personal information, 5 different proxy parameters are created to create the pseudonymised set.

Pseudonymisation preserves the legacy process created for identified information processing while "De-identification" may disrupt the legacy system of processing which needs to be re-calibrated for the processing of de-identified information.

Pseudonymisation mapping also can be preserved and used for re-identification and hence it is not "Anonymisation" unless the mapping is irrevocably destroyed.

De-Identification, Pseudonymization are technology controls that reduces the risk of data breach since it reduces the adverse impact on a real individual on account of a breach. Anonymisation may be considered as a control for eliminating the risk of re-identification all together so that the data breach risk is further reduced.

Technology sometimes may not be perfect in these three processes of data security. For example, in the case of de-identification and pseudonymization, a mapping document exists and if that is leaked, then the information can be re-identified. This is similar to an encrypted document which may not be secured if the keys to decryption are available along with the encrypted document.

However, there are instances where technology can be used by criminals at a higher level to re-identify a de-identified, or pseudonymised or even the anonymised information, by data analytics techniques.

For example, in a video, the face may be masked for privacy and disclosed. But the clothing or the voice or even the gait and hand gestures can be sufficient to identify an individual. In some such cases the anonymisation may be reasonably good but the re-identifier may use a higher-level technology to break the anonymisation just as hackers may use techniques to break a password or encryption by brute force.

In such circumstances law should define a "Reasonable level of security" which the de-identifier needs to follow and recognize breaking of anonymization beyond this "reasonable" level as a "Crime with malicious intent".

This kind of distinction is not found in GDPR or even the current version of DPDPA. Hence it is necessary to interpret the "Reasonable Standard of Anonymization" and "Criminality of Re-identification" with reference to other laws applicable in a country.

Tokenization:

Tokenization of data is a concept similar to Pseudonymization and may involve one more step of encryption or hashing of the pseudonymised data element.

Tokenization is the process of substituting a single piece of sensitive information with non-sensitive information. The non-sensitive substitute information is called a token. It can be created using cryptography, a hash function, or a randomly generated index identifier and used to redact the original sensitive information.

The operation of detokenization, or translating a token to its corresponding data, should only be done on a need-to-know basis (using the right permissions). To support various use cases, tokenization engines that are used for pseudonymization must account for the following possible requirements:

- Format-preserving tokens: These tokens preserve the format of the original data. They are often required in situations with strict storage formatting, such as when changing the database scheme is *impossible.*

- Deterministic vs. unique tokens: This refers to whether the same value is always mapped to the same token or if each value is mapped to its own unique token.
- Ephemeral tokens: These tokens are valid for a limited amount of time. Their expiry limits exposure.

Differential Privacy:

Differential Privacy is a technology Concept used as a tool of Anonymisation. It enables data processing companies to collect and share aggregate information about a community maintaining the privacy of individual users.

Essentially when a personally identifiable data base is to be published without endangering the privacy of individuals a suitable algorithm is used to generate a modified data set from which the probability of identification of an individual is reduced tending to zero. In other words, if an observer seeing the output created by an algorithm cannot identify if a person's data is contained therein or not, we say the algorithm is "Differentially Private".

Essentially Differential Privacy is a mathematical framework that processes an identifiable data set and generates an alternate data set where the use of the data set for a given requirement is preserved but the probability of identification of an individual is reduced to near zero.

The Seven Parameters of Data Protection:

As we briefly discussed in the previous paragraphs, Information Security starts with the CIA triad which represents the preservation of Confidentiality, Integrity and Availability of information as a necessary step towards Information Security. It then expands to Authentication and Non-Repudiation in the concept of Information Assurance. In the context of Data Privacy, the five parameters of Information assurance get modified with an addition of other parameters namely Legal Basis, compliance, and Governance while the scope of the CIA, Authentication and Non-Repudiation is focussed on the Personal Data instead of both Personal and Non Personal Data.

Confidentiality:

"Confidentiality" means that data should be available only to those persons who have a need to know. This is directly linked to the Data Access management and requires linking of data to a user. For this purpose, the data may have to be classified, people to access the data should be assigned certain permissions based on their roles and responsibilities and the access control system needs to be managed to prevent "Unauthorized Access".

"Resetting the password" and gaining access by those who donor have the permission to re-set a password of a user is like decryption of an encrypted information and hence can be considered as "Unauthorised" activity and a "Crime".

System admins who routinely carry out such actions as "Re-setting" information should ensure that their permissions are properly documented so that any user may not raise an objection.

From the managerial perspective one can also consider that the information asset of the company belongs to the company, and it is its prerogative to allow access to any of its employees or withdraw it.

While this appears very logical, in practice particularly in the data protection domain, there is often a debate on who owns an asset like "E-Mail ID @ company's name" or a "Laptop provided by a Company" and whether the assignee has the permission to store his personal information in the asset and later claim that he should have access to it exclusively or in derogation of the authority of the organization.

Some data protection laws specifically clarify that "Business E Mail ID is not personal ID" but many are silent and leave it for interpretations.

Most organizations consider that "@gmail" is not an acceptable business email ID and is always a "Personal email ID". This may not however be a correct interpretation since many users may use gmail ID for business purpose and there may be thousands of Google Employees for whom "gmail ID" is the corporate ID.

Business Managers need to therefore understand such conflicting interpretations and ensure that the organizational policies address such instances.

Confidentiality may also be extended to the information being read by unauthorised persons so that the IPR of the organisation may be adversely affected. Data Confidentiality therefore is controlled first by restricting the physical access to systems holding the information, then through logical access restricting access to the applications inside a computer and lastly through encryption restricting the access to the content in readable form.

The term "Data Privacy" aptly describes confidentiality though in practice we assign it a meaning related to protection of personal data.

Integrity:

Integrity refers to the control on data from the perspective of accuracy, completeness and from being unauthorizedly modified. When data is to be used for decision making it is imperative that it is reliable. Reliability comes from data being secure from being altered by persons who are not authorised.

Some technologies like "Hashing" specifically address capturing an electronic document in such a manner that any change made thereon is immediately detected.

Certain "Hashing Algorithms" calculate a "Message Digest" of a given electronic document which alters with change of any bit of data. MD5, SHA1, SHA256 etc are examples of such algorithms. At present Indian digital signature system does not recognize MD5 algorithm and considers it below the acceptable standard. SHA1 is used in the digital signatures to capture the hash value of a document to be signed.

When different versions of documents need to be maintained, they can be maintained along with their hash values and their distinctness can be certified.

Hashing algorithms are however not "Reversible" like encryption. In "Encryption", data is converted from plain text to cypher text using some encryption method so that persons who do not know the method (Key) will not be able to access the data. But those who have the decryption key can convert the encrypted text to plain text and hence the process is reversible.

The hashing process however calculates what is a "Checksum" for the given document and as long as no change is made to the document it will consistently return the same "Hash Result" or "Message digest". On the other hand, even if a dot or comma or space is changed, the hash will be totally different. Hence one can distinguish one version of the document to another though the document cannot be recreated from the hash value.

Hash tables are used as a part of document storage system for organizations to keep track of the different versions of a document as part of the Integrity Control.

Availability:

Availability of information means that it is necessary for information to be available to the decision makers when required and if interrupted, it will adversely affect the "Security".

Availability can be affected with a "Denial of Service" attack where without stealing a password and changing it, an attacker can prevent a user from accessing the system. In such cases the attacker may not get access to the information and hence there may not be a confidentiality breach but still the information may remain in accessible.

In our hierarchical pyramid approach to information security, Availability is kept as the first step since most organizations set up their systems in the first place to make information available for business decision making. There after the need for Integrity and Confidentiality arises.

Authentication:

As the concept "Information Security" is extended to the concept of "Information Assurance", the information is expected to be properly authenticated as an assurance of the source of information.

This assurance can be provided through identification of the source device or IP address etc and works through the Identity and Access Management system.

Non-Repudiation is a further extension of the need for authentication to a stage where the person/device which has authenticated an information cannot repudiate (refuse to own responsibility) for the information. In the Septagon model this is merged with Authentication.

"Digital Signature" is a means of such non repudiable authentication and law recognizes digital signatures as authentication equivalent to physical signature to a written document that binds a person in a Court of law.

In India, the Government through the Information Technology Act 2000 recognized a form of digital signature where the Controller of Certifying authorities' licenses Certifying authorities who in turn issue "Digital Certificates" to individuals or systems empowering them to affix non repudiable identity to digital documents.

In the Indian system, the hash value of the electronic document to be signed is first calculated using the approved algorithms and then it is encrypted using a "Public-Private Key" encryption system using the private key of the person who is signing the document. The Public key of the person is used for verification of the signature. In order to enable two unknown persons using the digital signing and verification, the "Digital Certificate" embeds the public key along with information of the holder of the private key corresponding to that public key and the identification of the hash and encryption algorithms used. The digital certificate of any person is publicly downloadable and is also forwarded when a digitally signed document is sent.

A Server may also use a system of encryption for the IP packets that are exchanged between the server and the browser which is a combination of the Public-Private key system called the Asymmetric Encryption system and the Symmetric Encryption system where one key is used both for encryption and decryption.

In Symmetric encryption, the encryption key has to be exchanged between the two parties who want to use them, and they need a trusted system for exchange of the key. In Asymmetric system private key is used for encryption of the hash vale to create the digital signature and public key is used for decryption of the digital signature to arrive at the original hash value. The decrypted hash value is compared with the hash value of the document as received and when both tally, it is considered that the document is authenticated.

On the webserver, in the initial handshake, the server sends its public key to the browser and the browser creates a symmetric key and sends it back to the server encrypted with the public key of the server which can be decrypted by the server using the private key. Subsequently all IP packets are encrypted using the symmetric key.

This system leads to the 'https' security on websites and without the need for the browser to have a digital signature capability data in transit between the browser and the server is encrypted.

In corporate communication, data in transit can be encrypted using the Asymmetric encryption of the sender of an information can encrypt the data with the public key of the recipient.

In India, the Government has also adopted an Aadhaar based "E-Sign" system where any document can be electronically signed on a case-to-case basis in real time using Aadhar based KYC. This is a onetime transaction as compared to the normal digital signature system where the digital certificate is issued as valid for a period like one or two years.

Some document exchange systems use digital signatures which donor fall into this legal requirement in India and such documents may be disputed in a court of law as "Un-digitally signed".

Digitally signed documents in India are considered "Non-Repudiable" in Courts. In some countries the system is not run by a government body like the Controller of Certifying authorities and users may use the Asymmetric crypto system without the backing of a Government body. In this scenario, the non-repudiation is through mutual agreement rather than a law of the state.

Legal Basis:

Processing of data has to be for a legally acceptable purpose. Hence establishing the legal basis of processing is an important criterion of Data Governance and Protection as per law. Consent is a mechanism by which a personal data holder (called the Data Subject or Data Principal in law) can share his personal data with another entity for the purpose of storage, processing or transmission. As long as "Privacy" is considered a "Right of Choice", "Consent" remains the main legal basis for processing of personal data. GDPR may recognize other aspects of establishing legal basis and Indian law may address a similar requirement as "Legitimate Use", but

"Consent" remains the basis of personal data processing in the Privacy protection domain.

Since the owner of the personal data may have his own choices of how the data has to be shared or used by others as part of his "Privacy Rights", before collecting or accepting any personal data for processing, the receiving organization which may be called a Data Controller or Data Fiduciary in different laws obtains the "Consent" of the person on what data is being shared, why it is being shared, how it is expected to be used and who all will have access to it etc.

This is normally done by exchange of the intention of the Data Fiduciary through a "Notice" and its acceptance by the Data Subject or Data Principal.

In the Non personal data protection regime, "Consent" could be considered as part of the B2B contract where one entity transfers data to another entity for further processing. Hence it can be considered as relevant even in non-personal data security domain.

Compliance:

Information Security originated as an industry best practice in a quest for improving "Quality". But now recognizing the criticality of information for Business and Governance and the increasing incidence of Cyber Crimes, different countries have framed laws that directly and indirectly affect Information Security Management.

"Compliance to Law" is therefore an important ingredient of an Information Security Program. In the Non-Personal Data Protection regime, laws such as "Information Technology Act 2000 (ITA 2000) prescribe specific information security regime. In the personal data protection regime, laws such as DPDPA or GDPR rule the requirements.

Non-Compliance of laws lead to heavy financial penalties as well as criminal punishments and lead to the potential financial loss or even discontinuance of business.

While noncompliance of business requirements can be managed by efficient managements by negotiating with their clients, offering financial discounts etc., noncompliance of law is a matter of greater concern since it can land the CEO in jail and frustrate the entire enterprise.

Law Compliance is therefore mandatory in Information Security. While "Consent" is also part of Law compliance, there are other compliance requirements such as "Obligations", "Principles of Processing", "Protection of Data Principal's Rights", "Data Breach Notification", " Restrictions on Cross border transfer" etc which are all compliance requirements that need to be part of Law Compliance.

Governance:

In the data protection scenario, Governance is essential to assign roles and responsibilities to different executives, appoint a Governance Committee or Steering Committee, designate a DPO, Designate internal Data Controllers etc. This needs to be supplemented with policies related to HR, Business Acceptance, Business Associate appointment, Management of internal and external communication etc. Use of Anonymization, pseudonymisation or de-identification as strategies of security and compliance and establishing of Data Valuation system within the organization are also related to the Governance, Risk and Compliance.

In the corporate scenario, Data Governance also includes managing the productivity of data in a data driven organization which may include strategies of monetization of data. Use of Profiling and Advertising which may also relate to Personal Data

In the Data Governance and Protection Standard of India (DGPSI) which has been elaborated later in this book integrates the data governance for productivity and data protection into a single framework.

Data In Process:

Data at rest or in transmission can be encrypted using symmetric or asymmetric encryption system. However, data in process requires a different treatment.

A kind of encryption called "Homomorphic encryption" is used for security of data under process. In this process it is not necessary for the process to call the encrypted data, decrypt it, process it and again encrypt it before storing it as a processed information. Instead, the process is carried out on the encrypted data itself without the need for temporarily holding it in unencrypted form.

There are three types of homomorphic encryption namely "Partially Homomorphic", "Somewhat homomorphic" and "fully homomorphic".

Homomorphic encryption is a cryptographic method that allows mathematical operations on data to be carried out on cipher text, instead of on the actual data itself. The cipher text is an encrypted version of the input data (also called plain text). It is operated on and then decrypted to obtain the desired output.

When processing of homomorphic encrypted data is conducted, it means that the algorithm is able to view the data in its original form, but it is not revealed in a form where it can be stored or observed by a human. This concept of "Viewing by an algorithm" but not by a human is a concept which distinguishes the definition of information privacy breach. Though not universally accepted, the author believes that data which is processed without a human having visibility is not a breach of privacy.

This concept of Privacy breach being recognized only when a human is able to view the data in an identifiable form is relevant when we have CCTVs capturing the videos which include individuals. When a human applies a face recognition software and identifies a person, it could be considered as a privacy issue. But if an algorithm filters the data with reference to a face recognition software and a linked data base of say known criminals and creates an exception list of the identified "Suspects", no human may have access to the identifiable data of the filtered-out individuals. Only the activity of the "Suspects" become visible and if this is covered by the powers of the law enforcement, it could be considered as an acceptable usage of CCTV footage without violation of Privacy.

Chapter XXI

Approach to Data Protection

Data Protection has many stake holders such as the "Company", "Employees", "Customers", "Business Associates", "Government" etc. The Wishlist of each of these stake holders can be different. Accordingly, the means used to satisfy the different stakeholders may also be different.

Company:

For the company, data is a valuable asset and like any other asset of the company, it needs to be protected. Its customers who depend on the timely service also need assurance that any data shared by them to the Company is safe and that the information handling system is good enough to ensure quality of service. Hence the Company approaches the security of data from the perspective of the "Best Industry Practice" to secure the data and to provide assurance to its customers. Their focus is for popular industry standards such as ISO 27001. If the data is "Sensitive" then like handling of a hazardous inventory, the Company has to have additional measures to protect the "Sensitive" data. Such "Sensitivity" can be because the loss of data may result in a large potential penalty or cause significant damage to the Company.

Government:

The Government of the country is another stake holder in the information processing and has a responsibility to prevent Cyber Crimes and protect the Right to Privacy of its citizens. Hence it requires all data handlers to have a reasonable security to prevent cybercrimes involving citizens. This expectation includes collection and preservation of log records, CCTV footages and other evidence to enable prevention and detection of crimes. In terms of protection of the Right to Privacy of the citizens, Governments also want appropriate measures to manage personal information of the customers and the employees. For this purpose, Governments enact Data Protection laws which prescribe certain Data Processing principles, protection of certain rights of the data subjects/data principals and penalize violations. The Companies need to therefore work for "Compliance of the laws" as prescribed.

Customers and Employees:

The Customers and the Employees are the other stake holders since it is their personal data that is being protected through data protection laws and it is their right to privacy that is being protected. Security lapses leading to identity theft and leaking of personal data can cause reputation loss, mental harassment as well as financial loss to the data principals. The basis for protecting the interests of the employees and the customers is mainly the law of the land. However, they can be further fine-tuned by the ethics of business or considerations of employee welfare or marketing that may require implementation of data management provisions better than what the law mandates. Both the industry best practices and the law need to be kept in mind to meet the expectations of these stakeholders.

Management Personnel:

The Management of an organisation is a stake holder both because data is an asset, and it has to be managed efficiently to increase its productivity but also avoid any adverse consequences of law that may result in financial penalties on the organization and criminal punishments for the executives. In pursuance of the Governance requirements managements need to innovate the use of data to generate new revenue streams and enhance existing revenue streams. In this process the Technology may give several options, but it would be necessary to make an assessment of the Security and Privacy Risks for the implementation of new technology and ensure that there are no uncovered risks leading to unmanageable penalties. This has to mostly follow the legal obligations since penalties come from the noncompliance of law. Opportunities need to be weighed against the Risks and Risk mitigation/absorption plans. A framework like DGPSI (Digital Governance and Protection Standard of India) which is oriented to meet the management needs of Governance more closely than a framework like ISO 27001/ISO 27701 would be appropriate to meet the requirements of this stakeholder.

Business Associates:

The business associates of the Company are the stakeholders who are interested in Business Continuity so that their own dependent businesses are not adversely affected by any developments at their associate Company. Their means of ensuring is through visible Certifications that the organisation can display. They look for certifications that are popular and sometimes ignore the relevance. As a result, sometimes a customer may be satisfied if you say you are "ISO 27001 certified" though the customer's requirement is more on "Data Protection under Indian Data Protection Laws", or a customer may be satisfied if you say you are "HIPA Compliant" or "GDPR Compliant" though the data you are handling has nothing to do with US or EU.

The responsibility of adopting the right framework for data protection is therefore that of the management of a company which has to take into account the different stake holders who need to be satisfied, the available resources and their capacity to convince the stakeholders that the framework adopted serves the stakeholders as they prefer. This requires the "Risk Assessment", "Designing of the compliance system" along with continuous review and improvement.

Considering the scope of this book, we shall focus more on the requirements of Data Protection laws in general as the basis for understanding the responsibility for implementation of an appropriate data governance framework. We shall consider some of the popular data protection laws such as the GDPR or CPRA and more specifically the Indian law DPDPA-2023 to discuss the data protection principles and designing a compliance system.

The Common Data Protection Principles:

In the "Non-Personal Data Protection" we have identified five principles of data protection namely

1. Confidentiality
2. Integrity
3. Availablity
4. Authentication
5. Non-Repudiation

In the "Personal Data Protection", we have two sets of principles.

First set is the set of principles required to safeguard the personal data and these are the same as above meant for Non-Personal Data Protection.

The second set of principles are related to the Privacy Protection related aspects. These are.

1. Establishing a Legal Basis for Processing (Lawful basis)
2. Collection of personal data based on a specified purpose (Purpose limitation)
3. Collection of only that information as is required for the purpose (Data Minimisation)
4. Keeping the data complete and accurate (Accuracy)
5. Retaining data only for the period necessary (Storage limitation)
6. Providing necessary information about the process (Transparency)
7. Accountability (Documentation)
8. Protection of Data Principal's Rights (Rights Protection)
9. Cross Border Processing of data
10. Data Breach Notification system.
11. Handling of Automated Processing and Decision Making
12. Handling of Children Data
13. Handling of Publicly Available Data
14. Handling of Data Processors and Subcontractors
15. Handling of Grievances

Since Privacy Protection is a legal requirement, the set of "Privacy Principals" that we discuss has to be related to the laws. Laws are not uniform in all countries, and we need to keep in mind that Privacy related activities have to be pegged to a chosen law. For Companies in India, the Indian law namely the Information Technology Act 2000 (ITA 2000) substantially amended in 2008 and the Digital Personal Data Protection Act 2023 are the basis of Privacy law.

For EU, GDPR or General Data Protection Law is the reference.

In US, there is no federal law of general data protection. But there are sectoral privacy laws such as HIPAA (Health Insurance Portability and Accountability Act) for Health Sector, GLBA (Gramm Bleach Liley Act) for Finance Sector etc. Slowly US states one by one are coming out with specific data protection laws applicable within their state. California pioneered this trend and at present about 11 states have similar laws.

Other Countries such as Singapore, Australia, UAE, Brazil etc all have their own laws. At present more than 130 countries in the world have data protection laws including China and Pakistan.

For the purpose of our study, we will take up the Indian law in detail, GDPR in moderate detail and the US State laws such as Californian law (CPRA) in a broad manner.

In all the laws there will be certain common principles and some differences in the way the law is interpreted. We need to therefore develop a Data Governance System which is encompassing all the requirements and at the same time maintain the flexibility that is required to manage the differences.

Globally organizations use frameworks such as ISO 27701(with ISO 27001). In India there is a more appropriate framework namely DGPSI (Data Governance and Protection Standard of India). We shall explore DGPSI in detail along with a comparison with ISO 27701 in subsequent chapters.

1. Establishment of Lawful Basis:

Every Data Protection law sets out the first condition that data need to be processed on a lawful basis. First of all, the specific law such as GDPR or DPDPA itself is the law that needs to be followed fully. Additionally, Data Processing is a business activity that cannot be permitted for any business which is illegal or lacks lawful basis.

The Data Protection law therefore will not apply for any unlawful processing such as processing for money laundering or processing by a Company which is not constituted legally.

GDPR sets out six conditions of processing that make it a lawful processing if any one of the conditions are satisfied.

They are.

a. Data Subject (the person to whom a set of personal data can be identified to) has given a "Consent" for processing his/her personal data for a specified process.

b. There is a contract to which the Data Subject is a party, and the processing is necessary for the fulfilment of the contract.

c. Processing is necessary for compliance of the processing of the personal data by the Data Controller (The processor who determines the purpose and means of processing of personal data and collects the same for that purpose as distinguished from a Data Processor who processes personal data on behalf of another data controller).

d. Processing is necessary for protecting vital (life threatening) interests of a data subject or any other natural person.

e. Processing is necessary in public interest or under an official authority.

f. Processing is necessary for the legitimate interests pursued where such interests are not overridden by the interests of fundamental rights of the data subject particularly if the data subject is a minor.

The Indian law on the other hand adopts "Consent" as the mandatory condition. Additionally, it allows processing for "Legitimate uses".

Though GDPR indicates that any one of the six conditions can be considered sufficient, there have been instances where some regulatory authorities have rejected the legal basis of "Contract" and held that specific consent is the preferred legal basis.

The concept of "Legitimate Interest" is also vague in the GDPR while it is clearer in the Indian law. (DPDPA 2023 is covered in greater detail in an earlier chapter).

Further, "Consent" may be provided either for single use for a given purpose or for multiple use for the same purpose over a specified or open time period. While obtaining the consent, these aspects need to be properly indicated in the notice so that the data subject/principal is aware of the scope of the consent that he is providing.

2. Collection for a specified purpose:

GDPR requires that the Data Controller (P.S: In India this role is called Data Fiduciary) provides a proper notice to the data subject (P.S: In India this role is called Data Principal) and collects the consent specifying the purpose for which it is collected. The rest of the requirements such as how much of data to be collected, how long it is to be retained etc are dependent on the purpose. If data once collected has to be used for a purpose other than the original purpose, then it is expected that a fresh consent is obtained unless the Data Controller can justify that the original purpose cannot be satisfied without the processing as required by the additional/ancillary purpose.

The purpose specific consent is a standard feature in all data protection laws.

3. Data Minimization:

When personal data is collected, different elements of data may be collected such as the Name, Gender, Age, Date of Birth, Social Security Number or Aadhaar number, PAN Number, Mobile Number, E Mail address etc. How many of these elements are required to be collected for a given purpose is what determines the criteria of "Data Minimization". Even when some data has been collected, for subsequent distribution of data within the organization, the data minimization principle has to be adhered to so that data is shared only on "Need to Know Basis" even within the organization.

This is also a standard principle common in all data protection laws.

4. Accuracy of Data:

A Data Controller/Data Fiduciary is expected to keep the personal data of an individual being processed updated periodically so that stale information does not get processed leading to sub optimal decisions based on outdated data.

Most of the data protection laws do not specify the period after which data may become stale. It is to be determined based on the purpose of processing.

In India, the Information Technology Act 2000 (ITA 2000) has provided that such consents need to be renewed at least once a year and this can be taken as the norm for DPDPA 2023 also unless specific guideline is provided to the contrary.

When data is processed automatically and applied for some decision making such as credit rating and determination of eligibility for a loan or a facility, it is important that the data used must be accurate and updated and in such cases the quality of data will become a critical parameter.

The DGPSI framework adopted for compliance in India and recommended by organizations like the Foundation of Data Protection Professionals in India suggest that Data should be valued in rupee terms and the Data Valuation Standard of India (DVSI) used for the purpose depreciates the value of data over a period of time. Hence the updating of data automatically is factored into the system through data valuation standards.

This principle is common in all data protection laws but the criteria, compulsion and the duration for updating may vary.

5. Storage Limitation or Data Retention limitation:

With the purpose oriented personal data collection, comes the automatic decision of discarding of the data after the purpose is over. This determines the "Data Retention period". The general preference is that after the purpose of processing as per the consent is completed, the personal data has to be erased.

However, the personal data which becomes part of the processed personal data may be an asset of the Company and while further processing for creation of additional processed data from the same raw personal data may be stopped, it may be necessary to retain the personal data for certain legitimate purposes such as the legal requirements. Hence the "Data Retention" period cannot be blindly set either for the completion of the purpose or for a specific period.

Once the purpose is completed, there has to be a review and a documented decision on whether the data can be or need to be erased or it needs to be archived for possible future requirement up to another time period after which the retention may be reviewed again.

Sometimes the data subject may alter his original consent and withdraw the permission or specifically request for erasure of the personal data.

The request for erasure is referred to as the "Right to be forgotten" in GDPR and recognised as one of the rights of the data subjects. However, many other data protection laws including Indian law does not recognize a right for personal data to be completely erased from the records of the company. Stopping of further processing and removing of the personal data from the production environment is considered necessary when a data principal withdraws consent for further processing and such data can be archived safely subject to the legitimate interest of the organization.

Hence any request for erasure has to be handled carefully and the decision should be documented.

In India the ITA 2000 also has certain provisions regarding minimal data retention period for certain types of personal data and they have to be complied with along with the requirements of DPDPA 2023.

6. Transparency:

Transparency is a measure of openness in informing the data subject about how his personal data may be processed, stored, shared etc by an organization.

Transparency is often ensured by making the "Notice" given to a prospective data subject before collection of data explicit, with itemized description and indicating the downstream processing etc.

Indian law even requires the notice to be provided in all the 22 scheduled languages and also recommends the use of accredited intermediaries called "Consent Managers" who can provide proper clarifications to the data subjects as required.

This is also a commonly stated requirement in all data protection laws, but details may vary.

7. Accountability:

All data protection laws expect that the Data Controller or Data Fiduciary is accountable for compliance of the requirements of the data protection laws. This may require designation of specific persons as Data Protection Officers, documenting the Record of Processing Activities (ROPA), creating a document of roles and responsibilities within the organization, conducting a Data Protection Impact assessment (DPIA), Having an incident recording system, etc.

In other words, all the compliance measures need to be documented for the purpose of accountability.

Most data protection laws impose heavy penalties for noncompliance of the laws and hence "Accountability" is the insurance against penalties.

While in case of a data breach, penalties are likely to be unavoidable, there are many instances where penalties are levied for mere noncompliance of the law though no data breach has occurred. Accountability is important to avoid such liabilities.

Some laws such as GDPR have penalties linked to "Turnover" and may go up to a maximum of 4% of global turnover or 20 million Euros whichever is higher. In India there is no maximum penalties set in the law.

8. Protection of Data Principal's Right:

The objective of all Data Protection Laws is to protect the Right to Privacy of an individual. In the context of "Data", the laws prescribe how personal data may be collected from an individual, how it can be processed, shared and disclosed. The person whose data is being protected is referred to as the "Data Subject" or "Data Principal". The organization which collects the data and determines the purpose and means of processing is referred to as the "Data Controller" or "Data Fiduciary".

As a means of protecting the Right to Privacy the laws in the data protection area identify certain subordinate rights and incorporate it as part of the objectives of the law and obligations of the entity collecting the personal information.

The Data Protection Obligations such as the Purpose oriented collection, providing a notice and collecting consent etc are all related to the protection of Rights such as "No Processing without Consent or appropriate legal basis" "Right to a Notice before collection of data"," Right to withdrawal of Consent", "Right to object to processing or for automated decision making", are all derivatives of the rights of the data principal.

Additionally, most laws specifically mention the following Rights that are guaranteed by the law and infringement of which could lead to penalties under the law.

The first such Right is the "Right to have information about whether the information of an individual is being processed by a company and if so, how the information is being processed, who are the data processors to whom the data is being shared" etc. This is referred to as "Right of Access".

Failure to provide such information within a reasonable time may result in the regulator imposing penalties to the organisation.

The second important right is to ensure that whatever data is being processed is accurate and if not, the data principal may require it to be corrected. This is called "Right to Correction".

The third Right is a right to Object to the processing and withdraw consent either partially or fully. The objection may be to restriction of processing in terms of the purposes to which it was originally consented to, or a clean withdrawal of the consent earlier given. This is called the "Right to Object". Sometime the objection may be only to "Automated Decision making" and not to the processing per-se. This would be like modification of the original consent.

Obviously when a consent has been given earlier and the company is processing the same, withdrawal of the consent needs to be associated with what has to be done with the processing already done and whether the organization has to bear losses on account of the withdrawal.

Further there is the issue of verifying whether the withdrawal of consent is being asked for by the same person who originally gave the consent or whether he has the right to speak on behalf of the data principal.

Such issues may arise when Children data is involved, and a guardian is trying to provide some instructions. The normal cybercrime risks such as phishing also affect such rights. Indian law specifies that losses arising out of unfair withdrawal of consent may have to be borne by the data principal so that any irresponsible attitude of giving a consent and withdrawing it without reason is not encouraged.

The Fourth major right is the "Right to be Forgotten". This right was introduced by GDPR and not available uniformly in all laws.

Since usage of personal data is linked to the purpose-oriented consent, once the purpose is over, the processing needs to be stopped. However, the data provided by the data principal and the processed data created by the organisation remains with the organisation.

Under the Right to correction, a data principal can cause wrong data about himself to be removed. Under the right to object, he can cause stoppage of further processing and consider the consent purpose as having extinguished.

Since it is an obligation of an organization that data should retained only for the period necessary, once the necessity vanishes, the data needs to be erased.

In addition to this automatic deletion requirement, most laws specify that the data principal has a "Right to Erasure" of his personal data. "Right to Erasure" may be limited to erasing the data provided by the data principal or extended to the data created by the organization with the use of the personal data. When the request extends to removal of all instances of personally identifiable data the right is referred to as "Right to be forgotten". In a way this entitles the data principal to be not traceable at all in any of the information processed by the organization.

Accepting such a right creates a serious security risk of the data principal has committed any offence and the information about him is required as "Evidence".

Further many of the transactional personal information such as information about buying or selling in an e-commerce website is a "Joint Information" which belongs both to the individual and the organization. Hence such information cannot be "Forgotten". Similarly, some data such as a telephone conversation of a group discussion is data belonging to more than one party and hence it may not be possible to protect the "Right to be forgotten".

In India some Courts have agreed to redact the names of individuals from judgements if they were proved innocent after being charged with a crime or they were only witnessing etc. These are not strictly "Forgotten" data. They are only "Restricted disclosure of data".

Hence the "Obligation to erase data", "Right to erasure" and "Right to be forgotten" all have some minor differences. Where data is requested to be erased but needs to be retained for legitimate interests, data can be de-identified and archived.

In EU however the right to be forgotten is considered seriously and may be aggressively enforced by data subjects.

In India all such requests need to be suitably documented and a proper decision is taken based on the legitimate interests of the company, the law enforcement as well as operation of other laws.

There are many instances where ITA 2000 may require certain personal data to be regained for 6 months or even 5 years. In such cases, if the right to be forgotten is exercised without judicial authority, the organization may expose itself to the charge of "Destruction of Evidence".

The fifth important Right that data protection laws like GDPR address is the "Right to Portability". This essentially means that the data subject may require an organization to transfer the personal data given by him to the organization either back to himself or to another organization. One school of thought believes that this right extends only to the information supplied by the individual and not to the data created over this by the organization since such data represents the trade secrets or the IPR of the organization. As usual EU pursues such rights aggressively while many countries don't attach such rights to beyond what the individual has provided.

In addition to these rights, India considers "Right to Grievance Redressal" as a specific right and the organization has to put in place some system for grievance redressal which includes designating a responsible person for the purpose and organizing mediation kind of efforts before the grievance can be taken as a dispute to the regulatory authorities.

In India an additional Right "Right to Nominate" is being recognized. This essentially means that the personal data belonging to a person shall vest with a nominee in the event of his death. There are legal hurdles in this regard since Right to Privacy is considered as the right of a living individual and the "Consent" given in electronic form is a contract that extinguishes on the death of a person. Further Information Technology act 2000 does not recognize validity of a document that transfers rights on death of a person like a will. Hence any nomination instrument should ideally be in physical writing.

Providing "Nomination" facility means that the organisation should have a mechanism to receive and confirm the death of its customer and then validate the claim of a person as the nominee or a legal heir.

Thus, the data subject or data principal has many rights recognised under the law and if the organization fails to protect any of these subordinate rights to Privacy may end up paying penalties.

In terms of management the business managers need to understand these rights not only for external persons but also for the employees and ensure that they are in a position to address these rights without jeopardizing the interests of the organisation.

9. Cross Border Processing of Data:

Internet is a borderless technology and data processing similarly is a global activity where data from one country is routinely processed in another country.

The reason why Cross border movement of data is common is because of the time difference advantage between USA and India or economy of people's time or even availability of skills and expertise. Hence data subjects of one country hand over their data-to-data controllers in the same country but data controllers will hunt for data processors across the globe for economic services including the simple data storage services.

Today companies access cloud technologies not only for data storage but also for data processing and hence data governance managers need to factor in the use of services that carry data from one country to another.

The Data Protection laws normally mandate that the data controller is responsible for the security of data as well as following the privacy requirements and they should also take the responsibility for security and privacy aspects when data collected by them is transferred to another entity either in the same country or outside.

Many of the laws prohibit transfer of data to countries which may not have adequate data protection laws or impose severe contractual responsibilities. GDPR has suggested a set of "Standard Contractual Clauses" (SCC) to be included in the contracts between GDPR stake holders in EU and others. If a Company transfers data for processing within itself but with units in other countries, GDPR expects Binding Corporate Rules to be drawn up in consultation with the regulatory authorities which determine adequacy of the security measures when data is transferred across the borders.

GDPR also enables the EU Commission to declare countries or specific territories or sectors in another country as having adequate security to be considered for automatic approval of data transfer of EU citizens without any restrictions.

At present The European Commission has recognised Andorra, Argentina, Canada (commercial organisations), Faroe Islands, Guernsey, Israel, Isle of Man, Japan, Jersey, New Zealand, Republic of Korea, Switzerland, the United Kingdom under the GDPR, the United States (commercial organisations participating in the EU-US Data Privacy Framework) and Uruguay as providing adequate protection.

EU is looking for not only "Security of Information" in the destination countries but is also expecting that EU Data Subjects will have adequate judicial remedy against the local data processors in case of any data breach.

They also have objections to the local Governments and law enforcement agencies (such as FBI in US) donor gain access to EU data subject's data without appropriate judicial safeguards though EU itself follows the Law Enforcement Directive under which competent authorities may gain access to personal data for purposes of prevention, investigation, detection or processing of criminal offences or the execution of criminal penalties.

India has not yet given out any list of adequate countries or blacklisted countries but may do so in due course. Until such a time, Indian companies need to work with SCC or BCR to secure the data sent out for processing.

Use of Pseudonymization or anonymisation before data is sent out can enable bringing down the bar on required security assurances at the destination country.

RBI as a sectoral regulator in India however expects Banks to store their data within India and this would be applicable as of now before the DPDPB may come up with its own regulation. This "Data Localization" in India is often opposed by Big Tech industries though the EU itself follows strict data localization under GDPR by imposing impossible conditions on SCCs.

10. Data Breach Notification System:

All data protection laws require a data controller/data fiduciary to report incidents of data breach to the regulator. Some of the data breach incidents are also reportable to the affected data principals.

Failure to notify data breach within the specified time (72 hours under GDPR) could be considered as a serious violation of the law and attract penalties.

However, before determining the liability of notification, the organization need to satisfy that there is a data breach which is reportable. A Breach is normally identified through a system of "Incident Management" where any occurrence that jeopardises the confidentiality, integrity and availability of information is considered as an "Incident". In the Privacy scenario, observance of violation of any of the compliance requirements should also be recorded as an "Incident".

When an incident is first observed there may be a need for checking if it is only a false alarm or it is a real incident resulting in damage of some kind. Then a report is in order along with additional investigation and remedial measures. During the investigation the extent of leak and sensitivity of information leaked may be assessed to determine if there is a need to notify the data principals.

Once the data breach is reported to the regulatory authority the authority may also advise remedial measures and also whether notification is required to the data principals.

Since most laws even under Information Security or Cyber Security require notification of data breach for both personal and non-personal data, it may be necessary for reporting the data breach to multiple authorities. In India CERT In is the authority to which data breach need to be reported under ITA 2000 and hence personal data breach needs to be reported both to CERT-IN and the Data Protection Board under DPDPA.

Personal data breach in India is also required to be notified to the individual data principal whose data is breached so that he can take up a complaint if he is aggrieved. Under GDPR, the notification to the individuals may not be necessary if the breach is unlikely to result in any risk to the data subjects. Indian law at present has not stated any such exemptions but may introduce similar exemption through subsequent notification.

In the event the data breach is of encrypted data, the regulatory authorities may consider that the data principal may not suffer any harm though the organization needs to take measures to prevent such data breaches in the future.

11. Handling of Automated Processing and Decision Making:

Data Protection laws can be of two types. One kind of law could be a law that protects the right of choice of an individual on how his personal data may be collected, used or disclosed. Such data can be in digital form or non-digital form. Most laws provide exemptions for processing of personal data for domestic purpose and other reasons such a law enforcement etc. GDPR applies not only to digital personal information but also to "file systems" or data in paper form. Indian DPDPA 2023 is a law specific to digital data.

Hence in laws such as DPDPA 2023, it goes without saying that data which is subject to processing by computers or in other words subject to automated processing is the subject matter of the law.

In cases such as GDPR, there can be some differences in the law as it applies to manual processing and automated processing. Hence Such laws have to make mention of "Automated Decision Making" distinct from "Automated Processing". Automated decision making could lead to decisions that affect the data subject and such as rejection of a service and hence the law prescribes that automated decision making is amenable to an objection from the data subject. Hence processing by manual intervention may be permitted but in the same instance processing leading to automated processing could be disallowed.

This means that use of AI in data processing can be disallowed by the data subject by restricting the permission for processing.

In view of this the choice of technology for processing may be dependent on the data protection law and have a direct bearing on whether a specific process or the associated business can be accepted or not.

It is for this reason that a Business Manager involved in marketing should before committing on a client's business proposition should be aware of what is feasible as per the data protection law.

A Consent provided for a specific purpose cannot be extended without explicit permission to a situation where the processing leads to automated decision making.

All such instances need to be subject to a documented Data Protection Impact Assessment before the business is accepted and costed.

12. Handling of Children Data:

Personal data of Children or "Minors is considered a sensitive data which requires a verifiable parental consent. Before obtaining such consent, it is imperative that the identity of the parent or guardian and whether he/she has the right to represent the minor needs to be verified.

Age verification is therefore required in all cases of personal data processing since without age verification one cannot determine if the customer is actually a minor or not.

Further once an account of a minor is taken up for service, it would be necessary to track the age so that once the minor attains the age of majority, the control for consent passes on from the parent to the erstwhile minor.

The actual age of cut off for determining the eligibility of a person to be excluded from parental consent may differ from country to country. In India a minor below 18 years of age cannot enter into a valid contract and hence any "Consent" provided by him would not be considered as a valid contract.

In many other countries the age above which parental consent is exempted may be 16 years or even less. In India.

Additionally, most laws restrict that the data of a minor shall not be used for profiling or targeted advertising to the minor. Hence companies engaged in services directed to minors such as the education industry must be careful in determining its marketing strategy as well as the use of profiling technology.

The need for parental consent may however be exempt in certain businesses involving counselling of children and prevention of child abuse.

13. Handling of Publicly Available Data:

Certain data protection laws such as the Indian DPDPA 2023 exempt publicly available data from the provisions of the Act.

In some cases, such data may be exempt from prior consent for collection but need to be brought under a valid consent before it is being used.

In either case the "Data Breach" may or may not be fully exempt from notification requirements or from causing penalty to the organization.

Hence before strategizing collection of personal data by scrapping the Linked in or Face Book or Google, business managers need to take adequate care that they are not violating aby data protection law.

In certain cases, the purpose for which an individual might have made the data public may be considered as an acceptable purpose for which it can be collected and used without further consent.

14: Handling of Data Processors and Subcontractors:

Processing of data by an organization is often a collaborative exercise with the help of one or more subcontractors. While the organization that determines the purpose and means of processing is considered as the "Data Fiduciary" (or Data Controller) and responsible for the compliance of data protection laws, the sub-contractors who are engaged for some part of the processing of the personal data constitute the "Data Processors".

Law mandates Data Fiduciaries to have a valid contract with the data processor to ensure that they comply with the law to the extent that they undertake processing only as per the contract and ensure that the data is held secure during processing. They are also required to destroy the data when not required, update the data as per the information provided by the Data Fiduciary and report data breaches if any.

The data processor is not expected to subcontract the work without the knowledge and permission of the Data Fiduciary.

In many cases the Data Processor develops their own proprietary technology for processing the data for the purpose the Data Fiduciary would like the data to be processed. But the technology may be kept confidential so that the Data Fiduciary does not know the "Means of Processing". In such cases the Data Processor should be considered as "Joint Data Fiduciary" at least to the extent processing takes place under his control.

There are also instances where a Data Fiduciary engages the services of an external entity to "Collect the Personal Data". If we assume that the Data Fiduciary determines the purpose of processing, he may mandate a specific consent form that describes the purpose, the retention requirements etc and treat the Data Processor as a dumb collector. But in practice, the Data Collector introduces his own data collection methodology and hence it would be better to treat him also as a Joint Data Fiduciary.

In all cases the Data Fiduciary needs to keep a permission to audit the processing of the processor and satisfy himself that the processing is as per the contract.

While the Data Processor collects information from a data principal, if he does not disclose that he is collecting information as an agent of the Data Fiduciary then in the eyes of the Data Principal, he would be considered as a Data Fiduciary. If, however he is a disclosed agent then he can take the stand that he is a data processor collecting the information on behalf of the data fiduciary.

In many instances of service such as when a Data fiduciary uses a special software for processing or uses cloud services for storage there is a need to identify the correct role of each of the parties whether the software supplier or cloud service provider is merely a Data Processor or a Data Fiduciary.

From the point of view of mitigating the risk of liability for noncompliance, it is better for the Data Fiduciary to treat the Data Processor as Joint Data Fiduciary and make a specific mention in the contract so that certain responsibilities for data protection rests with him.

15: Handling of Grievances:

The emerging trend particularly in the Indian legal scenario is to require every organization to have an effective "Grievance Redressal Mechanism" to attend to the complaints of the Data Principals. In the context of Data Protection, the Grievance Redressal system should be beyond the technical support system with a link to the Incident Management system.

The person attending the customer complaints should be capable of distinguishing a technical help requirement from a legally tenable grievance that could turn out to be a complaint about infringement of any of the data principal's rights. If the complaint has a hint of infringement of the privacy rights of the complainant, it may be necessary to log the complaint as an incident and also escalate it to the Data Protection officer or similar person.

In summary we have discussed different data processing principles that are required to be kept in mind by Data Managers as a direct result of the Data Protection Law.

Specific aspect of "Securing the Personal Data" which is also a responsibility of an organization will be discussed separately.

Chapter XXII

Concept of Privacy and Compliance by Design

Approach to Data Protection:

In the earlier chapters, we have discussed the laws related to Data Protection and how the laws mandate that an organization that determines the purpose and means of processing (Data controller or Data fiduciary) need to place technical and organizational measures to comply with the requirements of law.

The objective of the law like GDPR is expressly provided as to protect the "Right to Privacy" of data principals. Indian law however is expressed as a law for protection of Digital Personal Data though the underlying objective is to protect the Right to Privacy of an individual.

While certain aspects such as need to obtain consent, need to minimize collection, need to limit retention etc are directly mentioned in the law itself, as regards the security measures to be adopted, laws normally stop at stating that "Reasonable Security" measures shall be adopted.

One example of a law which goes into a lot more detail is the HIPAA (Health Insurance Portability and Accountability Act) of USA which applies to the health information. This law includes 52 different

"Security Standards and/or Implementation Specifications". ISO 27001 or ISO 27002 or similar standards supported by guidelines such as ISO 27701 provide the framework which is not law but is a "Recommended Business Practice". Some of these standards are declared by the Standards organisation as "Certifiable" and accredited and trained auditors evaluate an ISMS (Information Security Management System) or PIMS (Personal Information Management System) against the recommendations in the standard and issue "Certification" which an organization may use to provide assurance to its customers.

In USA, NIST (National Institute of Standards and Technology) issues standards/guidelines to the Government organizations and are often also used as a framework in the Private sector.

Additionally, there are Private Sector specialized organizations who also provide similar guidelines. One such framework in USA is a framework developed by the HITRUST (Health Information Trust Alliance. founded in 2007) which is a framework issued for HIPAA compliance developed by a consortium of Private organizations.

In India, Foundation of Data Protection Professionals in India or FDPPI (a Section 8, Not for Profit Organization) has developed a Compliance Management System that focusses on Data Governance and Data Protection based on Data Governance and Protection Standard of India (DGPSI). This framework assists organizations to set up what is referred to as Data Governance and Protection Management System (DGPMS). This is an integrated system concept which addresses the requirements of Compliance of Data Protection laws like GDPR or DPDPA as well as the industry standards such as the Bureau of Indian Standard (BIS) framework (Presently in draft stage) for Adequacy of Data Governance and Management which includes Data Protection, from the perspective of Business Management.

Additionally, DSCI (Data Security Council of India), an organization promoted by NASSCOM and its members also provide guidance for Privacy management in IT systems through its own "Privacy Framework".

The objective of all these frameworks is to provide an easy to follow guidance to achieve the objective of setting up an ISMS (ISO 27001) or PIMS (ISO 27701) or DGPMS etc. which should help an organization in its endeavour for Data Protection.

We shall discuss the frameworks in more detail separately in a subsequent chapter but discuss some principles of Privacy implementation in this chapter.

When a law specifies that an organization shall implement "Appropriate" or "Reasonable" Organizational and Technical Measures it means that the organization shall conduct a "Risk Assessment" and based on the findings implement what is considered as the necessary risk mitigation measures which should reflect in the system. The frameworks provide some template for such organizational measures.

Though many organizations expect their Compliance Officers who are legal personnel or CISO/CTO s who are Technology persons to understand and decipher these standard documents and make them responsible for their implementation, it is important for us to realize that they need as much of managerial skill as technical and legal. Hence "Data Governance" which is a managerial function in an organization where Data is considered a "Business Asset" should consider ISMS/PIMS/DGPMS as their responsibility.

In this chapter, we shall discuss what is normally referred to as "Privacy by Design" which is a concept that implementation of the Privacy or Data Protection controls should be part of the Information technology architecture. In the concept of "Compliance by Design" which is promoted by FDPPI under DGPMS, the objective is that it is the overall "Business Architecture" which includes IT architecture which should be conducive to compliance and the responsibility has to be borne by the Managerial personnel.

If we fail to consider that the responsibilities of DPO or CISO are within the responsibility of the CEO, we will have a difficulty in aligning the marketing, finance and research functions with the goals set by a DPO or CISO and create disharmony in the organization.

Considering "Compliance" as an objective and making it a "Managerial Function" is the biggest difference that FDPPI's DGPMS concept has brought to the industry which otherwise focussed only on ISMS or PIMS which were aligned with either the IT or Legal functions without a tight integration to the Managerial Function.

In our subsequent discussions we will discuss the concepts as are popularly understood in the industry but remember always that we are discussing a managerial function using Policies and IT controls as a tool of Data Governance for the purpose of Privacy and Data Security.

Data Protection as part of Data Governance:

Data Protection requires to be managed from the perspective of Policies, Procedures, Technology as well as building a culture of Privacy and Data Protection among the work force. For this purpose, Governance of Data Protection system is necessary and is often considered as part of Governance, Risk And Compliance (GRC) initiative.

We can however also approach the Governance from the perspective of "Data as an Asset" and look at "Protection" as part of the asset protection and "Compliance" as part of the risk management.

For Business Managers it is essential to keep the Data Governance as a key goal and consider Data Protection as part of the Data Governance responsibilities.

If we therefore look at the organization of the Governance structure, the following functionalities of Data Governance emerge.

Objectives of Data Governance

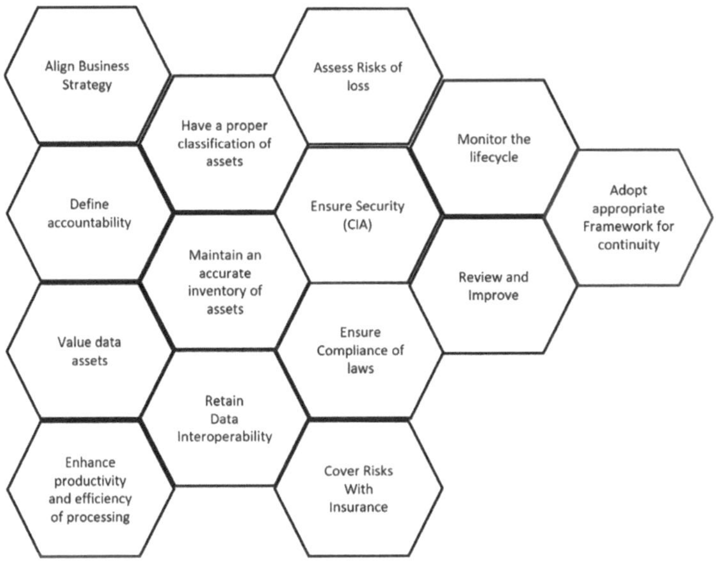

In order to meet the functionalities of Data Governance, an organization may consider the position of a Chief Data Officer who is responsible for strategizing use of data for aligning with the business strategy and organize accountability, valuation of data and enhancing the productivity of data. He will ensure with the assistance of the CTO maintenance of inventory of data with appropriate classification and data interoperability. The CISO and DPO will ensure assessment of risk, management of the Confidentiality, Integrity and Availability of data along with compliance of laws. The CFO will assist in the covering of risks with Cyber Insurance.

The Chief Data Officer (CDO) along with the CISO and DPO will insure monitoring the status of Governance, Security and Privacy throughout the life cycle of data processing, along with review and improvement as required. For this purpose, the CDO may use an appropriate framework such as the DGPSI. (Data Governance and Protection Standard of India).

Data Governance Hierarchy

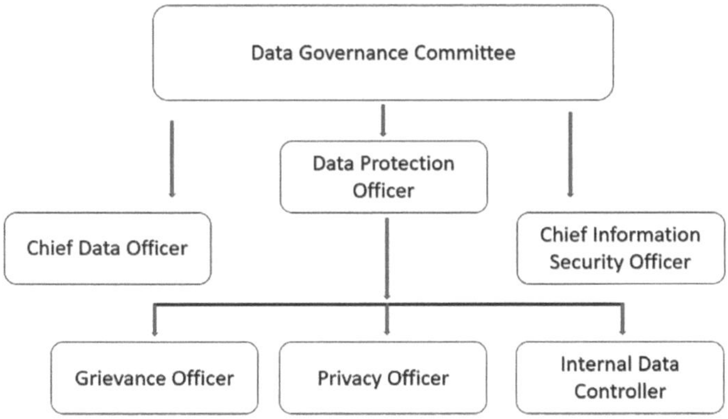

In this entire process whether CDO will lead the Data Governance with Data Protection or DPO will lead Data Protection with Data Governance is a matter of choice for the Companies based on whether it is a Data Driven company as a whole or Data is only a part of its overall business strategy.

The hierarchy of CxOs need to be organized based on the priorities and one such hierarchy could be as follows.

This structure places the overall responsibility for Data Governance and Protection with the Data Governance Committee which is ideally headed by an independent director with all stake holders as part of the committee. Most of the strategic decisions need to be taken by the committee so that implementation across the organization is smooth. At the next level of implementation, the CDO, DPO and CISO will function with their own teams. The DPO may use assistants for Grievance Redressal, internal privacy management and internal data control at process levels.

A good Governance structure is key to an effective management. Ideally it should cover end-to-end business structuring including the business identity and branding based on domain name availability, hosting and application usage, Data Monetization and Marketing etc.

Privacy Risk Assessment:

As a first step to implementing Privacy in an organization, it is necessary to conduct a "Privacy Risk Assessment". This is also referred to as "Privacy Impact Assessment" (PIA) or "Data Protection Impact Assessment" (DPIA). Risk assessment is essential to determine what is "Reasonable" in terms of security measures to be implemented.

Risks need to be assessed across the enterprise (Or any limited part of the business which is considered for assessment) taking into account the "Threats" and "Vulnerabilities". The intersection of threat with vulnerabilities is the "Risk". "Risk" so assessed is mitigated by some measures, avoided by making some business method changes and transferred through insurance to some extent. What remains after Risk avoidance, Mitigation and Transfer is the Residual Risk which needs to be absorbed by the organization. What is the extent of such absorption depending on the "Risk appetite" of the organization which is a management call.

In these four factors of Risk management namely Risk Avoidance, Risk mitigation, Risk transfer and Risk absorption, Risk avoidance is a management decision. Risk mitigation is the result of the Risk reduction process through implementation of the Privacy and Data Protection program. Theoretically Risk mitigation cannot reduce the residual risk to zero and hence part of it is covered through Insurance as risk transferred. This may still leave a portion of the risk as inevitable "residual risk" that has to be absorbed. To the extent insurance is a trade off with mitigation efforts, there is an element of management discretion involved in how much of risk is insured and how much is left for absorption as a contingent risk. Provisioning for "Absorbed risk" should be considered as a CFO responsibility.

When the contingent unabsorbed data protection risk is provisioned, it could reduce the free reserves of the Company. This has still not been adopted as an accounting principle and hence no such provision is made by auditors today. But in due course both valuation of data as well as the provision for data loss risk need to be brought into the account books.

Currently as a measure of caution, the DGPMS of FDPPI recommends that an organization has to have visibility to the value of data. If provisioning is considered, it can be in the form of below the line statement in the accounts rather than showing up as a reduction of free reserves. This is an area where accounting standards need to develop.

Gap Assessment:

When Risk is first assessed, we need to check with available risk mitigation and the difference is called the "Gap Assessment". The management looks at the "Gap Assessment" and creates an "Implementation Plan" on how much to invest in Risk mitigation and how much in Risk transfer and how much can be absorbed based on the Risk appetite of the organization. The "Implementation Plan" is considered as the "Implementation Charter" which should be owned by the top management. The DPO/ CISO or others engaged in the implementation are responsible for the implementation though the overall responsibility has to be taken up by the CEO/Top management which should sign off an Implementation Charter.

Under DGPMS, implementation charter is one of the necessary documents to be developed. While developing the gap assessment, DGPMS considers a set of Model Implementation Specifications (MIS) and maps the status of an organization against MIS. Similarly, Under ISO 27001, a similar document called the "Statement of Applicability" is developed in which the management adopts the limited set of controls from out of all the controls that may be listed in the ISO standard, by excluding what is not required.

Risk Register:

In Privacy Risk Assessment it is essential to consider the different aspects of risks that could affect the "Right to Privacy" and it includes the Confidentiality, Integrity and Availability risks associated with the personal data. The identification of threat as well as vulnerability has to be different from the norms that are applied for identifying threats and vulnerabilities in an ISMS scenario.

Threat relates to recognition of an intention to inflict damage to an IT resource. It could come from "Threat Actors" who could be insider employees or external hackers. When a security professional observes a threat, he should become alert and initiate measures to ensure that even if the threat materializes, it may not cause hurt.

An organization will be hurt if it has "Vulnerabilities" which can be exploited by threat actors. If the vulnerabilities are reduced the "Attack surface" available to a threat actor reduces.

Threats are mostly external to the system while vulnerabilities are mostly internal to the system. Exception is a malicious insider who becomes a threat to the organization or an external vulnerability like the zero-day vulnerability of the system or the "Manchurian Chips" in the mother board causing the injury to the organization.

For managing the Privacy Risk or Information Risk, the organization needs to have a system for gathering "Threat Intelligence", "Assess Internal Vulnerabilities" and develop a "Risk Register". The "Risk Register" should list the various scenarios which could result in the data compromise risk.

Data Inventory:

Before making any assessment of Risk, it is essential for an organization to understand where their risk lies in an organization. An organization may be located in multiple places, may have hundreds of computers, several data centres, several cloud storage contracts, thousands of employee devices all of which may have the corporate data in some form. It is like the data asset of the organization is spread across multiple systems controlled by multiple persons, some within a secure cooperate premises and some with contractual parties in their premises and some in employee places etc. Some data may be located in a virtual environment which cannot be placed in any physical location.

If we want to protect the data therefore, we need to first identify the data locations. One way by which data location can be tagged is to the "Processes". There are different business processes, and each process collects, processes and stores data. Hence "Process" can be a tag through which data location and data ownership for control purpose can be defined. The processes can also be further tagged to the physical location from which the process is controlled. This list of "Processes" is often referred to as "Record of Processing".

Each process either generates data or processes data or stores data or transmits data or destroys data. These could be considered as "Categories of Process".

"Generation of Data" could mean "Collection of data from outside", converting it into another form through processing. Sometime processes may convert a non-personal data to personal data or personal data to anonymised data etc and hence the nature of the data and the associated risks may change when data is processed.

If we take "Data Collection Processes" as one category, all these process owners need to be aware of the law regarding collection of personal data, the need for lawful basis for collection, obtaining purpose-oriented consent etc. These process owners deal with outside "Data Principals". At the gateway itself the process owners need to identify the data and classify them first as non-personal and personal and thereafter to subcategories as per the requirement.

This means that the organization need to have a "Data Classification Policy" to start with. It may classify non personal data as "Confidential",

Restricted", "Public" etc and personal data as "Employee-Nonemployee", "Minor-Adult", "Sensitive", "Critical" etc.

In the DPDPA 2023, India may adopt a policy of classifying organizations as "Data Fiduciaries", "Significant Data Fiduciaries", "Consent Managers" or "Data Processors" and the classification of information as "Sensitive" or "Critical" may be left to the organization based on the risks they need to bear.

Tagging data through Processes can be further subdivided within the process into different Computing devices each of which may have an owner.

In such an architecture, there can be a "Record of Processing" with say 100 different processes with a mapping of where the IT assets and the controllers are physically located and what classification of data lies within them.

This process can be called developing a "Data Inventory".

A Data Inventory needs to identify the data base which consists of a group of data sets, their classification, the computers where they are located, the owners of the individual computers and the owner of the process if designated etc. There needs to be an ID system to identify the database so that the organization has some idea of where their data assets lie.

A Data set is a collection of individual data identifiers which when together are related to a person whose "Core ID" is one of the ingredients of the data set. In addition to this "Core ID" it is essential to assign a Master Data Management ID (MDM-ID) to the data set for internal use. The data set therefore consists of MDM ID, Core ID, other identifiers, and associated data such as the health data or financial data etc. This entire set is one personal data set and has a certain depth, represents a certain sensitivity and is related to a particular jurisdiction. Additionally, each data set (for the core ID) has a source and consent attached with it. Probably there could even be multiple consents. The Consent represents the "Purpose" which also is part of the data set. Based on the purpose there would be a data retention requirement and data minimization obligation. If excess data is available, it can be pruned (if not required for other purposes as a part of cleansing of data). If data retention is limited the transfer of data from the staging environment to a secure archive has to be programmed and further an erasure process as per policy.

Assigning MDM-ID enables data to be stored in a central place so that all users are only provided access for processing on a thin client without storage. This will ensure that there could be only one instance of data in the organization. However, if every user downloads data to their computer and retains it after processing, there is a difficulty in tagging the data.

In Data Protection management there could be requests of data principals to access their data, withdraw consent, erase or port their data. In such instances, if the organization cannot locate all the relevant data and apply the condition of erasure or porting etc, there could be instances of noncompliance.

Some data may not even be in specific structured data base format. They may lie in unstructured format scattered all over the Company.

While a new process can be designed to be better organized with well-defined collection and storage norms, the existence of legacy data in an organization when a new data protection law becomes applicable to an existing set up poses a huge challenge.

DGPMS tries to address this requirement through the "Distributed Responsibility" concept which is the only practical method of handing the chaotic way data is distributed in organizations as of today making it impossible to apply some legal requirements with an assurance.

"Data Discovery" is therefore a technology process by which an automated process should scan all the corporate data devices and identify different types of data, their locations etc so that they can then be moved to different data stores for proper management after appropriate classification.

Hence one of the first steps in building a Data Protection Architecture is to run a "Data Discovery and Data Classification" process to generate a data inventory along with the mapping of ownership of individual data sets and the processes where they are used.

Access Control:

Once the data inventory along with the owners of the data locations are identified, based on the purpose classification, the organization may determine who all should be provided access to a given data set.

This will be documented as a policy to be implemented through the access controls which require specifications of how to grant access, how to maintain access and how to remove access at the appropriate contexts.

If the device controller is different from the information processing controller, organization may implement policies to provide an "Internal Data Controller" and "Internal Data Processor" type of role recognition to different persons. If there is a centralized storage of data, there may be a "Data Custodian" function that can be assigned.

If the security head decides on such role definitions, it becomes the obligation of the HR department to incorporate such responsibilities in the job specifications.

It is for this reason that the "Governance Committee" for Data Protection should have representation from different functional groups including the HR so that there is a focussed approach to the activity across the enterprise.

To implement appropriate access control, technology provides many tools in the family of "Identity and Access Management" (IAM). Current generation of IAM tools use AI to secure access particularly when an organization needs to provide access to its facilities from outside the corporate network or through BYOD (Bring your own devices) devices. Increased use of Cloud services for storage and processing has made remote access to data the norm rather than an exception.

In-Premise storage and processing today is only part of the data management strategies of an organization and used only for high security processing. But in high security processing such as in establishments where a security breach can have an adverse impact on national security, storing data and processing data within the four walls of the company with a network that is "Air-Gapped" with no Wi-Fi connection need to be considered.

The breaching of the security of the Iranian nuclear enrichment plants which were considered air-gapped systems set up 50 feet below ground was however a lesson that any system can be breached, and the risk is never zero.

The ISO 27001: 2022 framework adopts 93 controls of ISO 27002 through its Annexure which covers the requirements of information security from technical point of view. ISO 27701 tries to add the Privacy Controls to this list. DGPMS however is a single framework of 50 Model Implementation Specifications of which 8 are directly related to the protection of Confidentiality, Integrity and Availability of personal information corresponding to the controls in ISO 27001.

The Business Manager before embarking on a Privacy Protection Program should chose a proper framework which addresses all the concerns of an organisation and not go by the marketing hype of the Auditors.

In terms of the technology of Access Control, use of Single Sign on and Zero Trust along with Multifactor authentication, Pre-authentication and Adaptive authentication based on real time risk assessment is the norm. When used along with appropriate defining of "Roles and Responsibilities", access control can be integrated with the policy of "Access on a Need-to-Know Basis".

In the scenario of Personal Data Protection and Purpose oriented use of data, sometimes a single data set may have to be considered as multiple subsets with access on need to know basis to be distributed to different persons. The "Classification" of a data set and subsets will in such circumstances need to be recognized for appropriate allocation of access.

Policy Developments:

Once an organization is ready to implement Privacy Protection Controls and has identified the location of data assets, it can arrive at a Gap Assessment taking into consideration how the organization currently meets the identified Privacy Risks as documented in the Risk Register.

If the organization already has some polices in this regard, the extent these policies are being implemented may be verified and the Gap Assessment can be suitably modified.

Assuming that there are no policies at present, and it is a fresh approach to the data protection requirement, the organization needs to develop a variety of policies to cover the obligations of Privacy management as envisaged in an applicable law.

The set of policies my include the Comprehensive Privacy Policy and Comprehensive Information Security polies supported by different sub policies. Simultaneously some policies at the management level over and above the implementation of security controls and policy controls for the middle and lower management personnel will also be required.

The DGPMS therefore envisages a set of 50 Model Implementation Specifications (MIS) to be implemented by the organization out of which 15 are related to the top management of an organization while another 35 to be implemented by the middle and lower management which includes the Data Protection Officer, the Legal Compliance Team, the HR Team and the IT Team.

We shall cover both ISO 27001-27701 framework as well as DGPSI in greater detail in the subsequent chapters.

Chapter XXIII

Data Audit

Fundamentals of Data Audit:

In the earlier parts of this book we covered the law of DPDPA 2023 and its implementation. We have also briefly covered ITA 2000 and GDPR and the requirements of compliance under these laws. In the current part we shall discuss the topic of how a Data Management System is audited and Certified.

An "Audit" is essentially a system of "Verification" of a system to a given objective. It requires a frame of reference. For example, DPDPA 2023 compliance audit has to verify if an organization is compliant with what is required under DPDPA 2023 as a legislation.

On the other hand we also use a term called "Assessment" where we try to estimate how far an organization has travelled in the journey of compliance.

"Audit" is like whether a student has passed an examination by crossing the passing cut off marks or not, while assessment is whether the passed student has got 60% or 70% as marks. 'Audit" is a binary view of "Yes" or "No" where as "Assessment" is placement of a status on a "Continuous" scale.

An "audit" can be of different types like "Inventory Audit", "Financial Audit" etc. Data Audit is different from such audits as the focus here is whether the organizational measures are commensurate with what the law intends the organization to do. It is a "Due Diligence Audit".

Audit can be first party audit conducted by the organization such as the DPO conducting a periodical internal audit, or a second party audit when a customer conducts an audit of the vendor or third party audit when an external consultant conducts an audit for certification purpose or a regulatory audit when a regulator conducts an audit to find out if anything is wrong in a company.

In the specific context of personal data protection itself there are multiple types of audits such as

a. Enterprise level compliance audit to check if the organization is compliant to DPDPA 2023 and any other relevant law.

b. Data Breach audit when a suspected data breach incident is probed to validate if a breach has taken place and if so find the cause of the breach and its impact on the data principals.

c. Privacy Impact Assessment (PIA) or Data Protection Impact Assessment (DPIA) which is an audit of a process or project to identify the risks associated with it in terms of what harm/damage it may cause to a data principal along with the mitigation efforts taken etc

d. "Data Processor Audit" which is an audit of the data protection practices of a data processor or sub contractor engaged by a data fiduciary. This is a replication of the DPDPA 2023 audit which the Data Fiduciary undertakes for himself at the Data Processor level limited to the process related to the Data Fiduciary.

e. "Regulatory Audit" where the regulator examines a complaint of non-compliance and determines whether the complaint is sustainable and if so what is the root cause, what has been the steps taken by the organization to mitigate the risk before and after the identification of the breach, whether the notification of data breach was in time and what level of penalty has to be imposed etc.

f. An assessment audit to evaluate the maturity level of compliance implementation in an organization in the form of "Data Trust Score".

In all such audits there is an "Audit Reference framework". The audit reference framework in case of legal audits is the law itself. However, not all laws describe the requirements of compliance clearly. Law is a legal document and hence there is a scope for interpretation. The law has to therefore be interpreted and converted into technology or operational terms and "Compliance" requirements are to be defined.

The DPDPA or GDPR simply say that there shall be appropriate organizational and technical measures for compliance. If an audit has to be conducted by the management or an auditor at the request of the management, then the auditor has to determine what is "Appropriate". This depends on the assessment of Risk. After such an assessment, risks are further reduced through mitigation efforts reaching a level of "Residual Risk". The residual risk is then covered to the extent possible through insurance and what is left is considered as "Absorbed".

This risk impact assessment in the case of Compliance of DPDPA 2023 or GDPR is based on what risks can arise in terms of non-compliance of the Act.

The audit under ISO 27001 is based on the suggested standards/ mandatory requirements which is a "Best Practice" and not "Law". Under ISO 27001, the risk assessment is on the possibility of compromise of Confidentiality, Integrity and Availability of information (CIA Triad).

In the DPDPA 2023, the CIA risk is recognized in terms of the Personal data but there are many other privacy oriented risks that needs to be identified and acted upon. It is for this reason that the Threat,

Vulnerability or Risk or defining of an incident, defining of the sensitivity of information etc used in ISO 27001 audit does not apply to a DPDPA 2023 audit.

The ISO 27701 audit when undertaken along with ISO 27001 addresses some of the privacy risks but it is aligned with GDPR as the reference framework. Compliance to GDPR is not compliance to DPDPA-2023 and hence ISO 27001 as a framework fails in the case of DPDPA 2023.

At present, the only framework in India that addresses the DPDPA 2023 compliance is the DGPSI framework (Digital Governance and Protection Standard of India) about which we shall discuss in detail in a subsequent chapter.

However, considering that some of the companies are exposed to both Indian Data Protection law as well as the EU law, we have devoted some part of this book to explain what does an ISO 27001 and ISO 27701 as audit framework achieve before going over to DGPSI discussions.

The difference between a DPO and a Data Auditor:

At this point of time, we can try to understand the difference between a DPO and a Data Auditor and how their perceptions on Audit may differ slightly. A DPO is a senior executive of the Company reporting to the Board of Directors and representing the Company with the Data Protection Board. At the same time, he is the principal contact for Data Principals for grievance redressal. On the other hand, the Data Auditor is an independent auditor who conducts audit of the Company's compliance program.

Both the DPO and the Data Auditor need to be highly knowledgeable regarding the data protection laws particularly the DPDPA 2023 and the ITA 2000. If the organization is operating on the web, it will be necessary to be also aware of the international data protection laws particular the GDPR.

In terms of application skills, the DPO needs a higher level of technical skills since he has to advise the company and supervise the implementation of the compliance measures.

On the other hand, the auditor normally verifies an existing system as implemented by a Company and hence could manage with lesser technical skills but with an ability to understand technology. In terms of attitude, a Data Auditor would be more inquisitive while a DPO has to be more solution oriented. A greater level of creativity is required for the DPO while a greater level of skills in extracting evidences of compliance and non compliance is required by the Data Auditor.

A DPO is like a class teacher who guides the children while Data Auditor is like the head master who is focussed on disciplining the children.

Qualities of a Good DPO

- Should be an expert in Data Protection Laws
- Should be able to covert Legal Principles into Policy and Technology Controls
- Should have ability for parallel thinking
- Should have empathy
- Good be a good listener with skills of Negotiation and Mediation
- Should be a good communication expert
- Should be humble and a natural leader

There is one school of thought built by the ISO system which treats implementers as different class of professionals from auditors in the context of ISO 27001. The implementer implements the ISMS (Information Security Management System) in an organization which the auditor audits. There are certification programs for "Lead Implementer" and "Lead Auditor" which are conducted differently at different costs.

Additionally, there are certified "Quality Assessors" who may do a different function of quality assessment of an organization and conducts CMMI or Capability Maturity Model Integration audits, (developed by Carnegie Mellon University as a system and managed now by ISACA). It is a set of related "best practices" derived from industry leaders and relates to product engineering and software development. However, a professional must be accredited with a training to do CMMI Audit/Assessment.

Though the ISO implementation and audit are just two sides of the same coin and CMMI audit is s special instance of evaluation of a software system, that the industry has created.

Similarly, when an organization uses credit card information processing, irrespective of ISO audit, the organization has to go through PCI-DSS audits. If the business partner is from USA, he would not go with ISO audit but prefer SOC 2 audit.

Thus professionals and organizations need to work for multiple certifications all for a similar outcome. While this expands the business for consultants, it increases the cost of compliance to the organization and subjects an organization to an end-less sequence of audits.

FDPPI, as an organization of the data protection professionals therefore has been trying to develop a unified guidance system which combines the implementation, audit and assessment.

It also tries to consider whether the audit related to Data Protection (Including ITA 2000 with DPDPA 2023) may be integrated with the requirements of the BIS standard – Adequacy of Organizational Data Governance and Data Management Practices (Data Governance and Data Management standard) applicable to Data Privacy.

FDPPI has also recognized that Indian companies often deal with personal data with stakes in both DPDPA 2023 and GDPR. Hence the need for simultaneous certification to multiple data protection laws need to be also considered.

For this purpose, FDPPI has created a framework called DGPSI. (Data Governance and Protection Standard of India). This framework uses certain Model implementation Specifications and achieves compliance of DPDPA 2023, ITA 2000 and BIS draft guidelines on Data Governance and Data Protection together. Through its data classification system it also allows for separate implementation and audit of personal data which come under other data protection laws such as GDPR for which ISO 27701 may otherwise have to be used. The same system can also be used for DTS assessment for presenting the maturity of compliance management systems.

This unification of certification systems at the professional certification level and organizational compliance certification level substantially assists the organizations to simplify their compliance and for professionals to reduce the costs associated with multiple certifications.

As a part of creating an eco-system for DGPSI audits, FDPPI conducts accreditation program for professionals for Certified DPO and Data Auditor and also provides certified audit system for organizations obviating the need for multiple audits using DGPSI as the framework.

DGPSI is a revolutionary concept that brings down the need for compliance to multiple frameworks and certified by multiple certifiers into one common framework and is the framework of the future.

DGPSI is all set to disrupt the market of data protection audits and does confront opposition from established professionals. But over a period, Companies as consumers need to realize the value of such a framework and start convincing themselves and their customers about the need to adopt the new thought of DGPSI.

To make people understand and appreciate DGPSI, we cover in the subsequent parts of this book, the essence of ISO 27001 and ISO 27701 besides the details of DGPSI.

Chapter XXIV

Essence of ISO 27001 for Business Managers

(P.S: ISO 27001 is a copyright protected document and cannot be reproduced in its entirety)

ISO is the international organization for Standards composed of representatives from the national standards organisation of member countries. It has developed more than 30,000 standards and guidelines documents which industry may use for different purposes. ISO has also developed a system whereby some standards are "Certifiable" by accredited audit organizations on the basis of audits conducted by trained and accredited auditors.

ISO/IEC 27001 is an information security management system standard that provides a list of compliance requirements against which organizations and professionals can be certified. It helps organizations establish, implement, maintain, and improve an information security management system (ISMS).

ISO 27002 is a standard used to tailor information security management systems to the specific context of organizations by providing guidelines for selecting and implementing proper information security controls listed in

Annex A of ISO/IEC 27001. Furthermore, ISO/IEC 27002 offers much more detailed and thorough information regarding these controls.

Considering that ISO/IEC 27002 is a supporting standard containing guidance and not requirements, organizations cannot be certified against it.

The latest version of ISO 27001 is the 2022 version and referred to as ISO 27001:2022. The earlier version was ISO 27001:2013 and audit certifications made under this version need to be upgraded before 2025 into the new standards. Additionally, ISO 27002: 2013 is a document that prescribes the standards for "Controls" to meet the ISO 27001 requirements. These are also referred to as Annexure A in the ISO 27001 document.

ISO 27001 addresses the requirements of setting up an ISMS (Information Security Management System) in an organization which could be certified as per the standards and once certified, it is expected that the Company meets the expectations of information security in the industry. Most of the time when a company refers to ISO 27001 certification, they are referring to this Certification that their ISMS is in accordance with the Standards specified.

In many cases ISO 27001 is applied on ISMS with a limited scope of a division or system etc and not on the enterprise basis. A Scope limitation document in the form of "Statement of Applicability" documents the justification on why the scope as defined is acceptable.

ISO 27001: 2013 did not address the Privacy Issues but ISO 27001:2022 does address some Privacy Issues.

The annexure controls of ISO 27001:2022 has adopted the 93 controls of the ISO 27002:2019 as against the earlier 114 controls. The reduction has been brought mainly through merger of some controls and regrouping the controls under 4 groups instead of the earlier 14 groups.

The four groups are.

1. Organizational controls - contains 37 controls
2. People controls - contains 8 controls
3. Physical controls - contains 14 controls
4. Technological controls - contains 34 controls

The new standard has also added 11 new controls namely.

1. Threat intelligence
2. Information security for the use of cloud services
3. ICT readiness for business continuity
4. Physical security monitoring
5. Configuration management
6. Information deletion
7. Data masking
8. Data leakage prevention
9. Monitoring activities
10. Web filtering
11. Secure coding

Structure of ISO 27001:

ISO 27001 as a document Consists of 10 clauses of which the first 3 clauses are introductory.

Clause 4 is meant for auditors and implementors to keep the context of the system in focus and set the boundaries for the applicability of ISO 27001 implementation.

Clause 5 and 6 speak of "Leadership", or the management requirements and planning

Clause 7 and 8 relates to the support and Operations

Clause 9 speaks of Performance evaluation and Clause 10 speaks of need for review.

Annex A contains the list of controls that cover all the above requirements.

According to ISO 27001, the "Leadership" standard, it is expected that the top management shall demonstrate leadership and commitment with respect to the ISMS by

a. ensuring the information security policy and the information security objectives are established and are compatible with the strategic direction of the organization.

b. ensuring the integration of the information security management system requirements into the organization's processes.

c. ensuring that the resources needed for the information security management system are available.

d. communicating the importance of effective information security management and of conforming to the information security management system requirements.

e. ensuring that the information security management system achieves its intended outcome(s).

f. directing and supporting persons to contribute to the effectiveness of the information security management system.

g. promoting continual improvement; and

h. supporting other relevant management roles to demonstrate their leadership as it applies to their areas of responsibility.

ISO 27018:2019:

ISO 27018 is another Privacy related standard from the ISO stable and was recently updated in 2019. It is also intended as an extension to ISO 27001. This was the first privacy-specific international standard for cloud providers and contains extended controls and related implementation guidance that's particularly helpful to processors of PII using cloud computing.

27018 supplements the ISO/IEC 27001:2013 control set within Annex A with 25 extended controls unique to cloud service providers. (Needs updating to ISO 27001:2022)

These unique controls are associated with the 11 privacy principles within ISO 29100 and address topics such as consent, choice, data minimization and retention, and disclosure limitation.

While ISO 27018 is specific to the processing of PII in the public cloud, the controls and guidance in the standard can also be relevant to PII controllers, but we should be alert that it's possible this type of organization may also be subject to additional PII protection legislation, regulations, and obligations, which are not covered in ISO 27018.

Chapter XXV

ISO 27701

In 2019, ISO released a guidelines document namely ISO 27701:2019 to supplement ISO 27001 specifically to provide a guideline for compliance of GDPR. The Certifiable standard was still ISO 27001 and ISO 27701 when completed with ISO 27001 was eligible for certification.

While ISO 27001 was meant to be a standard for establishing an Information Security Management System, ISO 27701 was meant to provide guidelines for establishing "PIMS" or "Personal Information management System".

EU Council has not yet recognized any certification mechanism under GDPR though deliberations are going on in this regard. However, ISO 27701 could be a potential certification mechanism.

The essence of PIMS is to address the privacy related requirements of compliance such as

a. Establishing legal basis for processing

b. Complying with the Data Processing Principles

c. Protecting the Rights of Data Subjects

d. Ensuring Data Breach Notification

e. Ensuring cross border transfer as per compliance

f. Complying with other Compliance requirements of the applicable law.

The requirements of the standard can be separated in the following groups:

- PIMS requirements related to ISO 27001 are outlined in chapter 5.
- PIMS guidance related to ISO 27002 are outlined in chapter 6.
- PIMS guidance for Controllers are outlined in chapter 7.
- PIMS guidance for Processors are outlined in chapter 8.

PIMS requirements related to ISO 27001 (Chapter 5:):

This chapter aims to upgrade an already existing ISMS with privacy related requirements. Apart from applying this general change, all the chapters of ISO 27001 are covered. Below the most important changes will be discussed with reference to the ISO 27701 paragraph numbers (in brackets).

The organisational context (5.2):

ISO 27701 5.2 contains four sub-clauses that relate to privacy protection and the processing/control of PII, **each of which correspond to a linked clause within ISO 27001**

In addition, ISO 27701 contains extra guidance points for organisations seeking to implement a PIMS, with pointers on how to apply both the ISO 27701 and ISO 27001 guidelines to this specific topic.

Additional guidelines under ISO 27701 for determining the context includes.

1. Reviewing any prevailing privacy laws, regulations or 'judicial decisions'.

2. Taking into account the organisation's unique set of requirements relating to the kind of products and service they sell, and company-specific governance documents, policies and procedures.
3. Any administrative factors, including the day-to-day running of the company.
4. Third party agreements or service contracts that have the potential to impact upon PII and privacy protection.

When implementing a PIMS, organisations need to map out a list of interested parties that are either affected by a PIMS or have a role to play in processing PII. An interested party could be one of the following (but not limited to)

1. An employee.
2. A customer.
3. Regulatory, judicial, or supervisory authorities.
4. Other PII controllers and processors.

Under Chapter 6, PIMS requirements related to ISO 27002 are covered including protection of test data and Information security incident management. These controls state that personal identifiable information shouldn't be used for testing purposes and Incident management leading to breaches of personal data should be monitored.

Chapter 7 of ISO 27701 contains several GDPR compliance checks for Controllers of personal information. Most of these controls are mandatory on the basis of the GDPR, however. Themes covered are:

- Lawful basis for the processing of personal data
- Consent management
- Data Protection Impact Assessments (DPIA)
- Data Processing Agreements

- Facilitating data subjects' rights
- Implementing privacy by design and default principles
- Data export to third countries

Chapter 8 of ISO 27701 similarly contains several GDPR compliance checks for Processors of personal information. Most of these controls are mandatory on the basis of the GDPR, however.

Themes covered are:

- Conditions for processing
- Data protection principles
- Implementing privacy by design and default principles
- Data export to third countries

Annexure A of the ISO 27701 document lists 31 Control objectives and controls applicable to PII Controllers. Annexure B of ISO 27701 document lists of 18 control objectives applicable to PII processors. The list of these controls are as follows.

ISO 27701-Control Objectives for a PII Controller as per Annexure A

	7.2 Conditions for collection and processing (1-8)
1	Identify and document purpose
2	Identify lawful basis
3	Determine when and how consent is to be obtained
4	Obtain and record consent
5	Privacy impact assessment
6	Contract with PII processors
7	Joint PII Controller
8	Records related to Processing PII
	7.3: Obligations to PII principals (9-18)

9	Determining and fulfilling obligations to PII principals
10	Determining information for PII principals
11	Providing information to PII principals
12	Providing mechanism to modify or withdraw consent
13	Providing mechanism to object to PII processing
14	Access, Correction and/or Erasure
15	PII Controller's obligations to inform third parties
16	Providing copy of PII Processed
17	Handling requests
18	Automated decision making
	Privacy by design and default(19-27)
19	Limit collection
20	Limit processing
21	Accuracy and quality
22	PII minimization objectives
23	PII de-identification and deletion at the end of processing
24	Temporary files
25	Retention
26	Disposal
27	PII Transmission controls
	7.5: PII sharing, transfer and disclosure (28-31)
28	Identify basis for PII transfer between jurisdictions
29	Countries and international organizations to which PII can be transferred
30	Records of transfer of PII
31	Records of PII disclosure to third parties

ISO 27701-Control Objectives for a PII Processor as per Annexure B:

	8.2 Conditions for collection and processing (6)
1	Customer agreement
2	Organization's purposes
3	Marketing and Advertising use
4	Infringing instruction
5	Customer obligations
6	Records related to processing of PII
	8.3: obligations to PII principals(1)
7	Obligations to PII principals
	8.4: Privacy by design and default(3)
8	Temporary files
9	Return transfer or disposal of PII
10	PII transmission controls
	PII Sharing, Transfer and Disclosure (8)
11	Basis for PII Transfer between Jurisdictions
12	Countries and international organizations to which PII can be transferred
13	Records of PII disclosure to third parties
14	Notification of PII disclosure requests
15	Legally binding PII disclosures
16	Disclosure of sub-contractors used to process PII
17	Engagement of a subcontractor to process PII
18	Change of subcontractor to process PII

Though ISO 27701 can be considered flexibly to data protection laws other than GDPR, the standard is not as focussed as DGPSI in terms of compliance of Indian Data Protection laws. Further ISO 27701 can be certified only along with ISO 27001. ISO 27701:2013 is no longer being certified after 31st October 2023 and ISO 27701 is not yet aligned with ISO 27001: 2022. Hence there is uncertainty about the use of ISO 27701 for certification at present.

Also, this dual certification is not economical for SMEs/MSMEs. In view of the focus on Indian requirements and being more economical, DGPSI offers an alternative to SMEs/MSMEs as a framework for compliance.

The US market relies more on SOC 2 compliance instead of ISO particularly when service organizations are involved. SOC 1 reports focus on financial controls, while SOC 2 reports focus more broadly on availability, security, processing integrity, confidentiality and privacy. SOC 2 audit addresses the compliance requirement under the following 8 categories.

1. Notice
2. Choice and Consent
3. Collection
4. Use, Retention, and Disposal
5. Access
6. Disclosure and Notification
7. Quality
8. Monitoring and Enforcement

Notice:

The privacy notice encompasses the privacy practices the organization follows to meet its objectives over privacy commitments and system requirements that is communicated to data subjects. The privacy notice must be communicated to the data subjects at or before the time personal information is collected or shortly thereafter. Any changes to the privacy notice including changes in the use of personal information must be made timely by the organization to the data subjects. Privacy notices are commonly posted on an organization's public website so that they are readily accessible by anyone at any given time.

Choice and Consent:

Data subjects must be informed by the organization about the choices available to them and the consequences of each choice regarding the collection, use, retention, disclosure, and disposal of their personal information. Consent from the data subject must be obtained for the choices made regarding their personal information. The choices selected must be effectively implemented by the organization.

Collection:

Only personal information required to meet the organization's objectives should be collected by the organization that is consistent with the organization's privacy commitments and system requirements. The organization must have a process in place to evaluate the reliability of information collected from third-party sources and to be assured that the third-party sources collected their information fairly and lawfully. The data subject must provide implicit or explicit consent and this consent must be retained by the organization when sensitive personal information is collected, used, or disclosed unless a law or regulation requires otherwise.

Use, Retention and Disposal:

The use of personal information collected by the organization should only be for the intended purposes for which it was obtained. Personal information collected should not be retained any longer than needed to fulfil the stated purpose. Retaining personal information longer than needed raises the organization's risk for unauthorized access, unauthorized disclosure, or data breach. During the retention period, personal information must be protected from deletion, unauthorized modification, or destruction. Personal information must be securely disposed of in a manner to prevent unauthorized access or disclosure.

Access:

Data subjects must be authenticated by the organization prior to giving them physical or electronic access to their personal information for review and update. If their access is denied, the reason for denial must be provided timely. Data subjects must be given the ability to update their personal information. If the update is denied, the reasons for the denial and how they may appeal must be communicated by the organization.

Disclosures and Notification:

The organization may disclose personal information to third parties only with implicit or explicit consent from the data subject prior to disclosure. Personal information must be disclosed only to third parties who have agreements in place to protect the personal information consistent with the organization's own privacy notice or other specific instructions or requirements. A record of authorized and unauthorized (including breaches) disclosures must be created and maintained completely, accurately, and timely. An incident response plan should be documented by the organization to guide employees in the procedures when reporting security failures and incidents.

Privacy commitments from vendors and other third parties must be obtained by the organization and compliance assessments should be periodically performed either by the organization itself or through a third-party auditor. Corrective action to remediate any deficiencies noted must be taken, as necessary or other remedial action taken if the third party is in breach of the agreements. Commitments must be obtained from vendors and other third parties to provide notification to the organization in the event of an unauthorized disclosure of personal information.

The organization must have a process in place as part of their incident response plan to provide notification of breaches and incidents to affected data subjects, regulators, and others as required. The organization must maintain an inventory of the personal information held and of disclosures to third parties so that it may be made available to the data subject upon request.

Quality:

Personal information collected by the organization must be relevant, complete, and accurate for the purposes for which it is utilized to meet the organization's objectives. This is accomplished by allowing the data subject the ability to update their personal information as necessary and performing adequate due diligence on third-party sources utilized.

Monitoring and Enforcement:

Contact information must be provided to data subjects so that inquiries, complaints, and disputes may be communicated to the organization. The organization must have a process in place to address inquiries, complaints, and disputes in a timely manner. The effectiveness of controls over personal information and compliance with privacy objectives must be monitored by the organization and issues identified must be remediated timely. Having the ability to document and track inquiries, complaints, and disputes through to their resolution will help to achieve the criteria in this area.

While for Indian entities, the choice of ISO 27701 or SOC 2 audits may be driven by customer requests because they are aware of only these frameworks, Indian entities need to meet the requirements of Indian law for which DGPSI is more suited. Once the international market understands the DGPSI framework, perhaps the Indian entities would be avoiding the duplication of international frameworks which only serve marketing purpose whereas Indigenous frameworks like DGPSI provide the cover against legal liabilities to a better extent.

We discuss DGPSI the Personal Data Protection Compliance Standard of India on which DGPMS or Personal Data Protection Compliance Management system may be established, in a subsequent chapter.

Chapter XXVI

Essence of BIS draft Standard for Data Governance

Bureau of Indian Standards (BIS) has released a draft standard called "Information Technology-Adequacy of Data Governance and Management practices". The purpose of the standard is to define the core practices and processes which organizations must demonstrate in respect of data governance and management, as well as define the requirements and method of assessment to determine if those practices and processes being performed at a level that is defined to be adequate.

The document is intended for use primarily by the following actors:

a. Any organization wanting to undergo data governance and management adequacy assessment

b. Any organization wanting to provide Data Governance and Management Assessment Services

c. Conformity Assessment Bodies

The standard is generic and is intended to be applicable to all organizations, regardless of type, size or nature.

The document provides Four practice groups and within these practice groups there are 16 practice areas and a total of 71 expected outcomes to be achieved. If there is evidence that all outcomes for a given practice are being achieved, then the practice can be termed as operating at performed level. If there are documented processes that comprise the practice and there is documented evidence to show that these processes are indeed functioning as documented and are being regularly reviewed, then the practice shall be said to be operating at Managed level.

The four practice groups defined under this standard are as follows.

- Planning and Governance (10 expected outcomes)
- Data Value delivery enhancements (28 expected outcomes)
- Risk Management (25 expected outcomes)
- Foundation activities (8 expected outcomes)

Expected outcomes under DG and DM Standard of Bureau of Indian Standards (BIS)

Sl No	Requirement
	5.1.1: Data Governance Practice
1	A Data Governance Organization, (may be nimble) with appropriate roles and responsibilities
2	Data Governance Strategy, Policies, Processes at least for the prioritized business needs
3	Data Strategy, Data Principles at least for the prioritized business needs
4	Operating Model and Operations plan
5	Baseline Standards, Guidelines, Standard Operating Procedures, Review Process and Best Practice.
5.2.1: Data Planning Practice	
6	Established organizational key data assets
7	Established process to collate and manage data requirements from all business stakeholders (mostly for a rolling window of 1 year)

8	Established process to plan and budget for required initiatives for timely fulfilment of organizational data needs
9	Established process to plan infrastructural/capacity needs for existing and future data assets.
10	Established process to assess Key Data Asset Valuation
6.1.1: Decision Management Practice	
11	Understanding of the key decision needs of an organization.
12	Strategy, approach, plans, infrastructure requirements and roadmaps to meet the current and long-term decision needs
13	Established artifacts – data & analytics: business, application and technical architecture, and design patterns.
14	Productionized decision management capabilities
15	Established process to manage and continuously improve decision management capabilities and foster fact-based decision-making culture within the organization.
6.2.1: Data Architecture Practice	
16	Approach, data architecture master blueprints and roadmaps to meet the current and long-term data requirements of the organization.
17	Data architecture viewpoints, definitions and data models, at least for the key data layers.
18	Data architecture policies, standards, guidelines, and best practices.
19	Deployed organizational data architecture, integrated with overall enterprise architecture.
20	Established process and organization structure to govern and continuously improve organizational data architecture
6.3.1: Data Integration and Interoperability Practice	
21	DII approach, solution master blueprints and roadmaps for efficient data movements in a timely manner within and between systems, applications and organizations.
22	Deployed DII solutions to move data securely, fulfilling the information needs of the organization in a timely manner
23	Established DII standards and best practices

24	Established process and organization structure to govern and continuously improve DII capabilities.
6.4.1: Master and Reference Data Management Practice	
25	Availability of at least the key Master & Reference Data Assets and related capabilities
26	Approach, architecture blueprints and roadmaps to meet the current and long-term master & reference data requirements of the organization
27	Master & reference data artifacts - data models, architecture & design patterns, standards & guidelines, standard operating procedures
28	Utilization of master data assets through effective sharing.
29	Established process and organization structures to govern and continuously improve master & reference data capabilities/services
6.5.1: Document & Content Management Practice	
30	Compliance with regulatory requirements, primarily records management obligations and customer expectations
31	Deployed Document & Content Management Capability: Timely availability of consistent and current Document & Content type resources across the organization.
32	Approach, plans, architecture blueprints and roadmaps to meet the current and long-term Document & Content type requirements of the organization
33	Policies, procedures and standards
34	Established process and organization structures to govern and continuously improve master & reference data capabilities/services.
	6.6.1: Data Storage & Operations Practice
35	Established process to identify and manage data storage requirements
36	Data storage strategy, approach, plans, high level design and roadmap to meet the current and long-term data storage requirements of the organization
37	Established process and organization structure to govern and continuously improve organizational data assets throughout their lifecycle in terms of data integrity, availability and performance while optimizing storage cost
38	Established best practices, standards and guidelines and standard operating procedures.

7.1.1: Data Classification Practice	
39	Availability of a documented data classification policy
40	Availability of methods to label data in accordance with the classification policy.
7.2.1: Data Privacy Practice	
41	Availability of a documented privacy policy and consent management framework
42	Standardized process to assess whether information is PII and categorize PII based on associated privacy risks.
43	Limits the collection of PII to the minimum elements identified for the purposes described in the notice
44	Retention of PII for which the individual has provided consent
45	Compliance with privacy requirements
46	Management of privacy risks as part of managing the enterprise risk management function
	7.3.1: Data Confidentiality Practice
47	Availability of a documented encryption policy
48	Encryption Solutions deployment as per the document policy.
49	Enterprise-wide Key Management process in place including periodic rotation of keys.
7.4.1: Data Integrity Practice	
50	Documented policy describing the granularity for integrity protection and the periodicity for integrity verification
51	Standards for integrity protection such as checksums or digital signature
52	Documented process to be followed in case of actual or potential loss of data integrity.
7.5.1: Data Availability Practice	
53	Availability of a documented data backup policy
54	Backup done in accordance with the policy.
55	Data backup process is automated
56	Backup is protected at the same level as the live data
57	Backups periodically tested by being restored

58	Availability of documented data retention and disposal policy
7.6.1: Data Regulatory Practice	
59	Reporting metrics as required for compliance are documented
60	Instrumented processes for compliance metrics to be measured
61	Existence of formal incident response process which covers planning, communications, readiness, analysis, mitigation, and improvements
62	Periodic training for awareness of Data loss
63	Availability of established list of contact information for parties that need to be informed of any such incidents
8.1.1: Metadata Management Practice	
64	Organizational capability in terms of Business Glossary / Data Dictionary / Data Catalogue providing understanding on data attributes, business terms and usage.
65	Approach, technology enablement plans and roadmaps to meet the current and long-term metadata requirements of the organization.
66	Metadata artifacts - data models, design patterns, standards & guidelines, standard operating procedures.
67	Established process and organization structure to govern metadata quality, security, and usage.
8.2.1: Data Quality Management Practice	
68	Established approach to make data fit for purpose based on business requirements.
69	Approach, technology enablement plans and roadmaps to meet the current and long-term data quality requirements of the organization.
70	Established standards, guidelines, best practices and specifications for data quality controls as part of the data lifecycle.
71	Established process and organization structure to govern (measure, monitor, report) on data quality levels and improve the quality of data, through process and system improvements

The objective of Data Governance as per this standard is to ensure that all these 71 outcomes are adequately addressed and achieved with adequate documentation.

The organization shall implement measures required for achieving these outcomes with or without assistance from implementation consultants and Auditors may make an assessment and certify the achievement.

In as much as this standard includes 25 outcomes related to Risk Management under para 7, (referred to as BIS-G7 in subsequent discussions in this book) which includes Data Classification, Data Privacy, Data Confidentiality, Integrity, Availability and Data Regulatory Compliance, this standard is related to the compliance requirements under DPDPA 2023.

In assessing the compliance of "Reasonable Safeguards" under the law the best practice recommendation under this BIS document may assume importance to determine the "Due diligence" of an organization.

Recognizing this, the Data Governance and Protection Standard of India (DGPSI) discussed later in this book and endorsed for use by FDPPI, (Foundation of Data Protection Professionals in India) has adopted these 25 Risk Management Outcomes within the Implementation Specifications adopted under the DGPSI.

This is one of the most significant developments in the Indian data protection compliance management industry.

Chapter XXVII

Indigenous Framework for Data Protection Compliance – DGPSI

We have so far discussed the law related to Data Protection in India and identified the compliance requirements. At the same time, we have seen briefly what the ISO 27701 as a standard for establishing a Personal Information Management System proposes. We have also alluded to SOC2 as another framework applicable for service organizations.

ISO 27701 or PCI-DSS and SOC2 are customer driven choices and considered as good business practice. However, they may not be oriented to the requirement of compliance with Indian data protection law. Hence to cover the Privacy Risks in the Indian Context, it is necessary to look for a framework that addresses compliance with Indian data protection laws closely.

In India, Companies need to work on DPDPA Compliance along with ITA 2000 compliance whether they are already GDPR compliant or not.

The requirements to be compliant with DPDPA 2023 can be considered as the basic first level requirement of compliance to any organization in India processing personal data collected in India.

This requirement is codified as DGPSI-Lite and consists of 36 requirements listed below

Sl No	Section Reference	Cat-ID	Description
1	4	4.1	Establish whether the organization is processing personal data for a lawful purpose to which DPDPA is applicable and whether the organization is determining the Purpose and/or Means of processing.
2		4.2	Establish the legal basis as "Consent" or "Legitimate Use" for each process. *(Requires a Process Inventory covering also the data principals)*
3	5	5.1	Develop appropriate Notice/s indicating types of data collected, the purpose of collection with details of when the purpose terminates and how the data collected is related to the purpose.
4		5.2	Notice should indicate manner of exercising of Rights by Data Principals including power to withdraw consent, with a reminder of the duties of the data principal and consequences of withdrawal of consent
5		5.3	Notice should indicate manner of making complaint to DPB.
6		5.4	Notice should inform the availability of and manner of invoking the Grievance redressal mechanism
7		5.5	Notice should be available in 22 Scheduled Indian languages with an option for the data principal to chose.
8	6	6.1	Obtain consent which is Free, Specific, affirmative action, signifying agreement, *(Generates the inventory of Personal Data)*
9		6.2	Establish procedure for using consents received from a Consent Manager

10		6.4	Ensure documenting of the consent for prospective collection of personal data and tagging it with the relevant data set. *(Multiple notices and consent formats are required for multiple sources of collection)*
11		6.5	Ensure sending of notice to data principals of legacy holding of personal data, obtain consent and follow up for recording rejections, non-delivery, acceptances and no response. *(Requires discovery of personal data in the organization and its Data Processor's control)*
12	7	7.1	Establish policy for legitimate use of personal data, with monitoring and control. *(Needs validation from the Top Management)*
13	8	8.1	Ensure that the systems are in place to enable compliance with all aspects of the Act including the new the notifications that may be issued from time to time. *(The Data Fiduciary concept imposes a responsibility for compliance in letter and spirit)*
14		8.2	Ensure availability of appropriate contract for all downstream data processors and s with upstream vendors. *(Requires systematic review of every business contract)*
15		8.3	Establish appropriate technical and organizational measures for effective observance of compliance. *(This is an open ended and dynamic requirement and related to a risk assessment)*

16		8.4	Ensure protection of personal data with self and with data processor with reasonable security safeguards. *(This is an open ended and dynamic requirement and related to the preservation of confidentiality, integrity and availability of subject personal data.)*
17		8.5	Establish appropriate policy to identify, investigate, respond and report a personal data breach to the DPB/Data Principal. *(Requires an appropriate Incident Identification, Reporting, evaluation and response system)*
18		8.6	Ensure data retention is linked to purpose of collection. *(Requires erasure or archival of data when the purpose is terminated or consent withdrawn)*
19		8.7	Publish the business contact information of the DPO/Compliance officer.
20		8.8	Establish an appropriate Grievance Redressal mechanism. *(Requires a responsive complaint handling system with negotiation, intervention of ombudsman and mediation)*
21	9	9.1	In case of minors or persons with disability to provide own consent, obtain verifiable consent from the parent or guardian. *(Requires age-gating and identification of data principals to whom the tag of minor or disabled can be applied)*

22		9.2	Establish policies to restrict the behaviour monitoring or targeted advertising of the minor. *(Requires management of activities of Advertisers)*
23	10	10.1	Identify if the organization is a Significant Data Fiduciary (SDF) and document the reasons thereof. *(Err on the safe side)*
24		10.2	If organization is a SDF appoint a Data Protection Officer with relevant credentials. *(Requires understanding of what is required to be a good DPO in India. A qualification in GDPR compliance is not necessarily a qualification in DPDPA. It may be a good practice to retain access to external DPO consultants to meet exigencies to assist the DPO)*
25		10.3	If organization is a SDF, appoint an independent Data auditor with relevant credentials.
26		10.4	If organization is a, SDF, establish a policy for conducting periodic Data Protection Impact Assessment and Periodic audit for relevant processes.
27	11	11.1	Establish measures to provide right to access to a data principal and to respond promptly with appropriate response. *(Note that if any adverse information has been hidden in the notice, it may get revealed in the summary of processing to be revealed)*

28	12	12.1	Establish measures to provide right to correction and erasure, to a data principal and to respond promptly with appropriate response. *(Note that the data principal has a duty to provide correct information and correct wrong information if already held)*
29	13	13.1	Inform and educate the Data Principal on the existence and use of grievance redressal mechanism and its access through the consent manager.
30	14	14.1	Establish appropriate measures to provide right to nomination and necessary measures to act there on at the appropriate time. *(This requires an elaborate system of claims management)*
31	15	15.1	Ensure that the data principals are appropriately informed about their duties under the Act. *(It would be a good practice to obtain an undertaking)*
32	16	16.1	Ensure to keep track of any directions from Data Protection Board or relevant sectoral regulators about restrictions for personal data transfer outside India.
33	17	17.1	Establish appropriate measures to identify and avail exemptions available with strict observance of attached conditions and limitations. *(Note that all exemptions have their own individual limitations and a strict adherence is required)*

34	28	28.1	Establish measures to promptly receive and respond to any communication received from the Data Protection Board, participate in the inquiry process and avail of the voluntary undertaking benefit where available.
35	30	30.1	Establish measures to receive directives from Data Protection Board and respond appropriately and without delay to comply with the order or otherwise respond to it with appeal, or representation for review or for proposing voluntary undertaking
36	32	32.1	Establish measures to structure and propose voluntary undertaking where required

Now if BIS framework also gets traction, even under the limited personal data protection perspective, BIS-G7 (BIS-Practice Group on Data Privacy) compliance is required.

This means that being GDPR Compliant or being ISO 27001+27701 certified does not complete the Compliance requirements of Indian Companies. They need to be also DPDPA compliant with ITA 2000 and BIS-G7 compliance.

DGPSI or Digital Governance and Protection Standard of India based on which an organization may establish DGPMS (Digital Governance and Protection Management System) addresses this requirement and, in the process, encompasses an adoption of the best principles from ISO 27701 and SOC 2 as well as the BIS draft framework on Data Governance.

DGPSI is built on 50 implementation specifications. The 50 implementation specifications are referred to as MIS or Model Implementation Specifications. These are used for Gap Assessment after which the management will apply their Risk management strategies, decide their Risk absorption capability and determine whether any minor changes are to be made in adopting the MIS. If the management decides to adopt a lesser number of specifications, the set of adapted specifications are referred to as AIS or Adapted implementation specifications.

The AIS is converted into an "Implementation Charter" that the management hands out to the implementation team with a "Deviation Justification Document". This process is like the "Statement of Applicability" in ISO audits and brings the responsibility for leaving out any part of MIS to the management.

DGPSI also envisages mandatory assessment of the compliance maturity with a Compliance score called DTS or Data Trust Score which is computed on the basis of 50 Model Implementation Specifications and not on the lesser number of Adapted Implementation Specifications.

The Certification audit however is conducted on the basis of AIS. Certification is based on a binary response "Requirement met" or "Requirement Not Met" while the DTS calculation is based on an evaluation of each of the parameters of compliance on a continuous scale of 1-10. More about this methodology is provided in a separate chapter on DTS.

For immediate reference we provide below the requirements (implementation Specifications) of DPDPA 2023 compliance and ITA 2000 compliance that needs to be addressed by any Data Protection framework in India and there after look at the implementation specifications recommended by DGPSI

Model Implementation Specifications or Requirements

(Full DGPSI Framework)

[P.S: Lead Responsibility levels (LRL):

M=Management, D=DPO, H=HR, L=Legal, T=Technology]

No	Policies to be Documented, Implemented, Reviewed, and Refined periodically	LRL
MANAGEMENT (15)		
1	Organization shall designate/appoint DPO/Compliance Manager, with necessary credentials and provide support in terms of people, budget and technology and external consultancy.	M-1
2	Organization shall constitute the Data Governance and Data Protection committee under the chairmanship of a Board member, preferably an independent director, Designated DPO/Compliance officer as the Secretary and representation of key stakeholders such as the CEO,CFO, CMO CTO, CISO, Chiefs of Legal, HR.	M-2
3	Organizations which are Significant Data Fiduciaries shall appoint an independent external Data Auditor with necessary credentials.	M-3
4	All policies shall be subject to "Exceptions" and the Organization shall establish an appropriate exception handling policy and procedures with adequate checks and balances with appropriate documentation.	M-4
5	Establish a policy of distribute responsibility for data protection where every employee will be responsible for data protection within their domain of control of data.	M-5
6	Organization shall conduct a business impact assessment to determine the applicability of data protection laws to its operations with reference to the type of data processed, the volume and nature of processing and status as a data fiduciary, Significant Data Fiduciary.	M-6
7	Organization shall establish an appropriate policy for applying "Legitimate Use" provisions as legal basis for processing personal data including publicly available data, Anonymized personal data, personal data of data principals outside India etc.,	M-7

8	Organization shall establish an appropriate policy for identifying and availing Exemptions available under the data protection laws where available	M-8
9	Organization shall establish an appropriate policy to recognize the financial value of data and assign a notional financial value to each data set and bring appropriate visibility to the value of personal data assets managed by the organization to the relevant stakeholders.	M-9
10	Organization shall establish an appropriate policy for identifying and factoring the impact of data protection laws at all levels of business operations commencing from marketing of new business and through the data processing lifecycle.	M-10
11	The organization shall establish appropriate policy for using services of third-party contractors for data processing and enter appropriate enforceable contractual agreement with appropriate assurances towards data protection. Such contracts shall also enable audits and indemnities as may be required and cover all services related to personal data processing including manpower outsourcing, cloud services, shared services for hosting of website, e-mail, application development etc.	M-11
12	Organization shall establish a system for monitoring and managing the relations with regulatory agencies such as DPB, CERT IN and other sectoral and jurisdictional regulators.	M-12
13	Organization shall establish a Policy for Data Monetization in a manner compliant with law.	M-13
14	Organization shall establish an appropriate policy for maintaining digital presence on the web, mobile, Wearables, IoT etc with adequate security against misuse of applicable data protection laws including intellectual property and cyber crime laws.	M-14
15	The Organization shall establish policy for conducting a risk assessment identifying risks of non compliance under all applicable data protection laws including laws such as ITA 2000, establish a risk management strategy, to issue an implementation charter for compliance.	M-15

DPO (17)		
16	Organization shall establish an appropriate policy for continuing use of legacy personal data and for continuing use of personal data after the end of the purpose for which it was collected. Such policy shall include sending of notice, monitoring and documenting the response and initiating necessary follow up actions.	D-1
17	Organization shall establish appropriate policy for Internal and External Data Audit including DPIA, Audit of Data Processors/Business Associates, Audit of suspected data breach incidents etc.	D-2
18	Organization shall establish appropriate policy to issue privacy notice based on the Context and purpose. Such policies shall include appropriate policies for web or mobile or other applications.	D-3
19	Organization shall establish an appropriate policy for minimization of data collection based on purpose in each process.	D-4
20	Organization shall establish an appropriate policy for minimization of data retention based on the purpose and in compliance with retention requirements under applicable laws.	D-5
21	Organization shall establish an appropriate policy for keeping personal data updated, to maintain the completeness, accuracy, and relevancy as per all applicable laws.	D-6
22	Organization shall establish an appropriate policy for Identifying end of purpose of collection of any personal data or withdrawal of consent and initiating necessary action of deletion, archival, or anonymisation.	D-7
23	Organization shall establish an appropriate policy for managing relationship with Consent Managers including setting up technical measures for receiving and withdrawing consent or for exercising any rights of the data principal.	D-8
24	Organization shall establish an appropriate policy for handling unstructured personal data including discovery, merging with other structured collection of personal data, erasure in unstructured form etc.	D-9
25	Organization shall establish an appropriate policy for providing "Access" rights to data principals including verifiable identification	D-10
26	Organization shall establish an appropriate policy for providing Right to Correction to data principals including verifiable identification	D-11

27	Organization shall establish an appropriate policy for incident management in the context of Privacy with relevant incident identification, incident validation and incident management.	D-12
28	Organization shall establish an appropriate policy for data breach notification for timely recognition and notification to all stakeholders under data protection laws, other laws such as ITA 2000 or sectoral regulations or the law enforcement authorities as may be required. The policy shall include measures to be undertaken from time to time for prevention, and detection of privacy incidents and corrective measures.	D-13
29	Organization shall establish an appropriate policy for disclosure and destruction of personal data as per all applicable laws.	D-14
30	The Organization shall establish an appropriate policy for implementing security measures at different levels such as Physical, logical, application or data level access required to protect unauthorized access to personal data assets whether they are located in the organizational resources or with data processors or cloud operators or employees.	D-15
31	The Organization shall establish an appropriate policy for acquisition or disposal or sharing or licensing of hardware and software assets from reliable and verified sources with assurance on security.	D-16
32	The Organization shall establish an appropriate policy for documentation of all compliance activities	D-17
LEGAL (5)		
33	Organization shall establish an appropriate policy for providing "Nomination" facility to data principals including verifiable identification of the nominee and description of the data assets to which nomination is applicable.	L-1
34	Organization shall establish a policy for handling personal data of data principals "Reported Deceased" including verification of a report of death of a data principal, notification to a nominee, processing the nominee's request, resolving objections of other legal claimants etc.	L-2
35	Organization shall establish a policy for providing an appropriate Grievance redressal mechanism for data principals and other stake holders during the entire life cycle of the dispute resolution including complaint, appeals and resolution.	L-3

36	Organization shall establish an appropriate policy for collection and verification of status of a minor or other disabled data principals who are represented by legal guardians and to manage such consent along with restrictions such as behaviour monitoring or targeted advertising as well as transmission of consent control back to the minor/disabled person on termination of the power of the guardian.	L-4
37	Organization shall establish an appropriate policy for structuring contracts with business associates as instruments of ensuring compliance. Such policy shall ensure updating for data protection requirements, identifying inter-se responsibilities, contact persons, expiry etc.	L-5
HR (5)		
38	Organization shall maintain an inventory of people with relevant policy for assigning responsibility under distributed responsibility, providing privacy awareness training on a periodical basis.	H-1
39	Organization shall establish an appropriate Privacy policy for processing personal data of employees, including those who are in the recruitment process or have ceased to be employees, or working on manpower supply contracts, as per applicable laws.	H-2
40	Organization shall establish an appropriate augmented HR Policy for developing a Compliance Culture in the organization including imposition of duties, sanctions and incentives.	H-3
41	Organization shall establish a whistleblower policy covering employees and extending to external participants including the public with appropriate witness protection and incentives.	H-4
42	Organization shall establish an appropriate accepted usage policy of resources allocated by the organization including in the context of working from locations outside the office and using Own Devices with relevant sanctions for violation.	H-5

TECHNOLOGY (8)		
43	Organization shall develop an Inventory of Processes, which generate, Use, Disclose or Destroy Personal Data with unique process ID assigned to each process and tagging the purpose of processing... Each process shall also identify and tag the contextual role of the organization as Data Fiduciary, Data Processor or Joint Data Fiduciary. Each Process shall identify a process owner who shall as an Internal Data Controller be responsible for compliance within his area of operation. Each process shall identify the input output data, nature of processing, storage status and movement of data during processing and storage. Each process shall adopt dynamic access permissions on a need to know basis. Each process shall tag the restrictions on the rights of use as per contractual permissions covering data protection laws, IPR laws, sectoral regulations etc.	T-1
44	Organization shall create an inventory of personal data as a data set with a unique Master Data Management (MDM) with necessary attributes. The attributes shall include the source of the data and the legal basis of collection. Each personal data set shall be associated with classification attributes such as Minor, Employee, Sensitive, applicable jurisdiction etc. Organization shall establish a technology architecture that creates an inventory of personal Data Identifiers, and run continuous search for periodical updating, merger, de-duplication, and classification of data as personal data as combinations of data identifiers. Organization shall identify a unique ID as a Core ID associated with the MDM ID and establish a system for populating other personal data attributes on an ongoing basis	T-2
45	The Organization shall set up an appropriate policy for use of Pseudonymization, anonymization and data masking for secure disclosure of personal data between processes or for disclosure.	T-3

46	The organization shall create a Centralized Personal Data Store and secure remote access architecture with virtual processing.	T-4
47	The Organization shall establish an appropriate set of information security controls necessary for protecting the data prevention of unauthorized access, modification or denial of access applicable to personal data and also data leakage and data exfiltration along with Shall include policy for using encryption in storage, transit, processing along with required key management system. Shall include data integrity management and non-repudiable authentication of data with the use of appropriate techno legal tools. Shall also include system updating and malware etc.	T-5
48	The Organization shall establish an appropriate policy for handling transit of data across jurisdictional borders as per applicable law including sectoral laws	T-6
49	The Organization shall establish an appropriate policy for disaster recovery and Business Continuity to meet requirements during exigencies. Shall include escrow of encryption keys, critical software code etc. where appropriate.	T-7
50	The Organization shall establish an appropriate policy for adopting technical measures to segregate processing of personal data of different jurisdictions and to maintain arm's length relationship between service units belonging to different jurisdictions.	T-8

Note:

1. All policies mentioned above need to be supported with detailed operational procedures, communicated to employees, awareness created, and monitored for proper implementation. The word "Appropriate" with respect to policies indicate that they are based on suitable risk identification and assessment with an objective of mitigating the risks to the threshold level of risk absorption capability of the organization.

2. The above implementation specifications are considered the "Requirements" suggested as "Model". Organizations may through appropriate risk assessment and a considered risk management strategy create a "Deviation Justification Document" and defer adoption and/or modify of some of the implementation specifications, and create an "Implementation Charter" for the purpose of implementation.

The above requirements distribute the responsibility for compliance between the different responsibility centres as follows.

Management	15
DPO	17
HR	5
Legal	5
Technology	8
Total	50

It is necessary for organizations to develop policies and procedures for each of the MIS or the lesser number of AIS which has to be tuned to the context and Risk Assessment.

DGPSI is amenable to be used as a guidance for implementation by an organization as well as for Certification of assessment of compliance of an organization by an external auditor. It is possible to consider this as one of the most useful innovations of recent times in the field of data protection compliance.

Further DGPSI audit also can double up as an assessment of Data Trust Score which is a measure of the maturity of compliance and therefore obviates a need for yet another assessment exercise. (See next chapter for details)

One of the most interesting features of DGPSI is that it is a framework which can be owned by the Legal, Technical and Managerial professionals in an organization. Compliance to DGPSI creates a superordinate goal for the enterprise. This is preferable when compared to the BIS standard to be owned by the CDO, ISO 27001 by CISO, ISO 27701 by GDPR-DPO, DPDPA compliance by Indian DPO and ITA 2000 compliance by the CCO and Assessment by the Quality team.

DGPSI is therefore the future of Data Protection Audit frameworks in India.

Certifiable Audit system under DGPSI:

FDPPI has introduced a system for Certification of organizations under DGPSI. For this purpose professionals who can lead the DGPSI audit are being trained under a Certification program and organizations which handle the business side of Audit are also accredited.

Chapter XXVIII

Data Trust Score as a Measurement of Compliance

Measurability of a goal is always a desired approach for the management since it gives visibility to where we stand vis a vis where we want to go. Some of the goals can be easily measured in terms of specific numbers such as achieving a sales target or desired profit etc.

But there are many activities of the management where the measurement must be made in subjective binary terms such as "Satisfactory", "Not Satisfactory". There are also times when the measurement need not be in binary terms but graded over a scale which may extend across very much below average, below average, average, above average, much above average and outstanding. These subjective assessments can be captured in a heatmap for easy interpretation.

An organization often looks for an "Assessment" of where they stand, even after the auditor confirms that they have reached a satisfactory level based on the implementation of controls along with the "Statement of Applicability" or "Deviation Justification Document" (Under DGPMS) which allows companies to reduce their Compliance burden by absorbing some risks through risk management strategies.

Data Trust Score (DTS) a system developed by FDPPI, is a measure of the maturity of an organization in achieving a level of assurance through compliance of the data protection law. For DTS, the assessor would take the entire 50 model implementation specification into control and not restrict his assessment to only adapted implementation specifications.

In DTS, as applicable to compliance of Data Protection law, a hybrid approach is used to record subjective observations and then assign a specific value across a scale of 10 points.

For example, assessment grid may be like the following:

Very much below satisfactory/average expectation	0-2
Below satisfactory	3-4
On par with satisfactory	5
Above average	6-7
Much above average	8-9
Outstanding	10

The assessment is based on the observed compliance of the DPDPA 2023 read along with the notifications and related laws.

It is considered that " Non-Compliance" leads to a "Penalty Risk" and DTS is a measure of how well this "Penalty Risk" is covered.

To further refine this task of assigning a "Rating" to the complex function of Techno legal compliance, the overall compliance requirement is sub divided into 50 components and under each component a division of 10 different levels are designated to create a total of 500 different points. Then using a weightage, the points are converted into a single number as an index in the range of 0-100.

The 50 different subdivisions are the 50 model implementation specifications suggested in the DGPSI or the Data Governance and Protection Standard of India. These 50 "Model Implementation Specifications" (MIS) are divided into five responsibility centres such as

"Management", "DPO", "Legal", "HR" and "Technology" and different weightages are accorded to each of the responsibility centres.

The auditor who evaluates the compliance status would check the documentation of policies, the technical measures taken by an organization for compliance and the culture of the organization to convert the policies into practice and accords a value to each of the 50 MIS on a scale of 1-10. His assignment of value may be based on his perception of what is the par expectation and whether the achievement is above par or below par and further how much above par or how much below par.

This could still leave room for different auditors assigning different par values in their perception and this will remain as the subjective part of the process.

The DGPSI allocates 15 MIS to Management responsibility, 17 to DPO, 5 to Legal, 5 to HR and 8 to IT. Hence after the first level of allocation 150 points will be the maximum under management, 170 under DPO, 50 under legal, 50 under HR and 80 under IT. The actual scores will be less than the maximum as per the evaluation of the auditor. The scores will then be normalized with the maximum scores for each responsibility.

The FDPPI process then provides a discretion for the Accredited audit firm to allocate weightages to the five divisions and accordingly the weighted total score is created and indexed over a score of 100. For example, if the weightages are equal for all divisions and the total score is 250 then the weighted score would be 250 over 500 or 50% in index terms. The DTS score would therefore be 50.

If the index for each of the divisions are different such as Management 30%, DPO 25%, legal 5%, HR 10%, IT 30% then individual achievements in each responsibility levels will be first indexed at the responsibility level and there after weighted to calculate the aggregate level.

While allocation of responsibilities to different responsibility centres is suggested as a model implementation procedure, it is open to an organization to re-allocate the responsibility to different centres for implementation based on the organizational structure.

For Certification of an audit, the Adapted implementation specifications (AIS) are used while for DTS computation, the Model Implementation Specifications (MIS) is used. The difference between MIS and AIS is that the management based on its risk appetite would have created a Deviation Justification document to adopt a subset of MIS for their organization and issued an "Implementation Charter".

Further the Certification audit may consider a binary evaluation of "Satisfactory" or "Unsatisfactory" over the different AIS to arrive at the Certification eligibility. The auditor does not use MIS nor the 1-10 scaled evaluation of each of the MIS.

With this kind of approach, FDPPI has created the DGPSI as both a system of certifiable audit as well as a system for compliance maturity measurement.

Chapter XXIX

Business Opportunities under DPDPA 2023

New Professional Opportunities:

DPDPA 2023 mandates that a Significant Data Fiduciary shall appoint a Data Protection Officer within the organization at a senior level to represent the organization for all compliance purposes and a Data Auditor as an external auditor for conducting the audit of compliance. These two are the professional career opportunities created by DPDPA 2023 which may be used by people who are today functioning as CISOs or in similar positions in a Company or as auditors independently or in audit firms conducting ISO audits.

Additionally, those individuals who have the skill of "Mediation" and the knowledge of the law can develop themselves as "Mediators" for dispute resolution either as part of the grievance redressal mechanism of an organization or on suggestion from the Data Protection Board (DPB) on case to case basis when a dispute is referred to them. Since "Voluntary Undertaking" is an option to reduce the penalties, organizations facing inquiry from the DPB will benefit with sound advice from the mediators.

Grievance redressal setup is mandatory for all data fiduciaries and hence both under this Act and ITA 2000, 100% of all organizations using data or more particularly personal data will need to set up a grievance redressal mechanism and hence this is a huge professional opportunity for many advocates. Opportunities in litigation is always available in any law and they continue to be available for lawyers who may represent companies in DPB or in TDSAT when complaints are being inquired into.

Hence any professional with adequate awareness of DPDPA 2023 can leverage it with his other skills and build a professional career either as an employee of an organization or as an independent consultant.

Training as Business:

With a quest for knowledge arising from professionals, the first business that will take off is the business of "Education". Many educational institutions will introduce new courses in Data Protection and many private sector educators will offer their own training. Certain organizations will formalize such training into a "Certification" and depending on the reputation of an organization, "Certification of Data Protection Professionals in India" will be a huge business by itself.

At present Data Protection Certifications have been dominated by IAPP which conducts certifications for knowledge based on international data protection laws such as GDPR or CCPA etc. The certification exams cost about US$ 575 and may require further investment in trainings. ISACA has a certification of CDPSE which also costs around US$760 along with membership.

Unfortunately none of these programs are focussed on DPDPA 2023. We hope in future India specific programs may be introduced by such organizations. As at present these certifications are not relevant for DPDPA compliance by Indian Companies.

In the audit front the ISO audit system is an unquestionable leader and professionals can certify themselves as "Lead Auditors" which could cost around Rs 30000-50000 in the least.

Both ISO audits as well as CIPP certifications (Certificate from APIP, International Institution of Privacy Professionals) are well recognized in the industry circles and carry a reputation. However these reputations are built on a different context and they need to be re-built in the Indian context. Sooner the industry realizes that we need horses for courses and a Sunil Gavaskar is not the right person to choose for the World Cup team of 2023 despite being a king of his times, the reputation built in the European or US markets will be accepted by Indians.

What we need is indigenous models created for the needs of the Company in India now.

In India, there are two main alternatives for Privacy professionals to acquire recognized certifications. One option is the NASSCOM promoted DSCI which provides some privacy related programs which may in due course cover the Indian scenario. One must watch out what DSCI offers in terms of professional certifications in the post DPDPA 2023 context.

The more comprehensive option is from FDPPI (Foundation of Data Protection Professionals) is the one private organization which has developed certification programs related to Indian expertise for both knowledge and for audit purpose. FDPPI, in its training and certification programs provides coverage of both Indian laws and global laws and also training on a compliance framework which can be used for certification. Details can be explored on www.fdppi.in and www.naavi.org. (P.S: The author is the Chairman of FDPPI).

The same argument extends to organizations who need to choose an ISO 27701 audit over DGPSI audit. Just because my client knows only ISO 27701 and not DGPSI and adds it in his specifications, companies in India should not accept and need to educate my customer. Similarly if a recruiter of Indian Data Protection Officer mentions a GDPR qualification as a requirement to be a DPO in India, he is perhaps unaware of the Indian Certification scenario and the candidate should be confident enough to argue that his certification is more relevant for the context.

Reputations are built on familiarity over time and the quality of content. Individuals and Organizations need to exercise due diligence in choosing the Certification agency.

The right professional certifications could help in increased job opportunities and also individual entrepreneurial opportunities for Data Audit. They may be preparatory to the building up of business opportunities discussed below.

New Business opportunities:

What is of interest keen to business houses is the emergence of some unique business opportunities as a result of this law. Just as ITA 2000 gave raise to the business of Digital Certification Authorities DPDPA 2023 is likely to generate two new business opportunities apart from running training either for other Certification bodies or on their own.

One most prominent business that arises is the business of a "Consent Manager". Consent Manager is a data fiduciary who is registered as a special kind of data fiduciary for which detailed regulation has to be specified.

According to Section 6(9) of DPDPA 2023, the Government may prescribe technical, operational financial or other conditions for registration of an organization as a "Consent Manager". Since a Consent Manager is a representative of the Data Principal for providing or withdrawing of consent, it should be an organization which does not have vested interest in any Data Fiduciary. It should have the necessary security management system since it will be a repository of personal data from the public.

Additionally, it is important to avoid any fly by night operator to take on the role of a consent manager it is recommended that a minimum capital and net worth requirement may be fixed for consent managers just like the criteria used for Certifying Authorities under ITA 2000.

In the past we have observed that in the case of CIBIL which was once an Indian company owned by Indian Banks later was taken over by a US listed company namely TransUnion through share purchase from individual Banks. With this, the management control which was earlier with Indian Banks to the extent of 90% is now owned by TransUnion to the extent of 90%. The company has a vast asset based of over 500 million personal data set of financial transactions and the total value runs into several lakh Crores of rupees which is now in the hands of the new owners of the shares.

Since a similar transfer of ownership of a consent manager needs to be prevented, it is recommended that the Consent Manager should be an Indian Company with Indian promoters and controlling interest always with Indian shareholders.

The Consent managers will act as an "Intermediary" between the Data Principal and the Data Fiduciary, hold personal data of the subscribers in trust and release them on "Need to Know Basis" to the data fiduciaries.

There is one school of thought that believes that the "Consent Manager" under DPDPA 2023 will be similar to "Consent Manager" under the Account Aggregator scheme of RBI. But the author is of the opinion that the Consent Manager under DPDPA would be a data fiduciary who could provide some value added services to the data principal like such provision of "Pseudonymised" IDs t for disclosure to data fiduciaries if the purpose of processing does not require real IDs. They may also be the anonymisation gateways to release anonymised personal data for use for research and other applications which do not require identity.

At the same time, the Consent Managers can influence the compliance maturity of Data fiduciaries by insisting on a minimum Data Trust Score or similar maturity indicators. It is possible that some consent managers may develop their own methodologies for compliance maturity assessment or adopt available methods like the DGPSI based DTS system.

If rightly used, Consent Managers could become key instruments of compliance of DPDPA 2023 in India. This kind of a role is not available under other data protection laws.

The Consent Managers can extend their activity to two more business areas such as the Dispute Resolution support and Nomination and Claim management support.

Under Dispute Resolution, service would be required for small data fiduciaries for online dispute resolution with Ombudsman services and Mediation services. Such services had been earlier proposed by the author under ITA 2000 and they may now be taken up by other organizations.

Once an organization develops expertise in Data Disputes Mediation, then opportunities will open up for dispute resolution even under Arbitration between a Data Fiduciary and Data Principal.

When a Consent Manager represents a data principal and raises a complaint with the DPB, there may be a requirement for lodging a claim for compensation. However such claim has to be placed with the Adjudicator under ITA 2000 and hence the Consent Manager can use his expertise in ITA 2000 if available for providing such Adjudication support services.

The settlement of Claims of deceased data principals is another area of expertise where personal-Data Estate managers may develop who also can be "Consent Mangers" on power of attorney basis and manage the Data Property of an individual as part of the property settlement on death of a person. They can act as executors of will for data property and ensure that data is transferred to the nominee or the legal heirs as the case may be.

Thus "Training", "Consent Manager", "Dispute Resolution", "Data Estate Management", "Pseudonymisation service for Data Principals", "Anonymisation Service for data fiduciaries", etc could be different types of businesses that may emanate from DPDPA 2023.

We look forward to DPDPA 2023 developing not only as an instrument for protecting Privacy in India but also contribute to the economy of the country.

Appendix-The DPDPA 2023

INDEX

THE DIGITAL PERSONAL DATA PROTECTION Act, 2023

(No 22 of 2023)

Gazette Notification dated 11th August 2023

An Act

to provide

for the processing of digital personal data in a manner that recognises

both the right of individuals to protect their personal data and the need to process such personal data for lawful purposes and

for matters connected therewith or incidental thereto.

BE it enacted by Parliament in the Seventy-fourth Year of the Republic of India as

follows:—

CHAPTER I:

PRELIMINARY

1. Short Title and Commencement

1. This Act may be called the Digital Personal Data Protection Act, **2023**
2. It shall come into force on such date as the Central Government may, by notification in the Official Gazette, appoint and different dates may be appointed for different provisions of this Act and any reference in any such provision to the commencement of this Act shall be construed as a reference to the coming into force of that provision.

2: Definitions

In this Act, unless the context otherwise requires,—

a. "Appellate Tribunal" means the Telecom Disputes Settlement and Appellate Tribunal established under section 14 of the Telecom Regulatory Authority of India Act, 1997;

b. "automated" means any digital process capable of operating automatically in response to instructions given or otherwise for the purpose of processing data;

c. "Board" means the Data Protection Board of India established by the Central Government under section 18;

d. "certain legitimate uses" means the uses referred to in section 7;

e. "Chairperson" means the Chairperson of the Board;

f. "child" means an individual who has not completed the age of eighteen years;

g. "Consent Manager" means a person registered with the Board, who acts as a single point of contact to enable a Data Principal to give, manage, review and withdraw her consent through an accessible, transparent and interoperable platform;

h. "data" means a representation of information, facts, concepts, opinions or instructions in a manner suitable for communication, interpretation or processing by human beings or by automated means;

i. "Data Fiduciary" means any person who alone or in conjunction with other persons determines the purpose and means of processing of personal data;

j. "Data Principal" means the individual to whom the personal data relates and where such individual is—

   i. a child, includes the parents or lawful guardian of such a child;

   ii. a person with disability, includes her lawful guardian, acting on her behalf;

k. "Data Processor" means any person who processes personal data on behalf of a Data Fiduciary;

i. "Data Protection Officer" means an individual appointed by the Significant Data Fiduciary under clause (a) of sub-section (2) of section 10;

m. "digital office" means an office that adopts an online mechanism wherein the proceedings, from receipt of intimation or complaint or reference or directions or appeal, as the case may be, to the disposal thereof, are conducted in online or digital mode;

n. "digital personal data" means personal data in digital form;

o. "gain" means—

   i. a gain in property or supply of services, whether temporary or permanent; or

    ii. an opportunity to earn remuneration or greater remuneration or to gain a financial advantage otherwise than by way of legitimate remuneration;

p. "loss" means—

    i. a loss in property or interruption in supply of services, whether temporary or permanent; or

    ii. a loss of opportunity to earn remuneration or greater remuneration or to gain a financial advantage otherwise than by way of legitimate remuneration;

q. "Member" means a Member of the Board and includes the Chairperson;

r. "notification" means a notification published in the Official Gazette and the expressions "notify" and "notified" shall be construed accordingly;

s. "person" includes—

    i. an individual;

    ii. a Hindu undivided family;

    iii. a company;

    iv. a firm;

    v. an association of persons or a body of individuals, whether incorporated or not;

    vi. the State; and

    vii. every artificial juristic person, not falling within any of the preceding sub-clauses;

t. "personal data" means any data about an individual who is identifiable by or in relation to such data;

u. "personal data breach" means any unauthorised processing of personal data or accidental disclosure, acquisition, sharing, use, alteration, destruction or loss of access to personal data, that compromises the confidentiality, integrity or availability of personal data;

v. "prescribed" means prescribed by rules made under this Act;

w. "proceeding" means any action taken by the Board under the provisions of this Act;

x. "processing" in relation to personal data, means a wholly or partly automated operation or set of operations performed on digital personal data, and includes operations such as collection, recording, organisation, structuring, storage, adaptation, retrieval, use, alignment or combination, indexing, sharing, disclosure by transmission, dissemination or otherwise making available, restriction, erasure or destruction;

y. "she" in relation to an individual includes the reference to such individual irrespective of gender;

z. "Significant Data Fiduciary" means any Data Fiduciary or class of Data Fiduciaries as may be notified by the Central Government under section 10;

(za) "specified purpose" means the purpose mentioned in the notice given by the Data Fiduciary to the Data Principal in accordance with the provisions of this Act and the rules made thereunder; and

(zb) "State" means the State as defined under article 12 of the Constitution.

3. Application of the Act

Subject to the provisions of this Act, it shall—

a. apply to the processing of digital personal data within the territory of India where the personal data is collected—

i. in digital form; or

ii. in non-digital form and digitised subsequently;

b. also apply to processing of digital personal data outside the territory of India, if such processing is in connection with any activity related to offering of goods or services to Data Principals within the territory of India;

c. not apply to—

i. personal data processed by an individual for any personal or domestic purpose; and

ii. personal data that is made or caused to be made publicly available

by—

A. the Data Principal to whom such personal data relates; or

B. any other person who is under an obligation under any law for the time being in force in India to make such personal data publicly available.

X, an individual, while blogging her views, has publicly made available her personal data on social media. In such case, the provisions of this Act shall not apply.

CHAPTER II:

OBLIGATIONS OF DATA FIDUCIARY

4. Grounds for processing digital personal data

1. A person may process the personal data of a Data Principal only in accordance with the provisions of this Act and for a lawful purpose,—

  a. for which the Data Principal has given her consent; or

  b. for certain legitimate uses.

2. For the purposes of this section, the expression “lawful purpose” means any purpose which is not expressly forbidden by law.

5. Notice

1. Every request made to a Data Principal under section 6 for consent shall be accompanied or preceded by a notice given by the Data Fiduciary to the Data Principal, informing her,—

   i. the personal data and the purpose for which the same is proposed to be processed;

   ii. the manner in which she may exercise her rights under sub-section (4) of section 6 and section 13; and

   iii. the manner in which the Data Principal may make a complaint to the Board, in such manner and as may be prescribed.

Illustration:

X, an individual, opens a bank account using the mobile app or website of Y, a bank. To complete the Know-Your-Customer requirements under law for opening of bank account, X opts for processing of her personal data by Y in a live, video-based customer identification process. Y shall accompany or precede the request for the personal data with notice to X, describing the personal data and the purpose of its processing.

1. Where a Data Principal has given her consent for the processing of her personal data before the date of commencement of this Act,—

   a. the Data Fiduciary shall, as soon as it is reasonably practicable, give to the Data Principal a notice informing her,—

      i. the personal data and the purpose for which the same has been processed;

ii. the manner in which she may exercise her rights under sub-section (4) of section 6 and section 13; and

iii. the manner in which the Data Principal may make a complaint to the Board, in such manner and as may be prescribed.

b. the Data Fiduciary may continue to process the personal data until and unless the Data Principal withdraws her consent.

Illustration:

X, an individual, gave her consent to the processing of her personal data for an online shopping app or website operated by Y, an e-commerce service provider, before the commencement of this Act. Upon commencement of the Act, Y shall, as soon as practicable, give through email, in-app notification or other effective method information to X, describing the personal data and the purpose of its processing.

1. The Data Fiduciary shall give the Data Principal the option to access the contents of the notice referred to in sub-sections (1) and (2) in English or any language specified in the Eighth Schedule to the Constitution.

6. **Consent**

1. The consent given by the Data Principal shall be free, specific, informed, unconditional and unambiguous with a clear affirmative action, and shall signify an agreement to the processing of her personal data for the specified purpose and be limited to such personal data as is necessary for such specified purpose.

Illustration:

X, an individual, downloads Y, a telemedicine app. Y requests the consent of X for (i) the processing of her personal data for making available telemedicine services, and (ii) accessing her mobile phone contact list, and X signifies her consent to both. Since phone contact list is not necessary for making available telemedicine services, her consent shall be limited to the processing of her personal data for making available telemedicine services.

2. Any part of consent referred in sub-section (1) which constitutes an infringement of the provisions of this Act or the rules made thereunder or any other law for the time being in force shall be invalid to the extent of such infringement.

Illustration:

X, an individual, buys an insurance policy using the mobile app or website of Y, an insurer. She gives to Y her consent for (i) the processing of her personal data by Y for the purpose of issuing the policy, and (ii) waiving her right to file a complaint to the Data Protection Board of India. Part (ii) of the consent, relating to waiver of her right to file a complaint, shall be invalid.

3. Every request for consent under the provisions of this Act or the rules made thereunder shall be presented to the Data Principal in a clear and plain language, giving her the option to access such request in English or any language specified in the Eighth Schedule to the Constitution and providing the contact details of a Data Protection Officer, where applicable, or of any other person authorised by the Data Fiduciary to respond to any communication from the Data Principal for the purpose of exercise of her rights under the provisions of this Act.

4. Where consent given by the Data Principal is the basis of processing of personal data, such Data Principal shall have the right to withdraw her consent at any time, with the ease of doing so being comparable to the ease with which such consent was given.

5. The consequences of the withdrawal referred to in sub-section (4) shall be borne by the Data Principal, and such withdrawal shall not affect the legality of processing of the personal data based on consent before its withdrawal.

Illustration:

X, an individual, is the user of an online shopping app or website operated by Y, an e-commerce service provider. X consents to the processing of her personal data by Y for the purpose of fulfilling her supply order and places an order for supply of a good while making payment for the same. If X withdraws her consent, Y may stop enabling X to use the app or website for placing orders, but may not stop the processing for supply of the goods already ordered and paid for by X.

6. If a Data Principal withdraws her consent to the processing of personal data under sub-section (5), the Data Fiduciary shall, within a reasonable time, cease and cause its Data Processors to cease processing the personal data of such Data Principal unless such processing without her consent is required or authorised under the provisions of this Act or the rules made thereunder or any other law for the time being in force in India. Consent.

Illustration:

X, a telecom service provider, enters into a contract with Y, a Data Processor, for emailing telephone bills to the customers of X. Z, a customer of X, who had earlier given her consent to X for the processing of her personal data for emailing of bills, downloads the mobile app of X and opts to receive bills only on the app. X shall itself cease, and shall cause Y to cease, the processing of the personal data of Z for emailing bills.

7. The Data Principal may give, manage, review or withdraw her consent to the Data Fiduciary through a Consent Manager.

8. The Consent Manager shall be accountable to the Data Principal and shall act on her behalf in such manner and subject to such obligations as may be prescribed.

9. Every Consent Manager shall be registered with the Board in such manner and subject to such technical, operational, financial and other conditions as may be prescribed.

10. Where a consent given by the Data Principal is the basis of processing of personal data and a question arises in this regard in a proceeding, the Data Fiduciary shall be obliged to prove that a notice was given by her to the Data Principal and consent was given by such Data Principal to the Data Fiduciary in accordance with the provisions of this Act and the rules made thereunder.

7. Certain Legitimate Uses

A Data Fiduciary may process personal data of a Data Principal for any of following uses, namely:—

a. for the specified purpose for which the Data Principal has voluntarily provided her personal data to the Data Fiduciary, and in respect of which she has not indicated to the Data Fiduciary that she does not consent to the use of her personal data.

Illustrations:

I. X, an individual, makes a purchase at Y, a pharmacy. She voluntarily provides Y her personal data and requests Y to acknowledge receipt of the payment made for the purchase by sending a message to her mobile phone. Y may process the personal data of X for the purpose of sending the receipt.

II. X, an individual, electronically messages Y, a real estate broker, requesting Y to help identify a suitable rented accommodation for her and shares her personal data for this purpose. Y may process her personal data to identify and intimate to her the details of accommodation available on rent. Subsequently, X informs Y that X no longer needs help from Y. Y shall cease to process the personal data of X.

b. for the State and any of its instrumentalities to provide or issue to the Data Principal such subsidy, benefit, service, certificate, licence or permit as may be prescribed, where—

i. she has previously consented to the processing of her personal data by the State or any of its instrumentalities for any subsidy, benefit, service, certificate, licence or permit; or

ii. such personal data is available in digital form in, or in non-digital form and digitised subsequently from, any database, register, book or other document which is maintained by the State or any of its instrumentalities and is notified by the Central Government, subject to standards followed for processing being in accordance with the policy issued by the Central Government or any law for the time being in force for governance of personal data.

Illustration:

X. a pregnant woman, enrols herself on an app or website to avail of government's maternity benefits programme, while consenting to provide her personal data for the purpose of availing of such benefits. Government may process the personal data of X processing to determine her eligibility to receive any other prescribed benefit from the government.

c. for the performance by the State or any of its instrumentalities of any function under any law for the time being in force in India or in the interest of sovereignty and integrity of India or security of the State;

d. for fulfilling any obligation under any law for the time being in force in India on any person to disclose any information to the State or any of its instrumentalities, subject to such processing being in accordance with the provisions regarding disclosure of such information in any other law for the time being in force;

e. for compliance with any judgment or decree or order issued under any law for the time being in force in India, or any judgment or order relating to claims of a contractual or civil nature under any law for the time being in force outside India;

f. for responding to a medical emergency involving a threat to the life or immediate threat to the health of the Data Principal or any other individual;

g. for taking measures to provide medical treatment or health services to any individual during an epidemic, outbreak of disease, or any other threat to public

health;

h. for taking measures to ensure safety of, or provide assistance or services to, any individual during any disaster, or any breakdown of public order.

Explanation.—For the purposes of this clause, the expression "disaster" shall have the same meaning as assigned to it in clause (d) of section 2 of the Disaster Management Act, 2005; or

i. for the purposes of employment or those related to safeguarding the employer from loss or liability, such as prevention of corporate espionage, maintenance of confidentiality of trade secrets, intellectual property, classified information or provision of any service or benefit sought by a Data Principal who is an employee.

8. General Obligations of Data Fiduciary

1. A Data Fiduciary shall, irrespective of any agreement to the contrary or failure of a Data Principal to carry out the duties provided under this Act, be responsible for complying with the provisions of this Act and the rules made thereunder in respect of any processing undertaken by it or on its behalf by a Data Processor.

2. A Data Fiduciary may engage, appoint, use or otherwise involve a Data Processor to process personal data on its behalf for any activity related to offering of goods or services to Data Principals only under a valid contract.

3. Where personal data processed by a Data Fiduciary is likely to be—

    a. used to make a decision that affects the Data Principal; or

    b. disclosed to another Data Fiduciary, the Data Fiduciary processing such personal data shall ensure its completeness, accuracy and consistency.

4. A Data Fiduciary shall implement appropriate technical and organisational measures to ensure effective observance of the provisions of this Act and the rules made thereunder.

5. A Data Fiduciary shall protect personal data in its possession or under its control, including in respect of any processing undertaken by it or on its behalf by a Data Processor, by taking reasonable security safeguards to prevent personal data breach.

6. In the event of a personal data breach, the Data Fiduciary shall give the Board and each affected Data Principal, intimation of such breach in such form and manner as may be prescribed.

7. A Data Fiduciary shall, unless retention is necessary for compliance with any law for the time being in force,—

    a. erase personal data, upon the Data Principal withdrawing her consent or as soon as it is reasonable to assume that the specified purpose is no longer being served, whichever is earlier; and

    b. cause its Data Processor to erase any personal data that was made available by the Data Fiduciary for processing to such Data Processor.

Illustrations:

I. X, an individual, registers herself on an online marketplace operated by Y, an e-commerce service provider. X gives her consent to Y for the processing of her personal data for selling her used car.

The online marketplace helps conclude the sale. Y shall no longer retain her personal data.

I. X, an individual, decides to close her savings account with Y, a bank. Y is required by law applicable to banks to maintain the record of the identity of its clients for a period of ten years beyond closing of accounts. Since retention is necessary for compliance with law, Y shall retain X's personal data for the said period.

8. The purpose referred to in clause (a) of sub-section (7) shall be deemed to no longer be served, if the Data Principal does not—

   a. approach the Data Fiduciary for the performance of the specified purpose;

and

   b. exercise any of her rights in relation to such processing, for such time period as may be prescribed, and different time periods may be prescribed for different classes of Data Fiduciaries and for different purposes.

9. A Data Fiduciary shall publish, in such manner as may be prescribed, the business contact information of a Data Protection Officer, if applicable, or a person who is able to answer on behalf of the Data Fiduciary, the questions, if any, raised by the Data Principal about the processing of her personal data.

10. A Data Fiduciary shall establish an effective mechanism to redress the grievances of Data Principals.

11. For the purposes of this section, it is hereby clarified that a Data Principal shall be considered as not having approached the Data Fiduciary for the performance of the specified purpose, in any period during which she has not initiated contact with the Data Fiduciary for such performance, in person or by way of communication in electronic or physical form.

9. Processing of Personal Data of Children

1. The Data Fiduciary shall, before processing any personal data of a child or a person with disability who has a lawful guardian obtain verifiable consent of the parent of such child or the lawful guardian, as the case may be, in such manner as may be prescribed.

Explanation.—For the purpose of this sub-section, the expression "consent of the parent" includes the consent of lawful guardian, wherever applicable.

2. A Data Fiduciary shall not undertake such processing of personal data that is likely to cause any detrimental effect on the well-being of a child.

3. A Data Fiduciary shall not undertake tracking or behavioural monitoring of children or targeted advertising directed at children.

4. The provisions of sub-sections (1) and (3) shall not be applicable to processing of personal data of a child by such classes of Data Fiduciaries or for such purposes, and subject to such conditions, as may be prescribed.

5. The Central Government may, if satisfied that a Data Fiduciary has ensured that its processing of personal data of children is done in a manner that is verifiably safe, notify for such processing by such Data Fiduciary the age above which that Data Fiduciary shall be exempt from the applicability of all or any of the obligations under sub-sections (1) and (3) in respect of processing by that Data Fiduciary as the notification may specify.

10. Additional obligations of Significant Data Fiduciary

1. The Central Government may notify any Data Fiduciary or class of Data Fiduciaries as Significant Data Fiduciary, on the basis of an assessment of such relevant factors as it may determine, including

    a. the volume and sensitivity of personal data processed;

    b. risk to the rights of Data Principal;

c. potential impact on the sovereignty and integrity of India;

d. risk to electoral democracy;

e. security of the State; and

f. public order.

2. The Significant Data Fiduciary shall—

   a. appoint a Data Protection Officer who shall—

      i. represent the Significant Data Fiduciary under the provisions of this Act;

      ii. be based in India;

      iii. be an individual responsible to the Board of Directors or similar governing body of the Significant Data Fiduciary; and

      iv. be the point of contact for the grievance redressal mechanism under the provisions of this Act;

   b. appoint an independent data auditor to carry out data audit, who shall evaluate the compliance of the Significant Data Fiduciary in accordance with the provisions of this Act; and

   c. undertake the following other measures, namely:—

      i. periodic Data Protection Impact Assessment, which shall be a process comprising a description of the rights of Data Principals and the purpose of processing of their personal data, assessment and management of the risk to the rights of the Data Principals, and such other matters regarding such process as may be prescribed;

      ii. periodic audit; and

      iii. such other measures, consistent with the provisions of this Act, as may be prescribed.

CHAPTER III:

Rights and Duties of Data Principal

11. Right to access information about personal data.

1. The Data Principal shall have the right to obtain from the Data Fiduciary to whom she has previously given consent, including consent as referred to in clause (a) of section 7 (hereinafter referred to as the said Data Fiduciary), for processing of personal data, upon making to it a request in such manner as may be prescribed,—

    a. a summary of personal data which is being processed by such Data Fiduciary and the processing activities undertaken by that Data Fiduciary with respect to such personal data;

    b. the identities of all other Data Fiduciaries and Data Processors with whom the personal data has been shared by such Data Fiduciary, along with a description of the personal data so shared; and

    c. any other information related to the personal data of such Data Principal and its processing, as may be prescribed.

2. Nothing contained in clause (b) or clause (c) of sub-section (1) shall apply in respect of the sharing of any personal data by the said Data Fiduciary with any other Data Fiduciary authorised by law to obtain such personal data, where such sharing is pursuant to a request made in writing by such other Data Fiduciary for the purpose of prevention or detection or investigation of offences or cyber incidents, or for prosecution or punishment of offences.

12. Right to correction and erasure of personal data

1. A Data Principal shall have the right to correction, completion, updating and erasure of her personal data for the processing of which she has previously given consent, including consent

as referred to in clause (a) of section 7, in accordance with any requirement or procedure under any law for the time being in force.

2. A Data Fiduciary shall, upon receiving a request for correction, completion or updating from a Data Principal,—
    a. correct the inaccurate or misleading personal data;
    b. complete the incomplete personal data; and
    c. update the personal data.
3. A Data Principal shall make a request in such manner as may be prescribed to the Data Fiduciary for erasure of her personal data, and upon receipt of such a request, the Data Fiduciary shall erase her personal data unless retention of the same is necessary for the specified purpose or for compliance with any law for the time being in force.

13. Right of grievance redressal

1. A Data Principal shall have the right to have readily available means of grievance redressal provided by a Data Fiduciary or Consent Manager in respect of any act or omission of such Data Fiduciary or Consent Manager regarding the performance of its obligations in relation to the personal data of such Data Principal or the exercise of her rights under the provisions of this Act and the rules made thereunder.
2. The Data Fiduciary or Consent Manager shall respond to any grievances referred to in sub-section (1) within such period as may be prescribed from the date of its receipt for all or any class of Data Fiduciaries.
3. The Data Principal shall exhaust the opportunity of redressing her grievance under this section before approaching the Board.

14. Right to nominate.

1. A Data Principal shall have the right to nominate, in such manner as may be prescribed, any other individual, who shall, in the event of death or incapacity of the Data Principal, exercise the rights of the Data Principal in accordance with the provisions of this Act and the rules made thereunder.

2. For the purposes of this section, the expression "incapacity" means inability to exercise the rights of the Data Principal under the provisions of this Act or the rules made thereunder due to unsoundness of mind or infirmity of body.

15. Duties of Data Principal.

A Data Principal shall perform the following duties, namely:—

a. comply with the provisions of all applicable laws for the time being in force while exercising rights under the provisions of this Act;

b. to ensure not to impersonate another person while providing her personal data for a specified purpose;

c. to ensure not to suppress any material information while providing her personal data for any document, unique identifier, proof of identity or proof of address issued by the State or any of its instrumentalities;

d. to ensure not to register a false or frivolous grievance or complaint with a Data Fiduciary or the Board; and

e. to furnish only such information as is verifiably authentic, while exercising the right to correction or erasure under the provisions of this Act or the rules made thereunder.

CHAPTER IV:

Special Provisions

16. Processing of personal data outside India

1. The Central Government may, by notification, restrict the transfer of personal data by a Data Fiduciary for processing to such country or territory outside India as may be so notified.

2. Nothing contained in this section shall restrict the applicability of any law for the time being in force in India that provides for a higher degree of protection for or restriction on transfer of personal data by a Data Fiduciary outside India in relation to any personal data or Data Fiduciary or class thereof.

17: Exemptions

1. The provisions of Chapter II, except sub-sections (1) and (5) of section 8, and those of Chapter III and section 16 shall not apply where—

    a. the processing of personal data is necessary for enforcing any legal right or claim;

    b. the processing of personal data by any court or tribunal or any other body in India which is entrusted by law with the performance of any judicial or quasi-judicial or regulatory or supervisory function, where such processing is necessary for the performance of such function;

    c. personal data is processed in the interest of prevention, detection, investigation or prosecution of any offence or contravention of any law for the time being in force in India;

d. personal data of Data Principals not within the territory of India is processed pursuant to any contract entered into with any person outside the territory of India by any person based in India;

e. the processing is necessary for a scheme of compromise or arrangement or merger or amalgamation of two or more companies or a reconstruction by way of demerger or otherwise of a company, or transfer of undertaking of one or more company to another company, or involving division of one or more companies, approved by a court or tribunal or other authority competent to do so by any law for the time being in force; and

f. the processing is for the purpose of ascertaining the financial information and assets and liabilities of any person who has defaulted in payment due on account of a loan or advance taken from a financial institution, subject to such processing being in accordance with the provisions regarding disclosure of information or data in any other law for the time being in force.

Explanation.—For the purposes of this clause, the expressions "default" and "financial institution" shall have the meanings respectively assigned to them in sub-sections (12) and (14) of section 3 of the Insolvency and Bankruptcy Code, 2016.

Illustration:

X, an individual, takes a loan from Y, a bank. X defaults in paying her monthly loan repayment instalment on the date on which it falls due. Y may process the personal data of X for ascertaining her financial information and assets and liabilities.

2. The provisions of this Act shall not apply in respect of the processing of personal data—

a. by such instrumentality of the State as the Central Government may notify, in the interests of sovereignty and integrity of India, security of the State, friendly relations with foreign States, maintenance of public order or preventing incitement to any cognizable offence relating to any of these, and the processing by the Central Government of any personal data that such instrumentality may furnish to it; and

b. necessary for research, archiving or statistical purposes if the personal data is not to be used to take any decision specific to a Data Principal and such processing is carried on in accordance with such standards as may be prescribed.

3. The Central Government may, having regard to the volume and nature of personal data processed, notify certain Data Fiduciaries or class of Data Fiduciaries, including startups, as Data Fiduciaries to whom the provisions of section 5, sub-sections (3) and (7) of section 8 and sections 10 and 11 shall not apply.

Explanation.—For the purposes of this sub-section, the term "startup" means a private limited company or a partnership firm or a limited liability partnership incorporated in India, which is eligible to be and is recognised as such in accordance with the criteria and process notified by the department to which matters relating to startups are allocated in the Central Government.

4. In respect of processing by the State or any instrumentality of the State, the provisions of sub-section (7) of section 8 and sub-section (3) of section 12 and, where such processing is for a purpose that does not include making of a decision that affects the Data Principal, sub-section (2) of section 12 shall not apply.

5. The Central Government may, before expiry of five years from the date of commencement of this Act, by notification, declare

that any provision of this Act shall not apply to such Data Fiduciary or classes of Data Fiduciaries for such period as may be specified in the notification.

CHAPTER V:

Data Protection Board of India

18. Establishment of the Board

1. With effect from such date as the Central Government may, by notification, appoint, there shall be established, for the purposes of this Act, a Board to be called the Data Protection Board of India.

2. The Board shall be a body corporate by the name aforesaid, having perpetual succession and a common seal, with power, subject to the provisions of this Act, to acquire, hold and dispose of property, both movable and immovable, and to contract and shall, by the said name, sue or be sued.

3. The headquarters of the Board shall be at such place as the Central Government may notify.

19. Composition and Qualifications for Appointment of Chairperson and Members

1. The Board shall consist of a Chairperson and such number of other Members as the Central Government may notify.

2. The Chairperson and other Members shall be appointed by the Central Government in such manner as may be prescribed.

3. The Chairperson and other Members shall be a person of ability, integrity and standing who possesses special knowledge or practical experience in the fields of data governance, administration or implementation of laws related to social or consumer protection, dispute resolution, information and communication technology,

digital economy, law, regulation or techno-regulation, or in any other field which in the opinion of the Central Government may be useful to the Board, and at least one among them shall be an expert in the field of law.

20. Salary, allowances payable to and term of office.

1. The salary, allowances and other terms and conditions of service of the Chairperson and other Members shall be such as may be prescribed, and shall not be varied to their disadvantage after their appointment.

2. The Chairperson and other Members shall hold office for a term of two years and shall be eligible for re-appointment.

21. Disqualifications for appointment and continuation as Chairperson and Members of the Board

1. A person shall be disqualified for being appointed and continued as the Chairperson or a Member, if she—

    a. has been adjudged as an insolvent;

    b. has been convicted of an offence, which in the opinion of the Central Government, involves moral turpitude;

    c. has become physically or mentally incapable of acting as a Member;

    d. has acquired such financial or other interest, as is likely to affect prejudicially her functions as a Member; or

    e. has so abused her position as to render her continuance in office prejudicial to the public interest.

2. The Chairperson or Member shall not be removed from her office by the Central Government unless she has been given an opportunity of being heard in the matter.

22. Resignation by Members and filling of vacancy.:

1. The Chairperson or any other Member may give notice in writing to the Central Government of resigning from her office, and such resignation shall be effective from the date on which the Central Government permits her to relinquish office, or upon expiry of a period of three months from the date of receipt of such notice, or upon a duly appointed successor entering upon her office, or upon the expiry of the term of her office, whichever is earliest.

2. A vacancy caused by the resignation or removal or death of the Chairperson or any other Member, or otherwise, shall be filled by fresh appointment in accordance with the provisions of this Act.

3. The Chairperson and any other Member shall not, for a period of one year from the date on which they cease to hold such office, except with the previous approval of the Central Government, accept any employment, and shall also disclose to the Central Government any subsequent acceptance of employment with any Data Fiduciary against whom proceedings were initiated by or before such Chairperson or other Member.

23. Proceedings of Board:

1. The Board shall observe such procedure in regard to the holding of and transaction of business at its meetings, including by digital means, and authenticate its orders, directions and instruments in such manner as may be prescribed.

2. No act or proceeding of the Board shall be invalid merely by reason of

    a. any vacancy in or any defect in the constitution of the Board;

    b. any defect in the appointment of a person acting as the Chairperson or other Member of the Board; or

c. any irregularity in the procedure of the Board, which does not affect the merits of the case.

3. When the Chairperson is unable to discharge her functions owing to absence, illness or any other cause, the senior-most Member shall discharge the functions of the Chairperson until the date on which the Chairperson resumes her duties.

24. Officers and Employees of the Board

The Board may, with previous approval of the Central Government, appoint such officers and employees as it may deem necessary for the efficient discharge of its functions under the provisions of this Act, on such terms and conditions of appointment and service as may be prescribed.

25. Members and Officers to be public servants

The Chairperson, Members, officers and employees of the Board shall be deemed, when acting or purporting to act in pursuance of provisions of this Act, to be public servants within the meaning of section 21 of the Indian Penal Code.

26.Powers of the Chairperson

The Chairperson shall exercise the following powers, namely:—

a. general superintendence and giving direction in respect of all administrative matters of the Board;

b. authorise any officer of the Board to scrutinise any intimation, complaint, reference or correspondence addressed to the Board; and

c. authorise performance of any of the functions of the Board and conduct any of its proceedings, by an individual Member or groups of Members and to allocate proceedings among them.

CHAPTER VI:

POWERS, FUNCTIONS AND PROCEDURE TO BE FOLLOWED BY BOARD

27. Powers and functions of Board.

1. The Board shall exercise and perform the following powers and functions, namely:—

    a. on receipt of an intimation of personal data breach under sub-section (6) of section 8, to direct any urgent remedial or mitigation measures in the event of a personal data breach, and to inquire into such personal data breach and impose penalty as provided in this Act;

    b. on a complaint made by a Data Principal in respect of a personal data breach or a breach in observance by a Data Fiduciary of its obligations in relation to her personal data or the exercise of her rights under the provisions of this Act, or on a reference made to it by the Central Government or a State Government, or in compliance of the directions of any court, to inquire into such breach and impose penalty as provided in this Act;

    c. on a complaint made by a Data Principal in respect of a breach in observance by a Consent Manager of its obligations in relation to her personal data, to inquire into such breach and impose penalty as provided in this Act;

    d. on receipt of an intimation of breach of any condition of registration of a Consent Manager, to inquire into such breach and impose penalty as provided in this Act; and

    e. on a reference made by the Central Government in respect of the breach in observance of the provisions of sub-section (2) of section 36 (?) (ed: Should be 37) by an intermediary, to inquire into such breach and impose penalty as provided in this Act.

2. The Board may, for the effective discharge of its functions under the provisions of this Act, after giving the person concerned an opportunity of being heard and after recording reasons in writing, issue such directions as it may consider necessary to such person, who shall be bound to comply with the same.

3. The Board may, on a representation made to it by a person affected by a direction issued under sub-section (1) or sub-section (2), or on a reference made by the Central Government, modify, suspend, withdraw or cancel such direction and, while doing so, impose such conditions as it may deem fit, subject to which the modification, suspension, withdrawal or cancellation shall have effect.

28. Procedure to be followed by Board.

1. The Board shall function as an independent body and shall, as far as practicable, function as a digital office, with the receipt of complaints and the allocation, hearing and pronouncement of decisions in respect of the same being digital by design and adopt such techno-legal measures as may be prescribed.

2. The Board may, on receipt of an intimation or complaint or reference or directions as referred to in sub-section (1) of section 27, take action in accordance with the provisions of this Act and the rules made thereunder.

3. The Board shall determine whether there are sufficient grounds to proceed with an inquiry.

4. In case the Board determines that there are insufficient grounds, it may, for reasons to be recorded in writing, close the proceedings.

5. In case the Board determines that there are sufficient grounds to proceed with inquiry, it may, for reasons to be recorded in writing, inquire into the affairs of any person for ascertaining whether such person is complying with or has complied with the provisions of this Act.

6. The Board shall conduct such inquiry following the principles of natural justice and shall record reasons for its actions during the course of such inquiry.

7. For the purposes of discharging its functions under this Act, the Board shall have the same powers as are vested in a civil court under the Code of Civil Procedure, 1908, in respect of matters relating to—

   a. summoning and enforcing the attendance of any person and examining her on oath;

   b. receiving evidence of affidavit requiring the discovery and production of documents;

   c. inspecting any data, book, document, register, books of account or any other document; and

   d. such other matters as may be prescribed.

8. The Board or its officers shall not prevent access to any premises or take into custody any equipment or any item that may adversely affect the day-to-day functioning of a person.

9. The Board may require the services of any police officer or any officer of the Central Government or a State Government to assist it for the purposes of this section and it shall be the duty of every such officer to comply with such requisition.

10. During the course of the inquiry, if the Board considers it necessary, it may for reasons to be recorded in writing, issue interim orders after giving the person concerned an opportunity of being heard.

11. On completion of the inquiry and after giving the person concerned an opportunity of being heard, the Board may for reasons to be recorded in writing, either close the proceedings or proceed in accordance with section 33.

12. At any stage after receipt of a complaint, if the Board is of the opinion that the complaint is false or frivolous, it may issue a warning or impose costs on the complainant.

CHAPTER VII:

APPEAL AND ALTERNATE DISPUTE RESOLUTION

29. Appeal to Appellate Tribunal

1. Any person aggrieved by an order or direction made by the Board under this Act may prefer an appeal before the Appellate Tribunal.
2. Every appeal under sub-section (1) shall be filed within a period of sixty days from the date of receipt of the order or direction appealed against and it shall be in such form and manner and shall be accompanied by such fee as may be prescribed.
3. The Appellate Tribunal may entertain an appeal after the expiry of the period specified in sub-section (2), if it is satisfied that there was sufficient cause for not preferring the appeal within that period.
4. On receipt of an appeal under sub-section (1), the Appellate Tribunal may, after giving the parties to the appeal, an opportunity of being heard, pass such orders thereon as it thinks fit, confirming, modifying or setting aside the order appealed against.
5. The Appellate Tribunal shall send a copy of every order made by it to the Board and to the parties to the appeal.
6. The appeal filed before the Appellate Tribunal under sub-section (1) shall be dealt with by it as expeditiously as possible and endeavour shall be made by it to dispose of the appeal finally within six months from the date on which the appeal is presented to it.

7. Where any appeal under sub-section (6) could not be disposed of within the period of six months, the Appellate Tribunal shall record its reasons in writing for not disposing of the appeal within that period.

8. Without prejudice to the provisions of section 14A and section 16 of the Telecom Regulatory Authority of India Act, 1997, the Appellate Tribunal shall deal with an appeal under this section in accordance with such procedure as may be prescribed.

9. Where an appeal is filed against the orders of the Appellate Tribunal under this Act, the provisions of section 18 of the Telecom Regulatory Authority of India Act, 1997 shall apply.

10. In respect of appeals filed under the provisions of this Act, the Appellate Tribunal shall, as far as practicable, function as a digital office, with the receipt of appeal, hearing and pronouncement of decisions in respect of the same being digital by design.

30. Orders passed by Appellate Tribunal to ne executable as decree

1. An order passed by the Appellate Tribunal under this Act shall be executable by it as a decree of civil court, and for this purpose, the Appellate Tribunal shall have all the powers of a civil court.

2. Notwithstanding anything contained in sub-section (1), the Appellate Tribunal may transmit any order made by it to a civil court having local jurisdiction and such civil court shall execute the order as if it were a decree made by that court.

31. Alternate Dispute Resolution

If the Board is of the opinion that any complaint may be resolved by mediation, it may direct the parties concerned to attempt resolution of the dispute through such mediation by such mediator as the parties may mutually agree upon, or as provided for under any law for the time being in force in India.

32. Voluntary Undertaking

1. The Board may accept a voluntary undertaking in respect of any matter related to observance of the provisions of this Act from any person at any stage of a proceeding under section 28.
2. The voluntary undertaking referred to in sub-section (1) may include an undertaking to take such action within such time as may be determined by the Board, or refrain from taking such action, and or publicising such undertaking.
3. The Board may, after accepting the voluntary undertaking and with the consent of the person who gave the voluntary undertaking vary the terms included in the voluntary undertaking.
4. The acceptance of the voluntary undertaking by the Board shall constitute a bar on proceedings under the provisions of this Act as regards the contents of the voluntary undertaking, except in cases covered by sub-section (5).
5. Where a person fails to adhere to any term of the voluntary undertaking accepted by the Board, such breach shall be deemed to be breach of the provisions of this Act and the Board may, after giving such person an opportunity of being heard, proceed in accordance with the provisions of section 33.

CHAPTER VIII:

Penalties and Adjudication

33. Penalties

1. If the Board determines on conclusion of an inquiry that breach of the provisions of this Act or the rules made thereunder by a person is significant, it may, after giving the person an opportunity of being heard, impose such monetary penalty specified in the Schedule.

2. While determining the amount of monetary penalty to be imposed under sub-section (1), the Board shall have regard to the following matters, namely:—

    a. the nature, gravity and duration of the breach;

    b. the type and nature of the personal data affected by the breach;

    c. repetitive nature of the breach;

    d. whether the person, as a result of the breach, has realised a gain or avoided any loss;

    e. whether the person took any action to mitigate the effects and consequences of the breach, and the timeliness and effectiveness of such action;

    f. whether the monetary penalty to be imposed is proportionate and effective, having regard to the need to secure observance of and deter breach of the provisions of this Act; and

    g. the likely impact of the imposition of the monetary penalty on the person.

34. Crediting sums realised by way of penalties to Consolidated Fund of India.

All sums realised by way of penalties imposed by the Board under this Act, shall be credited to the Consolidated Fund of India.

CHAPTER IX:

MISCELLANEOUS

35. Protection of action taken in good faith.

No suit, prosecution or other legal proceedings shall lie against the Central Government, the Board, its Chairperson and any Member, officer or employee thereof for anything which is done or intended to be done in good faith under the provisions of this Act or the rules made thereunder.

36. Power to call for information.

The Central Government may, for the purposes of this Act, require the Board and any Data Fiduciary or intermediary to furnish such information as it may call for.

37. Power of Central Government to issue directions.

1. The Central Government or any of its officers specially authorised by it in this behalf may, upon receipt of a reference in writing from the Board that—

    a. intimates the imposition of monetary penalty by the Board on a Data Fiduciary in two or more instances; and

    b. advises, in the interests of the general public, the blocking for access by the public to any information generated, transmitted, received, stored or hosted, in any computer resource that enables such Data Fiduciary to carry on any activity relating to offering of goods or services to Data Principals within the territory of India, after giving an opportunity of being heard to that Data Fiduciary, on being satisfied that it is necessary or expedient so to do, in the interests of the general public, for reasons to be recorded in writing, by order, direct any agency of the Central Government or any intermediary to block for access by the public or cause to be blocked for access by the public any such information.

2. Every intermediary who receives a direction issued under sub-section (1) shall be bound to comply with the same.

3. For the purposes of this section, the expressions "computer resource", "information" and "intermediary" shall have the

meanings respectively assigned to them in the Information Technology Act, 2000.

38. Consistency with other laws.

1. The provisions of this Act shall be in addition to and not in derogation of any other law for the time being in force.

2. In the event of any conflict between a provision of this Act and a provision of any other law for the time being in force, the provision of this Act shall prevail to the extent of such conflict.

39. Bar of Jurisdiction

No civil court shall have the jurisdiction to entertain any suit or proceeding in respect of any matter for which the Board is empowered under the provisions of this Act and no injunction shall be granted by any court or other authority in respect of any action taken or to be taken in pursuance of any power under the provisions of this Act.

40. Power to Make Rules

1. The Central Government may, by notification, and subject to the condition of previous publication, make rules not inconsistent with the provisions of this Act, to carry out the purposes of this Act.

2. In particular and without prejudice to the generality of the foregoing power, such rules may provide for all or any of the following matters, namely:—

    a. the manner in which the notice given by the Data Fiduciary to a Data Principal shall inform her, under sub-section (1) of section 5;

    b. the manner in which the notice given by the Data Fiduciary to a Data Principal shall inform her, under sub-section (2) of section 5;

c. the manner of accountability and the obligations of Consent Manager under sub-section (8) of section 6;

d. the manner of registration of Consent Manager and the conditions relating thereto, under sub-section (9) of section 6;

e. the subsidy, benefit, service, certificate, licence or permit for the provision or issuance of which, personal data may be processed under clause (b) of section 7;

f. the form and manner of intimation of personal data breach to the Board under sub-section (6) of section 8;

g. the time period for the specified purpose to be deemed as no longer being served, under sub-section (8) of section 8;

h. the manner of publishing the business contact information of a Data Protection Officer under sub-section (9) of section 8;

i. the manner of obtaining verifiable consent under sub-section (1) of section 9;

j. the classes of Data Fiduciaries, the purposes of processing of personal data of a child and the conditions relating thereto, under sub-section (4) of section 9;

k. the other matters comprising the process of Data Protection Impact Assessment under sub-clause (i) of clause (c) of sub-section (2) of section 10;

l. the other measures that the Significant Data Fiduciary shall undertake under sub-clause (iii) of clause (c) of sub-section (2) of section 10;

m. the manner in which a Data Principal shall make a request to the Data Fiduciary to obtain information and any other information related to the personal data of such Data Principal and its processing, under sub-section (1) of section 11;

n. the manner in which a Data Principal shall make a request to the Data Fiduciary for erasure of her personal data under sub-section (3) of section 12;

o. the period within which the Data Fiduciary shall respond to any grievances under sub-section (2) of section 13;

p. the manner of nomination of any other individual by the Data Principal under sub-section (1) of section 14;

q. the standards for processing the personal data for exemption under clause (b) of sub-section (2) of section 17;

r. the manner of appointment of the Chairperson and other Members of the Board under sub-section (2) of section 19;

s. the salary, allowances and other terms and conditions of services of the Chairperson and other Members of the Board under sub-section (1) of section 20;

t. the manner of authentication of orders, directions and instruments under sub-section (1) of section 23;

u. the terms and conditions of appointment and service of officers and employees of the Board under section 24;

v. the techno-legal measures to be adopted by the Board under sub-section (1) of section 28;

w. the other matters under clause (d) of sub-section (7) of section 28;

x. the form, manner and fee for filing an appeal under sub-section (2) of section 29;

y. the procedure for dealing an appeal under sub-section (8) of section 29;

z. any other matter which is to be or may be prescribed or in respect of which provision is to be, or may be, made by rules.

41. Laying of rules and certain notifications.

Every rule made and every notification issued under section 16 and section 42 of this Act shall be laid, as soon as may be after it is made, before each House of Parliament, while it is in session, for a total period of thirty days which may be comprised in one session or in two or more successive sessions, and if before the expiry of the session immediately following the session or the successive sessions aforesaid, both Houses agree in making any modification in the rule or notification or both Houses agree that the rule or notification should not be made or issued, the rule or notification shall thereafter have effect only in such modified form or be of no effect, as the case may be; so, however, that any such modification or annulment shall be without prejudice to the validity of anything previously done under that rule or notification.

42. Power to amend Schedule.

1. The Central Government may, by notification, amend the Schedule, subject to the restriction that no such notification shall have the effect of increasing any penalty specified therein to more than twice of what was specified in it when this Act was originally enacted.

2. Any amendment notified under sub-section (1) shall have effect as if enacted in this Act and shall come into force on the date of the notification.

43. Power to Remove Difficulties

1. If any difficulty arises in giving effect to the provisions of this Act, the Central Government may, by order published in the Official Gazette, make such provisions not inconsistent with the provisions of this Act as may appear to it to be necessary or expedient for removing the difficulty.

2. No order as referred to in sub-section (1) shall be made after the expiry of three years from the date of commencement of this Act.

3. Every order made under this section shall be laid, as soon as may be after it is made, before each House of Parliament.

44. Amendments to Certain Acts

1. In section 14 of the Telecom Regulatory Authority of India Act, 1997, in clause (c), for sub-clauses (i) and (ii), the following sub-clauses shall be substituted,

namely:—

   i. the Appellate Tribunal under the Information Technology Act, 2000;

   ii. the Appellate Tribunal under the Airports Economic Regulatory Authority of India Act, 2008; and

   iii. the Appellate Tribunal under the Digital Personal Data Protection Act, 2023.".

2. The Information Technology Act, 2000 shall be amended in the following manner, namely:—

   a. section 43A shall be omitted.

   b. in section 81, in the proviso, after the words and figures "the Patents Act, 1970", the words and figures "or the Digital Personal Data Protection Act, 2023" shall be inserted; and

   c. in section 87, in sub-section (2), clause (ob) shall be omitted.

3. In section 8 of the Right to Information Act, 2005, in sub-section (1), for clause (j), the following clause shall be substituted, namely:—

   a. "(j) information which relates to personal information;".

Schedule

Sec 26

S No	Subject Matter of Breach	Penalty
1	Breach in observing the obligation of Data Fiduciary to take reasonable security safeguards to prevent personal data breach, under sub-section (5) of section 8	May extend to two hundred and fifty crore rupees.
2	Breach in observing the obligation to give the Board or affected Data Principals notice of a personal data breach, under sub-section (6) of section 8	May extend to two hundred crore rupees.
3	Breach in observance of additional obligations in relation to children, under section 9	May extend to two hundred crore rupees.
4	Breach in observance of additional obligations of Significant Data Fiduciary, under section 10	May extend to one hundred and fifty crore rupees.
5	Breach in observance of the duties under section 15	May extend to ten thousand rupees.

6	Breach of any term of voluntary undertaking accepted by the Board under section 32	Up to the extent applicable for the breach in respect of which the proceedings under section 28 were instituted.
7	Breach of any other provisions of this Act, or rules made there under	May extend to fifty crore rupees.

Notes on Clauses

Clause 1.—This clause seeks to provide for short title and commencement of the proposed Legislation.

Clause 2.—This clause seeks to define certain expressions occurring in the proposed Legislation.

Clause 3.—This clause relates to "Application of Act".: This clause seeks to clarify the application of the proposed Legislation about personal data.

Clause 4.—This clause relates to "Grounds for processing personal data".: This clause seeks to lay down grounds on processing of personal data in accordance with the provisions of the proposed Legislation and for a lawful purpose.

Clause 5.—This clause relates to "Notice".: This clause seeks to lay down the requirement of notice for collection or processing of personal data and description of notice.

Clause 6.—This clause relates to "Consent".: This clause seeks to expound the various aspects of consent which is necessary for processing of personal data.

Clause 7.—This clause relates to "Certain legitimate uses".: This clause seeks to expound the various aspects of certain legitimate uses which is necessary for processing of personal data.

Clause 8.—This clause relates to "General obligations of Data Fiduciary".: This clause seeks to lay down the general obligations on Data Fiduciary for processing personal data.

Clause 9.—This clause relates to "Processing of personal data of children".: This clause seeks to lay down the grounds for processing of personal data of children.

Clause 10.—This clause relates to "Additional obligations of Significant Data Fiduciary".: This clause seeks to lay down the additional obligations on Significant Data Fiduciary for processing personal data.

Clause 11.—This clause relates to "Right to access information about personal data".: This clause seeks to provide the data principal with the right to access information about personal data.

Clause 12.—This clause relates to "Right to correction and erasure of personal data".: This clause seeks to provide the data principal with a right to correct and erase his personal data.

Clause 13.—This clause relates to "Right of grievance redressal".: This clause seeks to provide the data principal with a right of grievance redressal.

Clause 14.—This clause relates to "Right to nominate".: This clause seeks to provide the data principal with a right to nominate.

Clause 15.—This clause relates to "Duties of Data Principal".: This clause seeks to lay down the duties of Data Principal for the exercise of the rights under the provisions of the proposed Legislation.

Clause 16.—This clause relates to "Processing of personal data outside India".: This clause seeks to lay down the Provisions related to processing of personal data outside India.

Clause 17.—This clause relates to "Exemptions".: This clause seeks to provide for exemption of certain provisions of the proposed Legislation and lay down the legitimate purposes for processing of personal data.

Clause 18.—This clause relates to "Establishment of Board".: This clause seeks to establish a Board to be called the Data Protection Board of India.: The Board shall consist of a Chairperson and such number of Members as the Central Government may notify.

Clause 19.—This clause relates to "Composition and qualifications for appointment of Chairperson and Members".: This clause seeks to list out the composition and qualifications for appointment of Chairperson and Members of the Board.

Clause 20.—This clause relates to "Salary, allowances payable to and term of office".: This clause seeks to list out the salary, allowances and other terms and conditions of service of the Chairperson and other Members of the Board.

Clause 21.—This clause relates to "Disqualifications for appointment and continuation as Chairperson and Members of Board".: This clause seeks to list out the disqualifications for appointment and continuation as Chairperson and Members of Board.

Clause 22.—This clause relates to "Resignation by Members and filling of vacancy".: This clause seeks to lay down the resignation by Members of Board and filling of vacancy.

Clause 23.—This clause relates to "Proceedings of Board".: This clause seeks to lay down the proceedings of Board. The Board is required to follow prescribed procedures for conducting its meeting and carrying out its business, including the use of digital means.

Clause 24.—This clause relates to "Officers and employees of Board".: This clause seeks to empower the Board to appoint officers and employees of Board for the effective execution of the functions under the proposed Legislation.

Clause 25.—This clause relates to "Members and officers to be public servants".: This clause seeks to deem Members and officers of the Board, while carrying out their duties in accordance with the provisions of the proposed Legislation, to be public servants as defined in section 21 of the Indian Penal Code.

Clause 26.—This clause relates to "Powers of Chairperson".: This clause seeks to provide the powers to be exercised by the Chairperson for the efficient administration of the Board.

Clause 27.—This clause relates to "powers and functions of Board".: This clause seeks to list the powers and functions of the Data Protection Board of India. The Board has the power to take prompt action in response to personal data breaches, investigate complaints, and impose penalties. Additionally, the Board can issue directions to ensure compliance and has the authority to modify or cancel its directions based on representations or references. Through these powers and functions, the Board aims to

safeguard the rights and interests of Data Principals and maintain the integrity of personal data processing activities.

Clause 28.—This clause relates to "Procedure to be followed by Board". This clause seeks to lay down the procedures to be followed by the Board pursuant to an inquiry.

Clause 29.—This clause relates to "Appeal to Appellate Tribunal".: This clause seeks to provide for appeal to the Telecom Disputes Settlement and Appellate Tribunal against any order of the Board.

Clause 30.—This clause relates to "Orders passed by Appellate Tribunal to be executable as decree".: This clause seeks to lay down to provide that the Appellate Tribunal shall have all the powers of civil court.

Clause 31.—This clause relates to "Alternate dispute resolution".: This clause seeks to lay down the alternate dispute resolution of the dispute through such mediation as the Board may deem appropriate.

Clause 32.—This clause relates to "voluntary undertaking".: This clause seeks to lay down the voluntary undertaking in respect of any matter related to observance to the provisions of the proposed Legislation from any person at any stage of a proceeding under clause 28 of the proposed Legislation.

Clause 33.—This clause relates to "Penalties". This clause seeks to provide monetary penalties by Data Protection Board.

Clause 34.—This clause relates to "Crediting sums realised by way of penalties to

Consolidated Fund of India". This clause seeks to lay down the crediting sums realised by way of penalties to Consolidated Fund of India.

Clause 35.—This clause relates to "Protection of action taken in good faith". This clause seeks to protect the Central Government, the Board, its Chairperson and any Member, officer or employee in case of action done under the proposed Legislation in good faith.

Clause 36.—This clause relates to "Power to call for information". This clause seeks to empower the Board to call for information from any Data Fiduciary.

Clause 37.—This clause relates to "Power of Central Government to issue directions". This clause seeks to empower the Central Government to issue directions to the Board.

Clause 38.—This clause relates to "Consistency with other laws". This clause seeks to provide for the overriding effect of this Legislation notwithstanding anything inconsistent with any other law.

Clause 39.—This clause relates to "Bar of jurisdiction". This clause seeks to lay down that no civil court shall have jurisdiction to entertain any suit on any matter which falls within the ambit of the Board.

Clause 40.—This clause relates to "Power to make rules". This clause seeks to empower the Central Government to make rules to carry out the purposes of the proposed Legislation.

Clause 41.—This clause relates to "Laying of rules and certain notifications". This clause seeks to require that rules and regulations made under the Legislation are to be laid before the Parliament.

Clause 42.—This clause relates to "Power to amend Schedule". This clause seeks to empower the Central Government to amend the Schedule to carry out the provisions of the proposed Legislation.

Clause 43.—This clause relates to "Power to remove difficulties". This clause seeks to empower the Central Government to issue an order for removal of any difficulty arises while during implementation of the proposed Legislation.

Clause 44.—This clause relates to "Amendments to certain Acts". This clause seeks to provide for related amendments to the Information Technology Act, 2000, the Telecom Regulatory Authority of India Act, 1997 and the Right to Information Act, 2005.

Financial Memorandum:

The Bill envisages the creation of a Data Protection Board of India. Since the structure of the Board is to be notified after enactment of the Bill, at this stage, the financial implication of the setting up and functioning of the Board is estimated to be about twenty-five crore rupees towards initial capital expenditure and ten crore rupees annually for recurring expenditure. The said expenditure is to be incurred from and out of the Consolidated Fund of India.

Memorandum Regarding Delegated Legislation:

1. Clause 40 of the Digital Personal Data Protection Bill, 2023 seeks to empower the central Government, by notification and subject to the condition of previous publication, not inconsistent with the provisions of the Act, to make rules for—

    a. the manner in which the notice given by the Data Fiduciary to a Data Principal shall inform her, under sub-section (1) of section 5;

    b. the manner in which the notice given by the Data Fiduciary to a Data Principal shall inform her, under sub-section (2) of section 5;

    c. the manner of accountability and the obligations of Consent Manager under sub-section (8) of section 6;

    d. the manner of registration of Consent Manager and the conditions relating thereto, under sub-section (9) of section 6;

    e. the subsidy, benefit, service, certificate, licence or permit for the provision or issuance of which, personal data may be processed under clause (b) of section 7;

    f. the form and manner of intimation of personal data breach to the Board under sub-section (6) of section 8; (g) the time period for the specified purpose to be deemed as no longer being served, under sub-section (8) of section 8;

    g. the manner of publishing the business contact information of a Data Protection Officer under sub-section (9) of section 8;

    h. the manner of obtaining verifiable consent under sub-section (1) of section 9;

i. the classes of Data Fiduciaries, the purposes of processing of personal data of a child and the conditions relating thereto, under sub-section (4) of section 9; (k) the other matters comprising the process of Data Protection Impact Assessment under sub-clause (i) of clause (c) of sub-section (2) of section 10;

j. the other measures that the Significant Data Fiduciary shall undertake under sub-clause (iii) of clause (c) of sub-section (2) of section 10;

k. the manner in which a Data Principal shall make a request to the Data Fiduciary to obtain information and any other information related to the personal data of such Data Principal and its processing, under sub-section (1) of section 11;

l. the manner in which a Data Principal shall make a request to the Data Fiduciary for erasure of her personal data under sub-section (3) of section 12;

m. the period within which the Data Fiduciary shall respond to any grievances under sub-section (2) of section 13;

n. the manner of nomination of any other individual by the Data Principal under sub-section (1) of section 14;

o. the standards for processing the personal data for exemption under clause (b) of sub-section (2) of section 17;

p. the manner of appointment of Chairperson and other Members of the Board under sub-section (2) of section 19;

q. the salary, allowances and other terms and conditions of services of the Chairperson and other Members of the Board under sub-section (1) of section 20;

r. the manner of authentication of orders, directions and instruments under sub-section (1) of section 23;

s. the terms and conditions of appointment and service of officers and employees of the Board under section 24;

t. the techno-legal measures to be adopted by the Board under sub-section (1) of section 28;

u. the other matters under clause (d) of sub-section (7) of section 28;

v. the form, manner and fee for filing an appeal under sub-section (2) of section 29;

w. the procedure for dealing an appeal under sub-section (8) of section 29;

x. any other matter which is to be or may be prescribed or in respect of which provision is to be, or may be, made by rules.

2. The matters in respect of which rules may be made under the aforesaid provisions are matters of detail and it is not practicable to provide them in the Bill itself. The delegation of legislative powers is, therefore, of a normal character.

Annexure

EXTRACT FROM THE TELECOM REGULATORY AUTHORITY OF INDIA ACT, 1997 (24 OF 1997)

* * *

CHAPTER IV

APPELLATE TRIBUNAL

14. The Central Government shall, by notification, establish an Appellate Tribunal to be known as the Telecom Disputes Settlement and Appellate Tribunal to—

* * *

a. exercise jurisdiction, powers and authority conferred on—
   i. the Appellate Tribunal under the Information Technology Act, 2000; and
   ii. the Appellate Tribunal under the Airports Economic Regulatory Authority of India Act, 2008.

* * *

EXTRACTS FROM THE INFORMATION TECHNOLOGY ACT, 2000 (21 OF 2000)

* * *

43A. Where a body corporate, possessing, dealing or handling any sensitive personal data or information in a computer resource which it owns, controls or operates, is negligent in implementing and maintaining reasonable security practices and procedures and thereby causes wrongful loss or wrongful gain to any person, such body corporate shall be liable to pay damages by way of compensation to the person so affected.

Explanation.—For the purposes of this section,—

a. "body corporate" means any company and includes a firm, sole proprietorship or other association of individuals engaged in commercial or professional activities;

b. (ii) "reasonable security practices and procedure" means security practices and procedures designed to protect such information from unauthorised access, damage, use, modification, disclosure or impairment, as may be specified in an agreement between the parties or as may be specified in any law for the time being in force and in the absence of such agreement or any law, such reasonable security practices and procedures, as may be prescribed by the Central Government in consultation with such professional bodies or associations as it may deem fit;

c. (iii) "sensitive personal data or information" means such personal information as may be prescribed by the Central Government in consultation with such professional

d. bodies or associations as it may deem fit.

* * *

81. The provisions of this Act shall have effect notwithstanding anything inconsistent therewith contained in any other law for the time being in force:

Provided that nothing contained in this Act shall restrict any person from exercising any right conferred under the Copyright Act, 1957 or the Patents Act, 1970.

* * *

87.(1)* * * * *

(2) In particular, and without prejudice to the generality of the foregoing power, such rules may provide for all or any of the following matters, namely:—

* * *

(ob) the reasonable security practices and procedures and sensitive personal data or information under section 43A;

* * *

EXTRACT FROM THE RIGHT TO INFORMATION ACT, 2005 (22 OF 2005)

* * *

8.(1) Notwithstanding anything contained in this Act, there shall be no obligation to give any citizen,—

* * *

(j) information which relates to personal information the disclosure of which has no relationship to any public activity or interest, or which would cause unwarranted invasion of the privacy of the individual unless the Central Public Information Officer or the State Public Information

Officer or the appellate authority, as the case may be, is satisfied that the larger public interest justifies the disclosure of such information:

Provided that the information which cannot be denied to the Parliament or a State Legislature shall not be denied to any person.

Epilogue

This book represents an effort to bring the Privacy and Data Protection topic to Lawyers, IT Personnel, Auditors and Business managers.

This book for the first time introduces the concept of Unification of multiple compliances into one DGPSI compliance framework and its unique advantage converting the individual compliances for ISMS, PIMS and Data Governance (BIS) into a super ordinate goal of the Company.

I hope that the effort would be appreciated by the Business Community as well as the professional communities.

Feedback is welcome at naavi@naavi.org

Naavi

About the Author

Na.Vijayashankar is popularly known as Naavi and is a pioneer in Cyber Laws in India. He is the founder of www.naavi.org a leading Cyber Law portal in India. He is also the Chairman of Foundation of Data Protection Professionals in India (FDPPI).

Naavi is an author of the first book on Cyber Laws in India in 1999 and has since then released many books on Information Technology Act and Data Protection Act.

He is a visiting faculty in a number of leading educational institutions including NALSAR, Hyderabad, IIMU, Udaipur and several law colleges in Bangalore.

Naavi is an experienced Techno Legal auditor and has extensive experience in HIPAA, GDPR, ITA 2000 audits.

Naavi is a thought leader having promoted many innovative thoughts including Theory of Data, Digital Value Standard of India (DVSI) and Digital Governance and Protection Standard of India (DGPSI).

Naavi is presently working on Neuro Rights law and AI regulation in India as an extension of his activities in Cyber Laws and Privacy.

www.ingramcontent.com/pod-product-compliance
Lightning Source LLC
LaVergne TN
LVHW052149210926
848482LV00019B/297
9798891868182